Reader's Guide
to
ROBERT BROWNING

Reader's Guide
to
ROBERT BROWNING

John T. Nichol

CENTRUM PRESS
NEW DELHI-110002 (INDIA)

CENTRUM PRESS
H.O.: 4360/4, Ansari Road, Daryaganj,
New Delhi-110 002 (India)
Ph.: 23278000, 23261597

B.O.: No. 1015, Ist Main Road, BSK IIIrd Stage
IIIrd Phase, IIIrd Block,
Bangalore - 560 085 (India)
Tel.: 080-41723429
Visit us at: www.centrumpress.com

Reader's Guide to Robert Browning

First Edition, 2009

ISBN 978-93-80106-86-1

PRINTED IN INDIA

Printed at Balaji Offset, Delhi.

Contents

Contents

Preface

The purpose of this Readers Guide is to afford some aid and guidance in the study of Robert Browning's Poetry, which, being the most complexly subjective of all English poetry, is, for that reason alone, the most difficult. And then the poet's favorite art-form, the dramatic, or, rather, psychologic, monologue, which is quite original with himself, and peculiarly adapted to the constitution of his genius and to the revelation of themselves by the several "dramatis personae", presents certain structural difficulties, but difficulties which, with an increased familiarity, grow less and less. The exposition presented in the Introduction, of its constitution and skilful management, and the Arguments given of the several poems included in the Guide, will, it is hoped, reduce, if not altogether remove, the difficulties of this kind. The study of poetry, in our institutions of learning, so far as I have taken note of it, and the education induced thereby, is almost purely intellectual. The student's spiritual nature is left to take care of itself; and the consequence is that he becomes, at best, only a thinking and analyzing machine. The spiritual claims of the study of poetry are especially demanded in the case of Browning's poetry.

No poetry in English literature, or in any literature, is more charged with discursive thought than his. But he is, at the same time, the most spiritual and transcendental of poets, the "subtlest assertor of the Soul in Song". His thought is never an end to itself, but is always subservient to an ulterior spiritual end — always directed towards "a presentment of the correspondency of the universe to Deity, of the natural to the spiritual, and of the actual to the ideal"; and it is all-important that students should be awakened, and made, as far as possible, responsive to this spiritual end.

Author

Chapter 1

Introduction

Robert Browning (7 May 1812 – 12 December 1889) was an English poet and playwright whose mastery of dramatic verse, especially dramatic monologues, made him one of the foremost Victorian poets. Browning was born in Camberwell, a suburb of London, England, the first son of Robert and Sarah Anna Browning. His father was a man of both fine intellect and character, who worked as a well-paid clerk for the Bank of England. Robert's father amassed a library of around 6,000 books, many of them obscure and arcane. Thus, Robert was raised in a household of significant literary resources.

His mother, with whom he was ardently bonded, was a devout Nonconformist as well as extremely musically talented. He had a younger sister named Sarianna, also gifted, who became her brother's companion in his later years. As a family unit they lived simply, and his father encouraged his interest in literature and the Arts. In childhood, he was distinguished by a love of poetry and natural history. By twelve, he had written a book of poetry which he later destroyed when no publisher could be found. After attending several private schools he began to be educated by a tutor, having demonstrated a strong dislike for institutionalized education.

Browning was a fast learner and by the age of fourteen was fluent in French, Greek, Italian and Latin as well as his native English. He became a great admirer of the Romantic poets, especially Shelley. Following the precedent of Shelley, Browning became an atheist and vegetarian, both of which he gave up later. At age sixteen, he attended University College

London, but left after his first year. His mother's staunch evangelical faith circumscribed the pursuit of his studying at either Oxford University or Cambridge University, both then open only to members of the Church of England. He had substantial musical ability and he composed arrangements of various songs.

In 1845, Browning met Elizabeth Barrett, who lived as a semi-invalid and virtual prisoner in her father's house in Wimpole Street. Gradually a significant romance developed between them, leading to their secret marriage and flight in 1846. (The marriage was initially secret because Elizabeth's father disapproved of marriage for any of his children.) From the time of their marriage, the Brownings lived in Italy, first in Pisa, and then, within a year, finding an apartment in Florence which they called Casa Guidi (now a museum to their memory).

Their only child, Robert Wiedemann Barrett Browning, nicknamed "Penini" or "Pen", was born in 1849. In these years Browning was fascinated by and learned hugely from the art and atmosphere of Italy. He would, in later life, say that 'Italy was my university'. The Brownings also bought a home in Asolo, in the Veneto outside Venice, and in a cruel irony the poet Browning died on the day that the Town Council approved the purchase. His wife died in 1861.

Browning's poetry was known to the cognoscenti from fairly early on in his life, but he remained relatively obscure as a poet till his middle age. (In the middle of the century, Tennyson was much better known.) In Florence he worked on the poems that eventually comprised his two-volume *Men and Women*, for which he is now well known; in 1855, however, when these were published, they made little impact.

It was only after his wife's death, in 1861, when he returned to England and became part of the London literary scene, that his reputation started to take off. In 1868, after five years work, he completed and published the long blank-verse poem *The Ring and the Book*, and finally achieved really significant recognition.

Based on a convoluted murder-case from 1690s Rome,

the poem is composed of twelve books, essentially comprising ten lengthy dramatic poems narrated by the various characters in the story showing their individual take on events as they transpire, bookended by an introduction and conclusion by Browning himself.

Extraordinarily long even by Browning's own standards (over twenty thousand lines), *The Ring and the Book* was the poet's most ambitious project and has been hailed as a tour de force of dramatic poetry. Published separately in four volumes from November 1868 through to February 1869, the poem was a huge success both commercially and critically, and finally brought Browning the renown he had sought and deserved for nearly forty years of work.

In the remaining years of his life he traveled extensively and frequented Manchester. Few of his later poems gained the popularity of *The Ring and the Book*, and they are largely unread today. However, Browning's later work has been undergoing a major critical re-evaluation in recent years, and much of it remains of interest for its poetic quality and psychological insight.

After a series of long poems published in the early 1870s, of which *Fifine at the Fair* and *Red Cotton Night-Cap Country* were the best-received, Browning again turned to shorter poems. The volume *Pacchiarotto, and How He Worked in Distemper* included a spiteful attack against Browning's critics, especially the later Poet Laureate Alfred Austin.

According to some reports Browning became romantically involved with Lady Ashburton, but did not re-marry. In 1878, he returned to Italy for the first time in the seventeen years since Elizabeth's death, and returned there on several occasions.

The Browning Society was formed for the appreciation of his works in 1881.

In 1887, Browning produced the major work of his later years, *Parleyings with Certain People of Importance In Their Day*. It finally presented the poet speaking in his own voice, engaging in a series of dialogues with long-forgotten figures of literary, artistic, and philosophic history. Once more, the Victorian public was baffled by this, and Browning returned to the short, concise lyric for his last volume, *Asolando* (1889).

He died at his son's home Ca' Rezzonico in Venice on 12 December 1889, the same day *Asolando* was published, and was buried in Poets' Corner in Westminster Abbey; his grave now lies immediately adjacent to that of Alfred Tennyson.

Browning's fame today rests mainly on his dramatic monologues, in which the words not only convey setting and action but also reveal the speaker's character. Unlike a soliloquy, the meaning in a Browning dramatic monologue is not what the speaker directly reveals but what he inadvertently "gives away" about himself in the process of rationalizing past actions, or "special-pleading" his case to a silent auditor in the poem. Rather than thinking out loud, the character composes a self-defence which the reader, as "juror," is challenged to see through.

Browning chooses some of the most debased, extreme and even criminally psychotic characters, no doubt for the challenge of building a sympathetic case for a character who doesn't deserve one and to cause the reader to squirm at the temptation to acquit a character who may be a homicidal psychopath. One of his more sensational dramatic monologues is *Porphyria's Lover*. The opening lines provide a sinister setting for the macabre events that follow. It is plain that the speaker is insane, as he strangles his lover with her own hair to try and preserve for ever the moment of perfect love she has shown him.

Yet it is by carefully reading the far more sophisticated and cultivated rhetoric of the aristocratic and civilized Duke of *My Last Duchess*, perhaps the most frequently cited example of the poet's dramatic monologue form, that the attentive reader discovers the most horrific example of a mind totally mad despite its eloquence in expressing itself. The duchess, we learn, was murdered not because of infidelity, not because of a lack of gratitude for her position, and not, finally, because of the simple pleasures she took in common everyday occurrences.

She is reduced to an objet d'art in the Duke's collection

of paintings and statues because the Duke equates his instructing her to behave like a duchess with "stooping," an action of which his megalomaniacal pride is incapable. In other monologues, such as *Fra Lippo Lippi,* Browning takes an ostensibly unsavory or immoral character and challenges us to discover the goodness, or life-affirming qualities, that often put the speaker's contemporaneous judges to shame.

In *The Ring and the Book* Browning writes an epic-length poem in which he justifies the ways of God to humanity through twelve extended blank verse monologues spoken by the principals in a trial about a murder. These monologues greatly influenced many later poets, including T. S. Eliot and Ezra Pound, the latter singling out in his *Cantos* Browning's convoluted psychological poem about a frustrated 13-century troubadour, Sordello, as the poem he must work to distance himself from.

Ironically, Browning's style, which seemed modern and experimental to Victorian readers, owes much to his love of the seventeenth century poems of John Donne with their abrupt openings, colloquial phrasing and irregular rhythms. But he remains too much the prophet-poet and descendant of Percy Shelley to settle for the conceits, puns, and verbal play of the Metaphysical poets of the seventeenth century. His is a modern sensibility, all too aware of the arguments against the vulnerable position of one of his simple characters, who recites: "God's in His Heaven; All's right with the world."

Browning endorses such a position because he sees an immanent deity that, far from remaining in a transcendent heaven, is indivisible from temporal process, assuring that in the fullness of theological time there is ample cause for celebrating life. Browning's is assuredly at once the most incarnate and dynamic of visions of Deity, in Christianity and perhaps in any of the world's great religions.

Browning was the first person to ever have his voice heard after his death. On a recording made by Thomas Edison in 1889, Browning reads "How They Brought the Good News from Ghent to Aix" (including apologizing when he forgets the words). It was first played in Venice in 1890.

COMPLETE LIST OF WORKS

- *Pauline: A Fragment of a Confession* (1833)
- *Paracelsus* (1835)
- *Strafford* (play) (1837)
- *Sordello* (1840)
- *Bells and Pomegranates No. I: Pippa Passes* (play) (1841)
- *Bells and Pomegranates No. II: King Victor and King Charles* (play) (1842)
- *Bells and Pomegranates No. III: Dramatic Lyrics* (1842)
  - "Porphyria's Lover"
  - "Soliloquy of the Spanish Cloister"
  - "My Last Duchess"
  - *The Pied Piper of Hamelin*
  - "Johannes Agricola in Meditation"
- *Bells and Pomegranates No. IV: The Return of the Druses* (play) (1843)
- *Bells and Pomegranates No. V: A Blot in the 'Scutcheon* (play) (1843)
- *Bells and Pomegranates No. VI: Colombe's Birthday* (play) (1844)
- *Bells and Pomegranates No. VII: Dramatic Romances and Lyrics* (1845)
  - "The Laboratory"
  - "How They Brought the Good News from Ghent to Aix"
  - "The Bishop Orders His Tomb at Saint Praxed's Church"
- *Bells and Pomegranates No. VIII: Luria* and *A Soul's Tragedy* (plays) (1846)
- *Christmas-Eve and Easter-Day* (1850) *Men and Women* (1855)
  - "Love Among the Ruins"
  - "The Last Ride Together"
  - "A Toccata of Galuppi's"
  - "Childe Roland to the Dark Tower Came"
  - "Fra Lippo Lippi"
  - "Andrea Del Sarto"
  - "A Grammarian's Funeral"

  - "An Epistle Containing the Strange Medical Experience of Karshish, the Arab Physician"
- *Dramatis Personae* (1864)
  - "Caliban upon Setebos"
  - "Rabbi Ben Ezra"
- *The Ring and the Book* (1868-9)
- *Balaustion's Adventure* (1871)
- *Prince Hohenstiel-Schwangau, Saviour of Society* (1871)
- *Fifine at the Fair* (1872)
- *Red Cotton Night-Cap Country, or, Turf and Towers* (1873)
- *Aristophanes' Apology* (1875)
- *The Inn Album* (1875)
- *Pacchiarotto, and How He Worked in Distemper* (1876)
- *The Agamemnon of Aeschylus* (1877)
- *La Saisiaz* and *The Two Poets of Croisic* (1878)
- *Dramatic Idylls* (1879)
- *Dramatic Idylls: Second Series* (1880)
- *Jocoseria* (1883)
- *Ferishtah's Fancies* (1884)
- *Parleyings with Certain People of Importance In Their Day* (1887)
- *Asolando* (1889)

The Laboratory

Timeline

Though Browning was eventually considered a premier Victorian poet, his critical reputation was hard won. Throughout his career, he honed the dramatic monologue, elevating the form to a new level. His experimentation with versification and with language, combined with the diversity and scope of his subject matter, forced Browning's critics to realise that this poet could not be evaluated by conventional literary standards.

Particularly devoted to dramatic characterization, Browning explored the human psychology through his characters and the dramatic situations he presented. Modern critics are concerned with Browning's poetic development, with the themes that unite the various poems in a particular volume, and with the unique elements of Browning's innovative style.

Born in Camberwell, a borough in southeast London, Browning was raised in a relatively affluent environment. His father was a well-read clerk for the Bank of England, and his mother was a strict Congregationalist. While Browning read widely as a boy, his formal education was somewhat irregular. Beginning in the early 1820s he attended the nearby Peckam School, where he studied for four years.

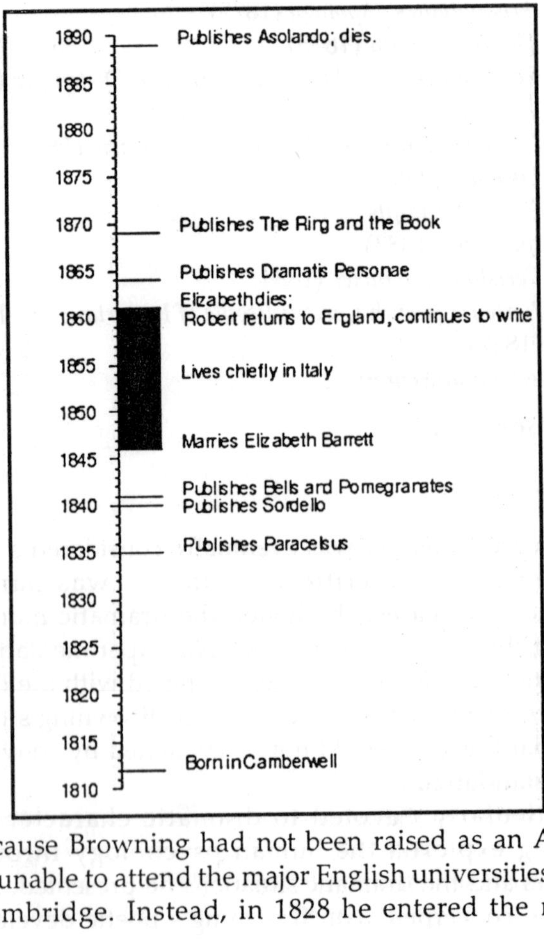

Because Browning had not been raised as an Anglican, he was unable to attend the major English universities, Oxford and Cambridge. Instead, in 1828 he entered the recently-founded London University but terminated his studies after less than one year. Browning decided to pursue a career as a poet and lived in his parents' home, supported by them, until 1846. He published his first poem, *Pauline: A Fragment of a Confession,* anonymously in 1833. Browning continued writing and publishing and experimenting with the dramatic monologue until 1845, when he fell in love with Elizabeth Barrett.

The pair secretly married in 1846, then departed for Italy where they settled in Florence and wrote until Elizabeth's death in 1861. Browning then returned to England, and after a period of literary inactivity, he began writing again. He remained highly prolific throughout the rest of his life. Browning died in 1889 while visiting his son in Venice. Browning's body was returned to England and buried in the Poets' Corner of Westminster Abbey.

After the anonymous publication of *Pauline,* which Browning later insisted was a dramatic piece, many readers speculated that the sentiments expressed were the poet's own. In his next work, *Paracelsus* (1835), Browning established the objective framework offered by a more dramatic form and was thus able to distance himself from the characters in the poem.

The dramatic monologue is based on the life of the Renaissance chemist Paracelsus, and the work received largely positive critical reviews. Browning then published *Sordello* in 1840, also based on a Renaissance subject, but the poem was less than favorably received by the critics, many of whom found it obscure and affected. In 1841, Browning began publishing a series of poems and dramas under the title *Bells and Pomegranates.*

The final volume appeared in 1846 and failed to restore Browning's reputation among critics. In 1855, with the publication of *Men and Women,* containing Browning's well-known love poems and dramatic monologues, Browning began to receive the respect of some of his critics, although popular success still eluded him. It was not until the 1860s, and in particular the publication of *Dramatis Personae* in 1864, that Browning achieved major critical and popular success.

The volume was followed shortly thereafter by his masterpiece, *The Ring and the Book* (1868-69).

A series of dramatic monologues spoken by different characters, the work was based on an Italian murder case. *The Ring and the Book* cemented Browning's reputation as one of the foremost poets of Victorian England.

Contemporary critical acclaim evaded Browning for many years. Gertrude Reese Hudson observes that the poet's critics required regular and frequent exposure to his unique dramatic method in order to recognize the excellence of Browning's art.

Hudson also notes that other factors contributed to Browning's winning over of his critics, including their changing opinion regarding the nature of poetry, as well as a growing appreciation for both the timeliness of Browning's writing, his intellect and originality, and the "totality of his achievement."

Browning's highly individualized style and his usage of dramatic monologue fascinate modern scholars as much as these elements troubled his early critics.

John Woolford and Daniel Karlin demonstrate that in using the dramatic monologue format, Browning was primarily interested in the creation and development of dramatic speakers and dramatic situations.

The two critics also analyze Browning's style, finding that his poetry, in its focus on the speaker, insists on being read aloud.

Woolford and Karlin further argue that Browning develops two distinct voices in his poetry, voices Browning himself described as "saying" and "singing" voices and which the critics contend result from the influence of the Romantics on Browning's work.

In a separate essay, Daniel Karlin examines Browning's use of binary oppositions, finding that "every Browning poem is oppositional in nature."

Karlin studies in particular the opposition between love and hate, maintaining that Browning explores hate not simply as the opposite of love, but as a force with its own purpose, a force which can lead to love as well as self-realization. Other critics review certain volumes of Browning's poetry as a whole, arguing that the individual poems support a larger theme or purpose.

Clyde de L. Ryals studies Browning's *Dramatic Romances and Lyrics* (1845) with this in mind. Ryals stresses that the theme of loyalty unites the poems in this volume, and that this theme is often expressed in an ironic manner.

Furthermore, Ryals argues that while the majority of the poems may concern national loyalties, the poems also explore other kinds of loyalties, including loyalty to one's self, to one's religion, and to one's beloved.

Similarly, Adam Roberts argues for the unity of the poems in Browning's *Men and Women* (1855), asserting that the volume demonstrates Browning's first successful attempt at balancing the subjective and objective impulses in his poetry. This synthesis is achieved, Roberts argues, through Browning's characterization.

Roberts explains that compared to the idiosyncratic, often insane characters in the earlier *Dramatic Romances and Lyrics*, the personalities in *Men and Women*, though complex, "communicate on something approaching our own level," and thus engender empathy and understanding among readers.

Roberts goes on to discuss how Browning's continued usage of "grotesque" style and imagery (including colloquial language, rough syntax, and precise but blunt forms of expression) helps to link the form of these poems to their content.

Considerable critical discussion of Browning's work pertains to his murder mystery, *The Ring and the Book*. The twelve dramatic monologues, delivered by different characters, have led critics to question which, if any, of these characters serves as the moral authority, or centre, of the poem.

Adam Potkay argues against assigning this position of moral authority to any one of the characters and instead considers the poem as a "decentered struggle of interpretations" in which the character of Guido leads the way in "decentering" the poem by questioning the very conception of identity. W. David Shaw likewise contends that there is no central viewpoint in *The Ring and the Book* and maintains that while Browning ranks the authority of the characters in the poem, the poet creates no central authority figure.

Additionally, Shaw explores the way in which deconstructionism and hermeneutics pervade Browning's masterwork, finding the Pope aligned with hermeneutical criticism and Guido and Tertium Quid aligned with the deconstructionists.

Chapter 2

Christmas Eve and Easter Day

The Italian period of Browning's life was comparatively barren. It has been suggested that this was due, in part, to the fact that the climate of Italy lowered his vitality; in part, to the unpopularity of his works.

Moreover, he took to drawing, and to modelling in clay, copying masterpieces with intense pleasure. Only two publications of verse marked this period—*Christmas Eve and Easter Day* (1850) and *Men and Women* (1855).

He also wrote at this time an essay on Shelley, by way of introduction to *Certain Letters of Percy Bysshe Shelley* (1852), which were afterwards found to be fabrications. The essay was evidently influenced by Milsand's article on Browning himself, in *La Revue des Deux Mondes*. It accentuates in the same way the distinction between subjective and objective poetry, and discusses Shelley's work with much skill and insight.

In *Christmas Eve and Easter Day*, critics discover clear evidence of the influence of Elizabeth Browning's devout Christian faith. Browning had been interested in religion all his life: for the "atheism" which he caught from Shelley was as superficial and temporary as the vegetarianism.

Pauline, Paracelsus, Pippa Passes, all the principal poems of the early period bear witness to his sense of the profound significance of religion. *Christmas Eve* deals with contemporary attitudes towards Christianity—dissent, the higher criticism, Roman catholicism—with a characteristic preference for the first. *Easter Day* is more restrained and stern, more full of lyric beauty and more searching in its truth.

It deals with the inner nature of the faith that is religious—religious and not epicurean or materialistic—not seeking its evidences in outward happenings or its worth in the complacency which it brings, the zest it gives to joy, or the bitterness it takes away from sorrow.

Both poems are dramatic; neither is to be regarded as the poet's confession of faith; nevertheless, they express the profoundest of his spiritual convictions, which centred upon the most sublime of all religious hypotheses, namely, that of the omnipotence and omnipresence of a Christlike God, the divine power and work of love.

Saul, especially the second part, which contains the prophecy of Christianity, *Cleon, Karshish,* bear witness to the same conceptions—the omnipresent wonder that transcends definition, and is yet the sole sure light whereby man can walk and find safe footing.

Elizabeth Browning's influence may be detected, also, in the poems which treat of love. The original *Dramatic Lyrics (the Dramatic Lyrics* as they stood before poems were transferred thereto from *Men and Women)* included Cristina and *In a Gondola,* and among *Dramatic Romances and Lyrics* there appeared *The Lost Mistress.*

But the collection which included *A Woman's Last Word, Any Wife to Any Husband, The Last Ride Together, One Way of Love,* among many more, was certainly a richer rendering of the marvel of love than any of his previous works.

It is probable that no single poet, in any country, so rendered the variety of its phases and the abundance of its power—its triumph, its failure; its victory over the world, its defeat by the world; its passion and poignancy; its psychical subtlety and its romance, and the immensity of its spiritual significance, whether in the life of the soul or in the outer cosmos.

Many of the poems in *Men and Women* of which the scene can be determined have reference to Italy. But it is doubtful whether his residence in Italy influenced Browning's choice of subjects to any great extent. "He was deeply Italianised before he went to live in Italy." To say nothing of *Sordello* and

Pippa Passes, there was an Italian group in the original *Dramatic Romances and Lyrics,* which is almost as conspicuous as that of the original *Men and Women*. After *The Ring and the Book,* Italian subject become both more rare and less important.

On leaving Italy, Browning settled in London. With the change of residence came a change of habit. His Italian life, quiet in the early years, had become gradually much more social.

In Florence, in Rome and during their visits to London, the charm of Elizabeth Browning, and Robert Browning's own genius for noble friendship, brought them into intimate relations with the most gifted of their time.

After her death, until the spring of 1863, he retired within himself, and his life, as he said, was "as grey as the London sky." Then, he thought that way of life morbid and unworthy, resolved to accept every suitable invitation and, thenceforth, his figure was familiar in the circles of the lovers of literature, although, except for a very few friends, all women, none ever saw of Browning more than "a splendid surface."

In 1863, he was much agitated by a proposal to publish a life of Elizabeth Browning, with letters. He turned savagely upon "the blackguards" who would "thrust their paws into his bowels," and he destroyed the greater part of his own correspondence.

But he preserved the letters that had passed between himself and his wife prior to their marriage; with the result that hardly anyone, except, perhaps, Carlyle, protested more strongly against the intrusion of spies into his life's intimacies, and had the inner shrine more ruthlessly laid bare. He, however, freely gave to the public what had been intended for them.

He republished Elizabeth Browning's prose essays on the Greek Christian poets and the English poets in 1863; and, two years later, made a selection from her poems, and expressed his delight at the popularity which made it necessary. For three years in succession, he spent the summer months at Ste. Marie, near Pornic, where he worked at his *Dramatis Personae,* published in 1864.

Part of 1866 and 1867 was spent at Croisic, the name of which is linked with *The Two Poets of Croisic*, as he linked that of Pornic with *Gold Hair, Red Cotton Night-Cap Country* and the gypsy woman of *Fifine at the Fair*.

The best explanation of a poet is to be sought in the best poem he has written, or in that theme which, at his touch, breaks out into the amplest music. There, his very self, the personality which he verily is and which, in a greater or lesser degree, subtly suffuses all that he does, finds fittest and fullest utterance; and the utterance itself, whether in phrase or figure, being faithful to fact, bears that stamp of inevitability which implies perfection.

There is little doubt as to the theme which called forth the fulness of the powers of Elizabeth Barrett and Robert Browning. It was love. It was love in the same cosmic sense as Wordsworth's duty, which "kept the stars from wrong," an omnipresent passion for the best in all nature and in all mankind. To Elizabeth Browning, there was no truth nor substance, save love.

It was the essence and wholeness of her being, and it expressed itself with unrestrained prodigality in *Sonnets from the Portuguese*. Everything in her life that went before—the beauty of her early home among the Malverns, the whole practice of her literary industry, the long lone years of illness and weakness, the heavy sorrow of the death-stricken home—is taken up, sanctified and dedicated in these poems; and everything that was to follow was but harvest-gleaning and aftermath. These sonnets, and, one is tempted to say, these sonnets only, of all that Elizabeth Browning wrote, the world will in no wise let go. They are equalled only by her life—in Milton's sense, they *are* her life.

Robert Browning cannot be so easily summed and surveyed. His skill was multifarious far beyond the wont even of great poets. There was hardly an instrument in the orchestra which he could not play, his touch was always unique and recognisable; and, within the domain of human character, there was hardly a bent or trait, a passion or propensity, which he did not celebrate.

Nevertheless, when, like his Arion, he "gathers his greatness round him," and "stands in state," and "harp and voice rend air" with his full "magnificence of song," the theme is almost certain to be some phase of love. And love had the same cosmic, constitutive character to him, the same, or even greater, moral worth and spiritual splendour. Speaking of *Sonnets from the Portuguese;* a critic has observed with truth that as piece of poetry they are not equal to the sonnets of Wordsworth or of Milton, yet it is not so unreasonable to question whether their removal would not leave a more irreparable gap in literature.

The removal of love from among Browning's themes would be, original as he was in everything, the removal of his most original, as well as his most massively valuable, contribution to our literature. It would have left the poet himself a man without a purpose in a universe without meaning. Love, in the last resort, was the only article in his creed. For these reasons, the convergence of these two lives into unity and their most intimate commingling ever after, have an artistic meaning no less than an ethical interest, and they concern the literary critic not less than the biographer.

Not that either of the two poets, when their 'prentice days were over, was content to be imitative, or could possibly be conceived as moving in the other's manner. There was no sacrifice of independence—there never is when the union is spiritual in character and complete. They even took precautions against influencing one another when a poem was in the making.

Nevertheless, what they meant for one another was more subtle and penetrating and pervasive than any direct and explicit borrowing, over which the critic could cry "Lo here," or "Lo there." It is easier to suggest and to instance than to describe their influence on each other: but a crowning example, I believe, is to be found in Browning's Pompilia. There are charms, and, above all, there are intensities, scattered abroad in *The Ring and the Book* which would not have been possible, even for him, had it not been for his "lyric Love."

No one was more eager to be dramatical than Browning,

or less willing to expose to a gaping world the pageant of his inner life. But, after all, a poet dips his pen in his own blood when he writes what the world *must* read; if he be robbed of experience as a man, he stands more bare as a poet; and, in the experience of both Robert and Elizabeth Browning, there was one event paramount, one sovereign fact that lent meaning to all that followed.

This was their discovery of one another and the unique perfection of their wedded life. Criticism of the Brownings and of their meaning to literature dare not disregard or discount a mutual penetration of personalities so intense as theirs, but must, in dealing with the one, be aware that it is dealing with the other as well. In this respect, what went before in their life and work was but preliminary, and what came after mere consequent.

Robert Browning was younger than Elizabeth Barrett by some six years. He was born in Southampton street, Camberwell, on 7 May, 1812. His father was a clerk in the bank of England, of literary and artistic tastes, and his mother the daughter of a Dundee shipowner of German extraction. It is more easy to read the acorn in terms of the oak than the oak in terms of the acorn; and the great man reveals and explains, rather than is revealed and explained by, the capacities that slumbered in his forefathers.

While none can deny the heredity of the features of the soul, any more than those of the body, it is idle to pretend that the lineaments of a great man's spirit can be traced back with any degree of accuracy to his ancestors.

Every man, even the most meagre in endowment, has so many ancestors! But the psychical structure and propensities of his *immediate* parents have a significance all their own: for these define and determine the environment within which the child's mind lives and moves and has its being.

The home, during the years when, most of all, the soul is being made, stands to the child for solid earth and starry firmament, and the influences operative therein are the air and the food and the drink, and,therefore, the very substance embodied in his personality. From this point of view, the simple piety of Browning's mother, her membership of an "Independent Church" in Walworth, her life-long class in the Sunday school, her box for contributions to the London Missionary society loses their insignificance. In these and other habits, the child saw the spirit of religion made real and ratified by his mother, and it remained with him, much modified it is true, but, owing to his mother's memory, permanently holy and always dominant.

Again, it must not be said that Browning's "genius was derived from his father." Genius is not derived. It is always a miracle and has no history. But the father's genius, that of a lover of art and of literature, made the son a lover of books and a collector of them. It led him to write verse—which he did fluently and after the manner of Pope; and he had a great delight in grotesque rimes.

Moreover, he was so skilful in the use of his pencil that Rossetti pronounced him to possess "a real genius for drawing." Now, "the handsome, vigorous, fearless child," unrestingly active, fiery of temper, crowded with energy of mind, observant and most swift to learn, naturally saw all these things and, not less naturally, imitated the ways of his parents and sought to acquire what they valued.

In Browning's case, no educational influence counts at all, in comparison with that of his father's tastes and habits and collection of books. That influence can be traced in the poet's choice of themes, all the way from *Pauline* and *Sordello* to *Parleyings* and *Asolando,* and it even marks his manner of dealing with many of them.

He read voraciously in his father's library, apparently without let or guidance, and his acquaintance was very early with the works of Voltaire, the letters of Junius and of Horace Walpole, the *Emblems* of Quarles and Croxall's *Fables.* The first book he ever bought with his own money was Macpherson's *Ossian.*

Side by side with this precocious literary omnivorousness went, from early childhood, careful training in music. "I was studying the Grammer of Music." he said, according to Mrs. Ireland, "when most children are learning the Multiplication

Table." Moreover, he was given permission, at an age lower than the rules allowed, to visit the Dulwich gallery, which was hard by his father's home. It became "a beloved haunt of his childhood." He was grateful all his life for the privilege and used to recall, in later years, "the triumphant Murillo pictures," "such a Watteau" and "all the Poussins" he had seen there.

He is "exploring passion and mind," he says, "for the first time," "dreaming not of restraint but gazing on all things." He is "borne away, as Arab birds float sleeping in the wind, o'er deserts, towers, and forests." He "nourishes music more than life, and old lore," and "knows the words shall move men, like a swift wind." In every way, *Pauline* must remain a supremely interesting poem to Browning's readers: it holds in bud many of Browning's qualities, powers and even convictions.

The wholesome and wealthy confusion of this seething period of the young poet's life is faithfully rendered or, rather, betrayed, in the brilliant and incoherent *Pauline*—Browning's earliest published poem. Pauline herself, except for the first half-dozen lines and a footnote, is the shadow of a shade—the passive recipient of the psychological confessions of a young poet: a young poet, who, not at all unaware of his curls and lace and ruffles, has been turning himself round and round before the mirror, and has found that he is too noble a being, too bold, reckless, unrestrained, sceptical, brilliant, intense, widesouled, hungry for knowledge and love for this work-a-day world.

The self-consciousness is not "intense," as J. S. Mill thought. It is picturesque. It is not "morbid" or unwholesome, as other critics have averred. It is only the frippery, the most serious mock-believe tragical outpourings of an extraordinarily handsome and innocent youth, who, in truth, had never known disappointment nor looked in the face of sorrow.

Browning's dislike of the poem in later years was entirely natural. He resented all prying into private life, and was, of all men, least willing to "sonnet-sing about himself." So, the drapery in which he had clothed himself in this early poem seemed to him to be almost transparent, and he felt as if he had been going about nude.

Pauline was published in January, 1833, anonymously, when its author was twenty years old. But that fine critic W. J. Fox discerned its merit and dealt with it in generous praise in *The Monthly Repository* for April in the same year. Allan Cunningham, also, praised it in *The Athenaeum.* Some years later (probably in 1850), Rossetti found and transcribed it in the reading room of the British Museum, and he wrote to Browning, who was in Florence, to ask him "whether he was the author of a poem called *Pauline.*"

Beyond this, the poem attracted no attention. Why, it is difficult to say. That it is mastered by its material, flooded by its own wealth, it true. Of all Browning's poems, it is the only one which owes its difficulty to confusion; and it is, in fact, to use the poet's own phrase, a "boyish work."

But what work for a boy! There are passages in it, not a few, of a beauty that exceeds so much as to belong to a sphere of being into which mediocrity never for a moment gains entry. So long as he has this theatrically earnest boy at his side, the reader is never safe from the surprise of some sudden splash of splendour:

The boy
With his white breast and brow and clustering curls
Streaked with his mother's blood, but striving hard
To tell his story ere his reason goes.

After the publication of *Pauline,* in 1833, Browning visited Petrograd with Benkhausen, the Russian consul general; and it was probably this contact with offical life which led him, shortly after his return to England, to apply—in vain—for a post on a Persian mission.

During this period, there is ample evidence of physical and mental exuberance, but little of poetic activity. It was many years later that the Russian visit yielded the forest-scene of the thrilling tale of Ivàn Ivànovitch, and his toying with the Persian mission (possibly) suggested *Ferishtah.*

But his interest in the complicated subtleties of diplomacy appeared in *Sordello* and *Strafford* as well as in *Prince Hohenstiel-*

Schwangau—not to mention *Bishop Blougram* and *Caliban upon Setebos.* In 1834, however, there appeared in *The Monthly Repository* a series of five poetic contributions of which the most noteworthy were *Porphyria,* afterwards entitled *Porphyria's Lover,* and the six stanzas beginning "Still ailing, Wind?

Wilt be appeased or no," which were republished in *James Lee's Wife.* Then, with a preface dated 15 March, 1835, when its author still lacked two months of completing his twenty-third year, there appeared one of the most marvellous productions of youthful poetic genius in the history of any literature.

Browning is said to have written *Paracelsus* in six months, meditating not a few of its passages during midnight walks, within sight of the glare of London lights, and the muffled hearing of its quieting tumult. This poem belongs to an altogether different altitude from that of *Pauline.*

Instead of a confused rendering of vague dreams and seething sentiments and passions, we have, in *Paracelsus,* the story of the lithe and sinewy strength of early manhood, the manifold powers of a most gifted spirit braced together and passionately dedicated to the service of an iron-hard intellectual ambition. Here is the "intensest life" resolute upon acquiring, at any cost, the intellectual mastery of mankind.

The subject was suggested to Browning by a French royalist and refugee, count Amédée de Ripert-Monclar, and the poem is dedicated to him. Browning was already acquainted with the career and character of Paracelsus—his works were in his father's library. Moreover, it is beyond doubt that, at this stage of his life, in particular, the poet was driven by a like hunger for knowledge and ambition for intellectual sovereignty. His reading of his subject implies affinity of mind and is altogether sympathetic.

The eccentricities of behaviour, the charlatanism, the boundless conceit, the miracles and absurdities with which Paracelsus was accredited by popular belief, either disappear or are sublimated into elements of a dramatic romance which has something of the greatness and seriousness of tragedy.

To assume that Browning, in this poem, was depicting "the fall of a logician," or of set design "destroying the intellectualist fallacy," is to misunderstand the spirit in which the poem was written. The adventurous alchemist was himself too much a poet to serve such an unpoetic purpose, even if Browning had been so little a poet as to form it. Paracelsus does not "fall": he "attains."

Far from convicting him of intellectual futility, Browning actually made him divine the secret he sought, and, in one of the most splendid passages of modern poetry, declare with his dying lips a faith which is no less Browning's than his own.True! knowledge without love is not even power; but neither is love without knowledge; and the consummation of the achievement of Paracelsus is that love becomes the means of knowledge and intelligence the instrument of love.

"The simultaneous perception of Love and Power in the Absolute" was, in Browning's view, "the noblest and predominant characteristic of Shelley"; and, for Browning, even in his most "metaphysical" days, when knowledge was always said to have "failed," it was still a power *Paracelsus* is the most miraculous and inexplicable of all the exhibitions of Browning's genius.

The promise it contained, with all the poet's lasting greatness, was not fulfilled. Its form and artistic manner, the lineaments and the movements of the mind which works within it, the noble passions which moved the poet and the faith which inspired and controlled him—these are pre-eminently illuminating to the student of Browning and by far the best introduction to all he strove to do.

Paracelsus is interesting, also, as touching the new times which were dawning around the young poet. In its closing pages, something of the spirit of modern science comes forth, for the moment, at least, wearing the garb of poetry. Never was the conception of the evolutionary continuity of nature more marvellously rendered, as successive zones

Of several wonder open on some spirit
Flying secure and glad from heaven to heaven.

The young poet had even grasped, what took the world

another half-century to perceive, that the idea of evolution levelled upwards and not downwards, spiritualised nature rather than naturalised spirit.

The minor characters of *Paracelsus* need not detain us. Festus is the commonsense foil of the hero, and the gentle domestic Michal, maiden and sorrowing mother, is only less of a shadow than Pauline. Aprile is an unsubstantial moonstruck "wraith of a poet," who "would love infinitely and be loved" but his *rôle* is most significantly derived and borrowed and accidental.

I saw Aprile—my Aprile there!
And as the poor melodious wretch disburthened
His heart, and moaned his weakness in my ear,
I learned my own deep error.

Paracelsus learnt from him "the worth of love in man's estate and what proportion love should hold with power." It was this new knowledge which made him wise to know mankind, be proud

Of their half-reasons, faint aspirings, dim
Struggles for truth, their poorest fallacies,
"all with a touch of nobleness ... upward tending,"
Like plants in mines which never saw the sun,
But dream of him, and guess where he may be,
And do their best to climb and get to him.

With this knowledge, this "splendour of God's lamp" on his dying brow, he is as secure of "emerging one day," as he was when he first set forth "to prove his soul." *Paracelsus,* on its publication, was hailed by the ever faithful and watchful Fox; but the most striking notice it received was from John Forster.

He predicted for the author a brilliant career, and, in a second article on the poem, said, with unusual daring as well as insight, "Without the slightest hesitation we name Mr. Robert Browning at once with Shelley, Coleridge, Wordsworth." But, by most journals, *Paracelsus* was simply neglected. In his letters to Elizabeth Barrett, Browning refers to the contemptuous treatment it received. It brought him neither money nor fame.

But it brought him, first, the acquaintance, and, then, the friendship, of the most distinguished men of the day—among them were Wordsworth, Dickens, Landor and Carlyle; and in nothing was the manly munificence of Browning's nature more evident than in his friendships. His affection for Landor, touched with sympathy as well as admiration, showed itself, in later years, in a care for him which was "one of the most beautiful incidents in a beautiful life."

The friendship with Carlyle was, on both sides, peculiarly warm and trustful. "I have just seen dear Carlyle," says Browning, "catch me calling people 'dear,' in a hurry"; and that Carlyle should cross over to Paris just to see and dine with Browning is, assuredly, eloquent of his regard and affection for the young poet.

"Commanded of me by my venerated friend Thomas Carlyle," says Browning of his translation of *Agamemnon,* "and rewarded will it indeed become if I am permitted to dignify it by the prefatory insertion of his dear and noble name." John Forster and William Macready were also added at this time to the group of Browning's friends and his acquaintance with the latter had, for a time, an important bearing upon his work. In *Pauline* and *Paracelsus,* it has been well said, Browning had "analysed rather than exhibited" character.

The soul, "the one thing" which he thought "worth knowing," was the psychologist's abstract entity, little more than a stage occupied successively by moods and passions: it was not the concrete, complex self, veined and blood-tinctured. Moreover (which signifies much), all its history fell within itself, and external circumstance, instead of furnishing it with the material out of which character is hewn, was but "decoration," to use Browning's own phrase, and was purposely put into the background.

These two poems were thus justly called "confessional": they were subjective and self-conscious. No sooner was *Paracelsus* finished than Browning contemplated another "soul-history." In it, once more, a greatly aspiring soul was to recognize, only at the last moment and after much "apparent failure," the mission which could save, fitting to the finite his infinity. The story that he wished to tell was *Sordello.*

In the preface to *Strafford,* Browning says that "he had for some time been engaged on a Poem of a very different nature, when induced to make the present attempt." This poem, as already hinted, was *Sordello,* Browning's second study of a poetic soul, but a soul, this time, caught in the context of large and imperious circumstance and quite unlike Aprile.

Many have explained *Sordello,* and some have comprehended it. It is uncompromisingly and irretrievably difficult reading. No historical account of the conflicts of Ghibelline and Guelph, no expository annotation of any kind, not even its own wealth of luminous ideas or splendour of Italian city scenes and solitudes, can justify it entirely as a work of art.

We may render its main plot in simple terms: how Sordello, endowed with powers that might have made him the Apollo of his people and victorious in a contest of song over Eglamor, his poetic foil, finds, unexpectedly, eminent station and political power within his grasp, but gains a victory of another kind, rising superior to the temptation doubly urged by the Ghibelline captain and the beauty of Parma; how the double victory has still left him a dabbler and loiterer, a Hamlet in both poetry and politics; how, clinging to his ideal, the cause of humanity, but failing to make it dominant over his "finite" world, he "dies under the strain of choice."

But no simplification of the story suffices. It is dark from the very intensity and multiplicity of the playing cross-lights; for the main ideas are reflected innumerably from the countless facets of the facts which the poet displays in confusingly rapid succession.

Brilliancy, swiftness of movement, the sudden exclamation made to convey a complex thought, the crowded intrusion of parenthetical antecedents, the elision of connecting relatives—such are the characteristics which make it difficult to decipher. It is no wonder that the appearance of *Sordello,* in 1840, destroyed the somewhat timid promise of public favour which

Paracelsus had brought to the poet. We are told that the "gentle literary public" of those days had found *Sartor Resartus* unintelligible, and frankly turned away from Browning. But the suggested comparison is misleading and the criticism is unfair.

The difficulties of *Sartor* have disappeared with the new times which Carlyle introduced; those of *Sordello* will stay so long as the mental structure of men remains the same. "I blame no one," said Browning, "least of all myself, who did my best then and since."

It was in no perverse mood of intellectual pride or of scorn for the public mind that he wrote *Sordello*. His error was, rather, the opposite. "Freighted full of music," crowded with the wealth of his detailed knowledge, rapt with the splendour of his poetic visions, he, in the simplicity of his heart, forgot his public so completely as to assume, as a matter of course, that his readers were able to wing their flight at his side.

There are evidences that the experience was painful and that its effects lasted. In *The Ring and the Book,* and elsewhere, there is, in the resolute simplification of the narrative and the painful iteration, a clue to the effect of the failure of *Sordello* upon his workmanship.

Both as he entered upon and as he closed that greatest of all his poetic adventures, there is a hint of a challenge and a touch of reproof, and even scorn, of the "British Public

ye who like me not,
(God love you!)—whom I yet have laboured for,
Perchance more careful whoso runs may read
Than erst when all, it seemed, could read who ran.

But it is time to turn to the outward events of this period of Browning's life. These were his journey to Italy and the removal of the family to Hatcham. He started for Italy on Good Friday, 1838, travelling as sole passenger on a merchantman.

On the voyage, he wrote the glorious story of the ride from Ghent to Aix, and *Home Thoughts from the Sea*. One of his objects was to gather materials for *Sordello;* but he harvested much more from his visit. It was, for him, "a time of enchantment." He saw Asolo and Venice and Padua; he visited mountain solitudes, and he brought home a passionate and enduring love for Italy. Italian themes were, henceforth, to be favourites of his imagination, and his life in that country was, for many years to come, to saturate his experience.

Browning himself, however, suggests two points of view from which the poems may be observed. He characterises them all as "dramatic." How far is this qualification accurate? Was Browing's genius verily dramatic in character?

The question is not easily answered, even although it can be profitably asked. In comparison with Wordsworth, who was both the most selfcontained and the most impersonal of all our poets, we must answer the question with a clear affirmative. But, compared with Shakespeare, or with Sir Walter Scott (as novelist), the difference is so great as to make the epithet "dramatic" positively misleading.

Of not one of Shakespeare's creations can we say "Here is the author himself"; of scarcely one of Browning's can we say "Here the author is not." Browning, in writing to Elizabeth Barrett, called the poems "Mere escapes of my inner power, like the light of a revolving lighthouse leaping out at intervals from a narrow chink." The analogy is true in more than one sense.

The poems carry suggestions of the abundance of riches within the poet's own living, alert, enterprising, sense-fraught, passion-fused soul; the motley throng of his *Dramatic Lyrics, Dramatic Romances* and *Dramatis Personae* also stand in the brilliant glare of his personality—not in the unobtrusive, quiet light of common day. There is hardly a stratum of society, an age of history, a corner of the world of man, which is altogether absent from these poems; nevertheless, we never escape the sense of the author's powerful presence. In all the diversities of type, race and character, there are persistent qualities, and they are the poet's own.

There is no quality of Shakespeare's mind which can be found in all his plays, except, perhaps, his gentleness; even as only the one epithet "gentle" satisfies when we speak of Shakespeare himself. But "gentleness" is just tolerance suffused with kindliness; and, where tolerance is perfect, preferences disappear, and the poet himself remains always revealing and never revealed.

To deny tolerance to Browning is impossible, and would utterly destroy his claim to be dramatic. There is a real sense in which he stands aloof from his creations, neither approving nor disapproving but letting them go. Bishop Blougram and Mr. Sludge; Caliban and the bishop of St. Praxed's; the lady of *The Laboratory* and of *The Confessional;* the lion of *The Glove* with "those eyes wide and steady,"

leagues in the desert already,
Driving the flocks up the mountain,

and the live creatures in *Sibrandus Schafnaburgensis*—"worm, slug, eft, with serious features," tickling and tousing and browsing him all over—all these are given a place in the sun, no less than his Valence or Caponsacchi, Colombe or Constance. It were unpardonable in a critic not to recognise that, for Browning, there was no form which the human soul could take that was too strange, complex, monstrous, magnificent, commonplace and drab, in its hate or love or in any other passion, to be interesting in the artistic and purely impersonal sense.

All the same, his tolerant universality is not like Shakespeare's in quality. There are, in Browning, no characters whom we must condemn and, also, must approve; whom we cannot justify and would not miss, but like beyond all speech or sense.

There is no Jack Falstaff, nor even a Dogberry, or Bottom, or Launce, far less a Touchstone. There is no Bob Acres, even, or Sir Anthony Absolute. Browning *will* persist in appealing to our reason. It is always a question of what accepts or refuses to accept its control. Morality, at rare moments, is allowed to see to itself, and the beautiful and ugly stand justified or condemned in their own right.

But truth always matters to him, and his intellectualising propensities never rest. The play of fancy is rarely quite irresponsible, and of humour more rarely still. There is no touch in Browning of the singing rogue Autolycus. Some of his lyrics, no doubt, are as light as they are lovely; and *The Pied Piper* is by no means the only first-rate example of joyous story-telling.

Nevertheless, Browning, many as are the parts he plays, is not like Bottom—he cannot aggravate his voice and roar us gently. He is never splendidly absurd, nor free of every purpose. Even at this period, he is plagued with problems, crammed with knowledge, crowded with mental energy, a revolving lighthouse bursting with light. In a word, he is intense and purposive, and his purposiveness and intensity had many consequences, not all of them favourable to his dramatic work.

A brief study of these is illuminative of his whole work as a poet. "Hold on, hope hard in the subtle thing that's spirit," he said, in *Pacchiarotto*. He laid stress "on the incidents in the development of a soul," he tells us, in his preface to *Sordello*, "little else is worth study." This was more than a fundamental idea to Browning, it was a constitutional propensity; and it drove him to the drama. But the confession of it implies the consciousness of a mission, and the artist, at his best, knows no mission of that kind.

He is in the service of no conception that the intellect can shape or express, or of no purpose that the will can frame and fix. His rapture is as fine and careless as that of the thrush, and he is snatched up and away by themes that define themselves only in the process of creation and, in the end, escape all definition and stand forth as miracles. But this absence of purpose we do not often find in Browning.

His dramatic pieces are not at leisure; the poet himself never strolls, but is always set upon some business, even among his *Garden Fancies*. For the same reason, there are no genuine little incidents in Browning's plays. Little things are apt to be symbolic—pinpoint rays of intense light coming from afar are imprisoned in them: they suggest grave meanings: possibly, for instance, the failure of the whole life, through making love, at some moment, a merely second-best.

Why did not you pinch a flower
In a pellet of clay and fling it?

Why did not I put a power
Of thanks in a look, or sing it?

The whole atmosphere ot the plays is heavily charged with significance; and many characters, in consequence, are, from beginning to end, in some highly-strung mood. There is tragic tension in the very first words that Mildred speaks: "Sit, Henry—do not take my hand."

The moral strain deepens with the next question, and it is never relaxed. No breath of fresh air from the unheeding outer world comes to break the spell, and, at the same time, to deepen, by contrast, the pathos and tragedy of Mildred's overmastering consciousness that she does not deserve, and will never hold in her arms, the happiness that seemed to stand close by.

It is, probably, this preliminary, purposive surcharging of the characters and incidents that led Dowden to say that the dramatic genius of Browning was in the main of the static kind; it studies with extraordinary skill and subtlety character in position; it attains only an imperfect or laboured success with character in movement.

As it stands, this dictum is unsound. Restless energy is always straining against the poet's control. His genius is dramatic, precisely in virtue of the sense of movement which it conveys, and the feeling that life is process and nothring else, a continuous new creation of itself carried on by itself.

Even in *The Ring and the Book,* where the poet not only knows but tells the end at the beginning, the dramatic quality of movement is present. The story expands at each telling, like circles in water.

The facts are transformed with each successive telling of them, by one and the other Half-Rome, Guido, Caponsacchi, Pompilia, The Pope and the lawyers. Not for a moment does the story stand still, nor does the reader feel that he is being told of past events, as in listening to an essentially epic poet, like Milton. Browning's poems are never stagnant: tragedy never hangs overhead, as in *Hamlet,* a black, motionless, delayed thundercloud; but the lightning is always ablaze. There are crowded happenings, and the heat and hurry of situations crashing into their consequences. Browning's genius is essentially dynamic, and there is abundant movement.

What Browning's characters lack is objectivity—if we may borrow a term from the philosophers. Such is the intensity of his interest in "the incidents in the development of a soul" that it transfuses not only the *dramatis personae* but the world in which they live. The outer world is not genuinely outer.

It does not exist for its own sake, carrying on its own processes, "going on just the same," whether men and women laugh or weep, live or die, utterly indifferent to every fate, distinguishing not in the least between great things and small, evil things and good, allowing "both the proudly riding and the foundering bark." It is not a world aloof from man, non-moral and, on surface reading, non-rational, the sphere of sheer caprice and the playground of accident. The world is the stage and background for Browning's characters and supplies the scenery they need.

What is done by his personages, therefore, is not the result of intercourse between human character and what, in itself, is an entirely natural world. And, consequently, what takes place lacks that appearance of contingency in collusion with necessity of which the true dramatist makes tragic use. When he is most completely under the spell of his muse, the true dramatist cannot tell beforehand what will happen to his men and women, or how they will behave. He is at the mercy of two unknowns: the inexhaustible possibilities of man's nature, and of the response which it will make to the never-ending contingencies of an indifferent outer world.

He has no preconceived theory, no scheme of life, no uniformities or necessities which can be labelled: the unity of his work, as a work of art, has some more mystic source than any of these things. But we cannot quite say this of Browning. His men and women cannot be called embodiments of *Ápriori* conceptions; meant to illustrate a doctrine or point a moral; and, yet, their intercourse with their fellows and interaction with the world have no genuinely fashioning potency.

Nothing quite new or quite unexpected ever happens to

them. They are not in a world where unexpected things are permitted to happen. Had not Macbeth *happened* to meet the witches on the moor, with the excitement of the battle not yet subsided in his blood, he might have lived and died a loyal and victorious general.

And what side-winds of mere accidents there are in *Othello* and *Hamlet!* These dramas are like life, because the fate which is irresistible comes clothed in accident and with its chaplet all awry and as careless as that of a Bacchic dancer. The accidents seem trivial, too, and might easily not have taken place or have been turned aside, until they *have* taken place.

Then, and not till then, do we feel that they were meant, and that they were as inevitable as destiny. But Browning's plays can be seen from afar to march straightforward to their consummation; and the world in which they take place is all too obtrusively "a moral order."

The personages are, from the first, inwardly charged with some dominant passion or propensity. They are dedicated, even when they are complex, to some one form of good or of evil; and some one misdeed stains the whole of life like ink in water.

They are enveloped in their own atmosphere, and outer incidents cannot affect their career; carried along by the powers within as if by a driving storm; freighted full from the first with their destiny: Pym with his love of England; Mildred with the guilt of her innocence; Luria with his "own East"; Tresham with the pride of family and the 'scutcheon without a blot; Valence with his stormy rectitude and great heart.

This is the only sense in which Browning's dramas lack movement, and his method may be called static. His characters are impervious to outward influence, except in so far as it serves to discharge what is already within. Within the inner realm of passions, emotions, volitions, ambitions, and the world which these catch up in their career, there is no lack of movement.

A plenitude of powers all active are revealed by him: they co-operate, sever, mingle, collide, combine, and are all astrain—but they are all psychical. Browning places us in the parliament of the mind. It is the powers of mind to which we listen in high debate. And we are reminded by them of the fugues of Master Hugues of Saxe-Gotha:

One dissertates, he is candid;
Two must discept-has distinguished;
Three helps the couple, if ever yet man did;
Four protests; Five makes a dart at the thing wished:
Back to One, goes the case bandied.

And they require scope to declare themselves, as they reveal the wonder-world of the human soul. Now, we have stated these points somewhat fully because they seem to throw light upon the whole of Browning's work as a poet.

The tendency towards dwelling upon ideal issues rather than upon outer deeds, on the significance of facts for souls, and the insignificance of all things save in the soul's context, was always present in Browning; so, also, was the tendency towards monologue, with its deliberate, ordered persistency.

And both of these tendencies grew. External circumstance became, more and more, the mere garb of the inner mood; deeds, more and more, the creatures of thoughts; and all real values were, more and more, undisguisedly ideal ministrants to man's need of beauty, or goodness, or love and happiness.

But to say this is to admit not only that the dramatic element in his poetry was on the wane, but that his poetry was itself becoming more deliberately reflective. And the spirit of reflection which rejects first appearances, sublimates sense and its experience into meanings, is, to say the least, as characteristic of philosophy as it is of art. It is philosophy rather than art which concentrates upon principles, and which allows facts and events to dwindle into instances of general laws.

Art must value a thing for what it is in itself, not for the truth which it exemplifies. The reference of the beautiful object beyond itself to a beauty that is eternal must be, for art, as undesigned as the music of a harp swung in the wind.

And, when a poet takes to illustrating themes, or the unity of his poems, instead of being a mystic harmony of elements mingling of themselves, comes of a set purpose which can be stated in words, then, indeed, is the glory of art passing into the grey. The poet outlived the dramatist in Browning, and, if the poet did not succumb to the philosopher, it was because of the strength of the purely lyrical element in his soul and the marvellous wealth of his sensuous and emotional endowments.

His humanity was too richly veined for him to become an abstract thinker; and certain apparent accidents of his outer life conspired with the tendencies of his poetic genius to lead them away from the regular drama.

One of these was his quarrel over *A Blot in the 'Scutcheon* with Macready, for whom and at whose request this play was written. But Macready's affairs were entangled; he would withdraw from his arrangement with Browning, was not frank with him, but shuffled: and Browning was angered, imperious and explosive.

The play was produced but "damned," apparently not by the audience but by Macready's own stage and press arrangements. *The Times* pronounced it "one of the most faulty dramas we ever beheld," and *The Athenaeum* called it "a puzzling and unpleasant business," and the characters inscrutable and abhorrent. This was in 1843.

The quarrel with Macready was not the poet's only unpleasant experience of the stage. Soon after this incident, Charles Kean negotiated with Browning for a suitable play, and, in March, 1844, *Colombe's Birthday* was read to him and approved. But Kean asked that it should be left with him, unpublished, till the Easter of the following year. Browning, however, thought the long delay unreasonable, was, possibly, doubtful of the actor's good faith and resolved to publish the play at once.

It was not acted till 1853, when it was produced by Phelps with Helen Faucit as heroine and ran for a fortnight. But it was reviewed on publication by Forster—who said that he abominated the tastes of Browning as much as he respected his genius. Forster repented, called on Browning and was "very profuse of graciocities"; but their friendship had received a fatal injury. Browning concluded that there was too much "spangle" and "smutch" in connection with actors, and wrote no more for the stage.

During the years 1844-5, Browning made a series of contributions to *Hood's Magazine.* The series included *The Flight of the Duchess* and *The Bishop orders his Tomb at Saint Praxed's Church.* The poet, having gone to Italy in 1844, and having visited the grave of Shelley, had turned into the little church of Saint Prassede near Santa Maria Maggiore.

Browning was at the height of his power during this period. Nowhere is his poetic work so uniformly great as in *Dramatis Personae* (1864); and there is no doubt that *The Ring and the Book* is the most magnificent of all his achievements, in spite of its inequalities.

Critics miss in *Dramatis Personae* something of the lightness and brightness and early morning charm of *Pippa Passes* and of some of his earlier *Men and Women;* and they find in it, not any trace of the pathetic fallacy, yet a lingering echo of the brooding sorrow for his life's loss.

It was later in the day; the world was more commonplace; the outlook more desolate and man's failure less tinged with glory; women were more homely, love was less ethereal; and the stuff to be idealised through being better known by a wiser love was more stubborn.

"The summer had stopped," and "the sky was deranged." But the autumn had come, bringing a richer harvest in *Dramatis Personae.* The significance of man's life, and of the clash of circumstance which elicited it, was deeper as well as more grave.

The world's worn look disappears when it is seen in the great context in which it stands—"All we have willed or hoped or dreamed of good shall exist," says Abt Vogler. Man has himself "a flash of the will that can," for he can use its distraught elements of life to a moral purpose, and weld them in a spiritual harmony—out of three sounds make, "not a fourth sound, but a star."

Prospice, Rabbi Ben Ezra, A Death in the Desert, even Mr. Sludge, "The Medium" and *Caliban upon Setebos,* are strong with a controlled ethical passion for what is real and true as things stand, and by interest in the issues which are ultimate; and, with realism, natural and spiritual, in both kinds, there is blended an imaginative splendour which transfigures even "the least of all mankind," when we "look at his head and heart"; and see what I tell you—nature dance

About each man of us, retire, advance,
As though the pageant's end were to enhance
His worth, and—once the life, his product, gained—Roll away elsewhere.

It is a permanent theme, its echoes are to be heard all the way to *Asolando*—this wash of circumstance around man's soul which yet maintains its mastery over all the play of the waves; and nowhere is it rendered more finely than in *Dramatis Personae* and its *Epilogue. The Edinburgh Review* found it a "subject of amazement that poems of so obscure and uninviting a character should find numerous readers"; and there were other critics besides Frederick Tennyson who still thought Browning's poetry "the most grotesque conceivable."

But the situation had, in truth, changed. Browning's admirers were no longer confined to pre-Raphaelites and "young men at the Universities." A second edition of *Dramatis Personae* was called for within the same year as the first. And the reception accorded to *The Ring and the Book* was still more favourable. At last, Browning was coming into his kingdom. It had taken long: so late as 1867, he spoke of himself as "the most unpopular poet that ever was."

There was an interval of four years between *Dramatis Personae and The Ring and the Book.* But the theme had interested him from the moment when he came upon the "old, square, yellow book" on an old bookstall in Florence—the parchmentbound tale of the trial of an Italian noble for the murder of his wife. He saw its dramatic possibilities when he stood on the balcony of Casa Guidi, in June, 1860, at night, watching the storm.

But it lay long working in his mind, and the sorrow of the following year led him to abandon the idea of writing, and he suggested the subject to two of his friends. In September, 1862, he recurred to it, spoke of "my new poem that is about to be," "the Roman murder story." He began to write it about 1864, and the poem grew steadily, for it became his crowning venture and he gave it regularly every day "three quiet, early morning hours."

It was published in four volumes, the first of which appeared in November, 1868; and the others during the three months following.

Many things concurred to make the story attractive to Browning. He had inherited a taste for tales of crime from his father; the situation was ambiguous and, as regards the priest and the girl-wife, it left room for a most beautiful, as well as for a sordid, explanation, and, therefore, it appealed both to Browning's love of argument and to his ethical idealism; moreover, opinion in Rome was divided, and the popular mind was on its trial; there was the possibility that the truth "told for once for the church, and dead against the world, the flesh, and the devil"; and the story, in its essence, was not a common drab, but glorious—the romance of the young priest and Pompilia was "a gift of God, who showed for once how he would have the world go white."

It was inevitable that such a theme should set free all the powers of Browning's spirit; but it borrowed sublimity and a sacred loveliness from another quarter. For, undoubtedly, the "poem which enshrined Pompilia was instinct with reminiscence." "With all its abounding vitality it was yet commemorative and memorial."

When he wrote of "the one prize vouchsafed unworthy me"; of "the one blossom that made me proud at eve"; of a "life companioned by the woman there"; of living and seeing her learn, and learning by her, can there be doubt as to who lent to these utterances their pathetic beauty. Nor is it fanciful to find in Caponsacchi something of the poet himself—more, perhaps, than in any other character he created.

There was his own tempestuousness, much that a wise old pope could find "amiss," "blameworthy," "ungainly," "discordant," "infringement manifold" of convention; but there was also a "symmetric soul within," "championship of God at first blush," "prompt, cheery thud of glove on ground," answering "ringingly the challenge of the false knight." What are these qualities, with the ardour of a great love and the headlong and utter devotion of a large-hearted manhood, except the poet's own? Caponsacchi's

> I am, on earth, as good as out of it,
> A relegated priest; when exile ends,
> I mean to do my duty and live long,

is inspired by the manly recoil of Browning and his refusal to be crushed by his sorrow. But the dream of having his "Iyric Love" by his side has been broken; and the bereaved poet is not perceptible in the "drudging student," who "trims his lamp," "draws the patched gown close" and awakes "to the old solitary nothingness."

The last words are a promise of this priest to "pass content, from such communion"; and Browning would fain have come back into the world of men as if his wound had healed. But the truth breaks out—

> great, just, good God! Miserable me!

There was, for both priest and poet, the rule in the world of a love that wrapped all things round about, and yet, somehow, also, there were sorrows that knew neither shores nor shoals.

To pass all the parts of this great poem under review is not possible, and to estimate the relative poetic worth of its several parts—*Caponsacchi, Pompilia, The Pope and Guido*—is not necessary; there are kinds as well as degrees of perfection, and comparison is sometimes absurd.

The possibility of justifying the structure of the poem as a whole will remain doubtful; and the macaronic speeches of the lawyers, and some parts of what Rome said, have no real artistic value. But the poem is unique in its excellence as well as in its defects. The text of 1888-9, set it against Browning's corrections to earlier editions and errors by typesetters and made 108 emendations of which nineteen were substantive changes and the rest, minor.

The four final 'books' of the poem are individually introduced and there is the now standard plethora of footnotes explaining the editors' changes. Of great use to students and scholars are the three appendices. The first, 'The Cadaver Synod' was taken from Browning's father's notebooks and gives us a new insight into Browning's historical basis for the poem.

The second concerns the variants between his edition and the Yale version whilst the third gives a list of compositors. The Afterword somewhat surprisingly comes after the Appendices and is by Michael Meredith (the general editor) and Signora Simonetta Berbeglia and is entitled 'The Truth behind the Franceschini Murder Case'.

This is a fascinating piece of research which shows the relationship between Browning's poem and the facts behind Guido Franceschini's murder of his wife, Pompilia. As before the editors are to be heartily congratulated on a masterly piece of editing.

Chapter 3

From Derrida to Browning

"I am involved," declares John Schad, "in an experiment of reading, an experiment that is best described as an extended version of the seventeenth-century poetic conceit". The conceit appropriately characterizes the capricious design of Schad's ambitious study. His critical aim, he says, is to put into practice a radical form of "poststructuralist intertextuality". This method involves "not so much making connections as discovering them" between pairings of poets and theorists: Christina Rossetti and Luce Irigaray; Matthew Arnold and Michel Foucault; Robert Browning and Jacques Derrida; Gerard Manley Hopkins and Jacques Lacan; and Elizabeth Barrett Browning and Helene Cixous.

Schad states that these poetic and theoretical combinations remain "in some sense arbitrary," since they are the result of "interpretive ingenuity".

His book, after all, "is concerned with accidents of meaning which take place between two bodies of writing that are usually thought of as being separated by language, genre and period". Such accidents, Schad acknowledges, certainly lead him toward the extremity of what one of Robert Browning's most satirized monologists-the boozy Bishop Blougram —styles "the dangerous edge of things."

Schad is fully aware that his hermeneutic procedures, for all their ingenuity, "place some strain on a conventional sense of literary history". This strain, Schad readily admits, suffers greatest torsion when he asserts that Hopkins (in poems like "The Bugler's First Communion") "anticipates the First World War that so concerns The Waste Land that so concerns Lacan in 'The Insistence of the Letter'". These otherwise unrelated texts, as he points out, share a direct or indirect interest in types of military conflict. Schad justifies showing how these writings accidentally anticipate one another on the grounds that "such a transhistorical reading is ... internal to both Victorian and poststructuralist writing".

According to this logic, the Victorian poets were always already caught up in the same mentalite as their loosely grouped poststructuralist heirs. To support this idea, Schad recalls Foucault's observation, in the first volume of The History of Sexuality, that "we" (persons of the late twentieth century) are the "other Victorians."

Schad makes these truly large claims about history, theory, and Victorian poetry in an introduction that terminates abruptly after four breathless pages. And he is probably wise not to have subjected these claims to detailed examination because it would have undoubtedly impeded the interpretive ingenuity that animates much of his ensuing discussion. An altogether more convincing book, however, would surely have emerged had Schad chosen to withdraw at times from the dangerous edge where arbitrary accidents frequently come to grief.

No matter how openly unconventional in his approach, Schad requires firmer argumentative ground on which to more rationally than randomly elaborate his authoritative knowledge of Victorian poetry and poststructuralist theory. Unquestionably, Schad possesses a vigilant critical eye that is always quick to identify complex textual features. He is acutely sensitive, for example, to the suggestive ways in which Hopkins's "The Wreck of the Deutschland" represents the body "asunder"-a word that may, he says, be read as "as-under," since the body "functions as a fragmented subtext, or unconscious" in the poem.

Schad is equally adept at accentuating moments of dazzling wordplay—such as the counter-pointing of "all" and "fall" that creates such a powerful dialectic in Hopkins's "Pied Beauty." Indeed, Schad's responsiveness to these linguistic intricacies, ones that bear traces of meaning that can remain obscure to commonsense reading, yields occasional benefits—but only if and when one can keep up with his often reckless maneuvering.

Without explaining the order in which he has arranged his chapters, Schad opens with a study of femininity in Irigaray's Speculum (on the Platonic cave as "hystera") and Rossetti's "The Lowest Room" (where her speaker occupies the "place assigned" her, which she terms the "lowest place"). Schad tells us that for both poet and theorist "the place that is woman ... is below". With this conceit in place, he promptly launches into a sequence of accidental observations that sometimes prove illuminating.

He remarks, for instance, how Rossetti's representation of femininity concurs with Irigaray's assertion that women remain suspended "between the lines," in a space where the patriarchal letter inscribes the sexual law. (In Rossetti's poem, he reminds us, the speaker describes her life as "Line graven on line and stroke on stroke") This is a thought-provoking link, one that raises many ideas about Rossetti's manner of textualizing femininity's "lowest place."

As he later comments, Rossetti's women speakers frequently appear to inhabit a realm of quotation, where they are compelled to cite—while desiring to subvert—the fathers' cultural script.

Schad, however, remains so determined to discover countless correspondences between the poet's and theorist's interest in femininity's "lowest place" that his sprightly critical movement back and forth between the two writers often prevents him from producing little more than a list of themes. He maintains, for example, that "Rossetti's daughterly concern with the 'I' of a woman recently dead" in "A Chilly Night" "is paralleled by Irigaray's philosophical concern with Descartes' 'eye of a man recently dead'".

To be sure, Schad upholds this parallel-itself quite tenuous but potentially engaging-by stating that Irigaray's attempt to visualize the Cartesian cogito from behind its mirrored screen resembles Rossetti's fascination with giving voice to dead female personae who occupy a realm on the other side of the mortal "L" But once he has conjured the conceit, Schad's ceaseless metonymic spirit urges him to connect Rossetti's detestation of the "vulgar optic" with general crises within "Victorian optics."

At this juncture he lists famous quotations from Ruskin on the "innocent eye" and Dickens's Mr. Sleary on the "fixed eye of Philosophy" before mentioning "the period's scientific fascination with the physiology of the eye" and Rossetti's "thyroid disorder which left her with bulging eyes".

Even though this startling chain of associations sustains at least some thematic continuity, it is pretty difficult to know how or why he arrives at the illness (Graves' disease) that seriously disfigured Rossetti's face in middle age. Eager to discover further thematic links, Schad instantly catches sight of yet another accident waiting to happen: namely, the proximity between Graves' disease and how "Rossetti's relationship to the eye is marked by death in much the same punning way as is Irigaray's".

"[F] or `Graves,'" Schad instructs us, "read 'Kore'—the bride of Hades" ("kore represents for Irigaray a dark opening to the concave back of the eye"). In my (no doubt restrictive) view, his imperative that we must read one thing for another "in much the same ... way" can only deepen the mystifying darkness of his metaphorical abyss. But maybe that is Schad's point.

The remaining four chapters run hastily into comparable methodological hazards. In his discussion of Arnold's poetry and Foucault's theory, Schad begins by placing well-known lines about "The Sea of Faith" from "Dover Beach" next to remarks about "man" as a "recent invention" that might at some time be "erased, like a face drawn in the sand at the edge of the sea" from The Order of Things.

Schad contends that the oceanic movement in both writings belongs "in a sense" to "the same sea". What is more, he insists, "it is this same man, man produced by the retreat of faith, who is threatened with disappearance on Foucault's beach a hundred years later". Even though one might concede that Arnold and Foucault are grappling with analogous conceptual problems (such as the fragility of the category "man" in an era when agnosticism and atheism gather strength), Schad's method, again, is able to do little more than describe the fact that these writers draw on a similar metaphorical resource—one whose flattened-out sameness, I feel, is open to some question.

In any case, Schad's tracing of the seas that ebb and flow in "Dover Beach" and The Order of Things, in 1867 and 1966 respectively, does not add significantly to our understanding of familiar aspects of both works.

Elsewhere, however, Schad's comparative method points toward intriguing insights, if still refusing to explore what they might imply. In the chapter on Browning and Derrida, Schad mentions the racialized metaphors of blackness that appear in both the poet's anti-spiritualist satire "Mr. Sludge, 'The Medium'" and the theorist's post-Cold War Specters of Marx.

We learn that Sludge (Browning's far from subtle moniker for the United States medium-cum-con-man Daniel Dunglas Home) is at one point "accused of being a 'hybrid,' literally the child of a slave and a freeman". Schad immediately remarks that "to mediate between the living and the dead is, it seems, to mediate between master and slave".

But rather than investigate the fascinating link between mediumship and "medial[ing] between master and slave,"Schad speeds ahead to make fresh connections with cultural context: "'Mr. Sludge' is not only written by the son of a former master of a West Indian plantation but published within eighteen months of Abraham Lincoln's emancipation of slaves".

Perhaps these pieces of biographical and historical information are supposed to elucidate the momentousness of slavery to Robert Browning. Yet Schad's characteristically brisk run of sentences chooses not to comment on Browning Sr.'s horror at plantation life at St. Kitts and Browning Jr.'s response to the abolitionist struggle. Instead Schad observes that "the poem makes its ghosts work as a metaphor for slaves".

He has, it seems, only passing interest in the historical forces that energize those metaphorical specters with such satirical glee.

It should be abundantly clear that Schad's book strikes me as misconceived. Yet, on occasion, one cannot help but admire his eager intelligence and compendious grasp of the field. Moreover, his scholarship certainly deserves better treatment from his pubfisher, which has allowed more than a few typographical howlers to creep into the text. The first name of Wilfred Owen, for instance, appears—ironically enough in a book celebrating verbal play—as "Wildred".

This kind of negligence encouraged me to think about why I had felt (perhaps appositely) "wildered" by a study that ends not with a conclusion but with an unexplained verse from the Acts of the Apostles: "These have turned the world upside down have come hither also".

This "wildered" reading-effect, however, is one of the book's unhappier accidents since it suggests that Schad's enthusiasm for topsy-turvy meanings can prove dangerously infectious. All the more reason, then, to contest Schad's marked resistance to analyzing the intellectual consequences of his experimental conceit.

Chapter 4

Brownings Prophyria's Lover

In Robert Browning's early dramatic monologue "Porphyria's Lover," first published as "Porphyria" in the Monthly Repository for January 1836, the speaker describes how he murders the woman he loves. Michael Mason discovered two related sources for the murder in John Wilson's "Extracts from Gosschen's Diary" (published in Blackwoods for 1818) and Bryan Procter's poem "Marcian Colonna" (1820), which Procter acknowledged to be based on Wilson's narrative. Both pieces deal with the murder of a woman by her lover, sensationalizing the erotic aspects of the crime and the woman's dead body.

Browning retains elements of both texts. The claimed absence of suffering and details of the woman's white flesh, fair hair, and blue eyes are taken from Wilson; the all-night vigil and the appearance of animation after death are taken from Procter. However, I think there is also another text that underlies Browning's monologue, which suggests some details not found in either Wilson or Procter. Furthermore, this subtext and Browning's revisionary allusions to it provide a critical yardstick by which the speaker can take the measure of this monologist.

When Browning explored the type of the jealous and possessive male in "Porphyria's Lover" and "My Last Duchess," he drew on Shakespeare's treatment of this type in the character of Othello and also Leontes in The Winter's Tale. The drama of Othello, in which the misguided hero murders his wife, seems to me particularly important to "Porphyria's Lover."

In Othello, the eponymous protagonist is a romantic and passionate figure whose active and impressionable imagination is easily stimulated by Iago's calumny against Desdemona. Othello's romanticism is glimpsed early on in the play in a lyrical speech made as he disembarks after a stormy voyage and is reunited with his bride. Addressing Desdemona, he says,

O my soul's joy!
If after every tempest come such calms,
May the winds blow till they have waken'd death! ...
If it were now to die,
'Twere now to be most happy; for I fear
My soul hath her content so absolute
That not another comfort like to this
Succeeds in unknown fate. (2.1.184-93)

Othello's idealization of the death-in-bliss, a kind of sustained erotic consummation, precedes the later evolution of that figure in romantic poetry such as Keats's: "Now more than ever it seems rich to die, / To cease upon the midnight with no pain."

As a Victorian reacting against his romantic heritage, Browning parodies precisely this kind of romantic idealization in "Porphyria's Lover," where "that moment"-the moment in which the lover witnesses the woman's apparently wholehearted love-is also the moment that he attempts to preserve by killing her.

Browning, de-idealizing the romanticism of his predecessors, exposes the fatuity of this attempt, echoing Keats ironically in the lover's assurance: "No pain felt she, / I am quite sure she felt no pain".

In Othello, Desdemona's commonsensical response to her husband's inauspicious words-"The heavens forbid / But that our loves and contorts should increase / Even as our days do grow!"-suggests a maturer perspective that is unfortunately disappointed by the eventualities of the plot; for, like the storm that heralds the murder of "Porphyria's Lover," the storm clouds of Othello are already gathering.

Browning inflates and explodes romantic egotism: the

lover kills the woman, not himself. But the death that preserves the woman's imputed compliance is, Browning implies, but a formalization of the romantic male speaker's desire to fix and possess the female beloved. Romantic poetry idealizes the woman who is subject to the male gaze; she is the reflector and guarantor of male identity.

Hence the male anxiety about woman's independence, for her liberty puts masculine self-estimation at risk. Porphyria's lover wants her to remain "pure"; Othello, a prototype of the romantic male, believing Desdemona an adulteress, accuses her of being a corrupted text: "Was this fair paper, this most goodly book, / Made to write 'whore' upon?" He had thought he owned that original "pure" text which secured his sense of self.

The death of the innocent Desdemona is almost less scandalous than Othello's assumption that her adultery justifies his murdering her. His self-condemnation is provoked only by the discovery of her blamelessness.

Iago's malignity furnishes another feature of Browning's monologue. Having provoked Othello into murderous fury against his wife, Iago slyly suggests, "Do it not with poison; strangle her in her bed, even the bed she hath contaminated".

Strangulation does not occur in Wilson or Procter's texts, where the woman is stabbed or poisoned, but it is the method of murder preferred by Porphyria's lover, probably because it ensures that the all-important appearance of the woman remains unblemished. In point of fact, Othello resorts to smothering rather than strangling his wife, but the preservation of Desdemona's loveliness is a key factor in his decision:

Yet I'll not shed her blood,
Nor scar that whiter skin of hers than snow,
And smooth as monumental alabaster. (5.2.3-5)

As the lover fondly surveys his mistress's corpse after the murder, Othello eroticizes the soon-to-be-monumentalized body of Desdemona. However, unlike Porphyria's lover, Othello does have an understanding of the irrevocability of his action. He does not confuse life and death: "When I have pluck'd thy rose / I cannot give it vital growth again, / It needs must wither" (5.2.13-15). Othello's misgiving functions as an ironic echo in the lover's self-deluded, objectifying description of Porphyria's drooping head: "The smiling rosy little head, / So glad it has its utmost will".

The subtext of Othello presents us with certain admonitory reading cues that help us construe the reality of the situation and give us an index to the indulgent self-deception of the lover. Mason suggests that Browning uses source-texts that portray insanity, not to prove his monologist a lunatic, but to give "an illustration of how an act conventionally referable to insanity might be the act of a rational being."

I would contend that the pattern of Othello offers us another way of understanding a supposedly "rational" behaviour that is founded on dangerously idealized notions of love and an endorsement of male selfdetermination at the expense of female autonomy. The "lunacy" that Browning exposes is that his monologist's crime can be regarded as "rational."

The lover's act of violence thus casts it shadow on all those other less-dramatic acts of domination and appropriation that manage to pass unnoticed under the cover of rational male behavior. Browning uses Othello as the archetype of the deluded lover, the one who can declare himself "An honorable murderer, . .. / For nought I did in hate, but all in honor" (5.2.294-95).

We are only too aware that "honor" is a face-saver; "honor" represents Othello's attempt to protect his identity when under seeming threat. Browning shows us how apparently reasoned justification is founded on misprision, on fantasy, jealousy, fear, and aggression. The paradigm of Othello alerts us to the emotional disorder that underlies the logic of Browning's controlled and controlling lover.

Browning was born in Camberwell, south London, in 1812; the son of a banker father and a devoutly religious mother; he had one younger sister, Sarianna. The family were financially comfortable, and he was never troubled with having to earn his own living; but Browning looked about for something to do with his life. He enrolled in the newly formed London University in 1828 (as only the sixteenth entrant), but dropped out after a year; in 1834 he travelled to Saint Petersburg as the secretary of the Chevalier de Benkhausen, possibly contemplating a diplomatic career.

But by this stage his heart was already given to poetry. Reading in his father's extensive library throughout his youth, he had first fallen in love with Byron, producing a volume (now lost) of Byronic verses called *Incondita* in the mid 1820s.

A deeper and more lasting passion for Shelley followed, and Browning's first published poem, *Pauline* (1833), dramatises his own youthful struggles with religious faith and doubt, and his hero-worshipping of Shelley. It was privately printed, little noticed, and sold no copies at all, which discouraged its author a little.

Deciding that *Pauline* had been too personal and confessional, or as he put it too "subjective", Browning planned a more "objective" poetic work. This was *Paracelus* (1835), a lengthy poetic-drama based on the life of the Renaissance alchemist, which brought him some public attention.

After meeting the actor-manager William Macready (1793-1873), Browning was persuaded that he ought to write for the stage; a development that takes the "objectivity" he sought to a logical extreme. But of the seven theatrical tragedies he wrote over the next few years only one was performed and it was not a success.

He published a long-gestated epic poem *Sordello* in 1840, a version of the life-story of a medieval Italian poet; but the poem was greeted with astonishment, incomprehension and even outrage. Jane Carlyle, for example, declared she had read through the whole thing and had never worked out whether Sordello was a man, a city or a book.

With *Sordello* Browning established a reputation for obscurity and poetic affectation that dogged his career; although the poem was to some extent rehabilitated in the twentieth-century by the enthusiastic endorsement of Ezra

Pound. Learning from his setbacks, this period also saw Browning experimenting with the form of the shorter poem, and his is the most significant claim to having invented the dramatic monologue, in some senses the most important Victorian poetic form. Here, for example,is an extract from "Frà Lippo Lippi":

You speak no Latin more than I, belike;
However, you're my man, you've seen the world
- The beauty and the wonder and the power,
The shapes of things, their colours, lights and shades,
Changes, surprises, - and God made it all!
- For what? Do you feel thankful, ay or no,
For this fair town's fac

Iain Finlayson's hefty study of the private life of Robert Browning is the biographical equivalent of the equally bulky literary concordance, Berdoe's Browning Cyclopoedia, which apeared in 1891: each represents an enormous amount of work and thought.

Mr. Finlayson, very sensibly, has both consulted, and freely admitted to so doing, the plethora of works which has gone before him. He has been criticised for this, but how in all conscience could he not do so? This is a well-tilled field. How could he not? What he makes of it, what new shapes, is the point.

The plain truth is that biographically there is really little left to be done. One central incident apart, Browning's life was not an exciting one. It was, frankly, dull. His abduction of the frail, laudanum over-dosed and addicted, forty-year-old, marcescent spinster of Wimpole Street was his apogee, and it has been so ceaselessly replicated theatrically and filmically as to have become a virtual folkloric stereotype.

The real continuing interest in Browning revolves about the untangling of the complex of theologico-philosophical notions that fizzed in his brain. His poetry was his attempt to externalise that inner dialogue, but his obscurity of expression, as opposed to his expression of obscurity, provided a most daunting translative challenge.

Carlyle famously reported that his wife, Jane, wished to

know whether Sordello was a man, a city or a book. Douglas Jerrold, who started reading Sordello while recuperating from an illness, threw it down almost at once, exclaiming 'My God! I'm idiot. My health is restored, but my mind's gone. I can't understand two consecutive lines of an English poem'.

It was only when he discovered that none of his family could, either, that his equanimity was re-established. And Tennyson confided that the only lines that he understood were the first and the last of the poem.

It was not only his obscurantism, but his syntactical curiosities, eccentric versification and lack of clarificatory Tennysonian mellifluities, that set on edge the teeth of the critics of his day.

Browning's earliest poetic work, written under the spell of Shelley, was treated as a not very good joke. Pauline (1833), published anonymously, sold not a single copy. Its successor, Paracelsus (1835), fared little better.

Appreciation came in the wake of Men and Women (1855) and Dramatis Personoe (1864). He published his greatest work, The Ring and the Book, in 1869, twenty years before his death in Venice.

With Elizabeth dead, ensepulchred in Florence, their son, Robert Weidemann Barrett Browning, known, for some unknown reason, as 'Pen', provided the sustaining focal point of his father's remaining twenty-eight years of life.

Pen, of the cascade of shoulder-length golden curls, tiny 'trowsers', and bedecked with blue and white satin ribbons, had become a 'beefy and beery' middle-aged man in knickerbockers, with a reputation as a promiscuous Don Juan. Not just too pernickety in his personal habits, his Venetian home was christened 'Palazzo Pigsty'.

I would, and do, recommend this as the best book for the tyro, the student, the general reader, and even, in a revisionary context, for the expert. Mr. Finlayson is a superior stylist, albeit somewhat over inclined to self-indulgence in an obvious taste for Anglo-Saxon alliterative; but this is a mote rather than a beam.

The book is well, often beautifully, written, and contains,

as well as a summation, a reader's digest, a considerable amount of worth-while original thought and a perfectly splendid index.

While no book-length studies on Browning have appeared during this review period, the year has seen a healthy number of articles which apply a variety of critical approaches to individual poems.

They demonstrate how well the poet lends himself to many current critical paradigms, including queer and feminist interpretations, cognitive psychology, and readings informed by material culture and narratology. I will begin with articles which focus on gender.

In "Increasing Suspicion about Browning's Grammarian", Arnd Bohm adds another name to the list of possible inspirations for "A Grammarian's Funeral": Brunetto Latini, whom Dante's Inferno places in the circle of sodomites, although there is no clear evidence that the scholar was a homosexual.

Having explained that Brunetto may have been linked with sodomy through the suspicion of homosexual relationships between teachers and pupils and the medieval association of scholars interested in grammatical deviations with sexual deviance, Bohm reads Browning's poem as preoccupied with the grammarian's and the speaker's ambiguous gender identity.

The evidence he proposes ranges from the arresting revelation that medieval scholars associated dactylic feet (which are prominent in Browning's poem) with the male genitalia and that the kinds of grammatical particles in which the grammarian is interested can be read as encoding homosexual tendencies, to a predictable reading of the speaker's use of the term "erect" and the rather unconvincing claim that the text is "blatantly reticent" about confirming the speaker's gender and therefore that his gender is ambiguous.

By the same token, many other monologists whose gender is perfectly obvious but not explicitly stated would be confused about their sexuality. Although the grammarian's renunciation of his sexual identity certainly needs to be considered, the article did not leave me fully persuaded that the grammarian's "research was deeply rooted in his [homosexual] desires".

The discussion of "the narrator's contempt for the city" also left me slightly puzzled, as the grammarian is not carried away from the cities in the plain, as Bohm states, but from a pastoral setting in the plain toward a city on top of a mountain, playing on the associations of urbanity with culture and of prophets with the mountaintop (albeit probably ironically).

In a similar vein, Ernest Fontana's "Gender and Sexual Anxiety in Browning's 'Waring' and 'The Guardian-Angel,'" in the same issue of Victorian Poetry, offers a queer interpretation of these two poems as encoding Browning's feelings about an unrealized homosocial relationship or same-sex intimacy with Alfred Domett before his friend left for New Zealand.

As in Bohm's article, the reading of a virile Waring seen in a boat in the company of a boy as evidence that "Waring has come out and is revealed in a tableau of festive homosociality" seems to me to rely on an overinterpretation of detail. Fontana's analysis of "The Guardian-Angel" as negotiating the transition from Browning's companionship with Domett to that with Elizabeth is more convincing, although it is not necessary to understand this in terms of "same-sex amatory feelings".

As the bicentenary year of Elizabeth Barrett Browning's birth, 2006 saw, of course, a substantial amount of critical material on her, but reference to Robert in these publications has as usual been quite sparse.

This reluctance to consider the Brownings in conjunction may arise from the fact that, as Corinne Davies puts it, critics "over the years have felt the mutual influence, but found the proving elusive" ("Two of Elizabeth Barrett Browning's Pan Poems and Their After-Life in Robert Browning's 'Pan and Luna,'" [VP 44, no. 4 (Winter 2006): 562]).

It may also be a result of the different critical positions from which the two poets tend to be approached. Judging from some recent publications—Mary Saunders Pollock's monograph of 2003 and Corinne Davies and Marjorie Stone's "'Singing Song for Song': The Brownings 'in the Poetic Relation,'" in Marjorie Stone and Judith Thompson (eds.),

Literary Couplings: Writing Couples, Collaborators, and the Construction of Authorship (Madison: Univ. of Wisconsin, 2006), pp. 151-174—it would seem that Robert lends himself more readily to comparative analyses from a feminist stance than Elizabeth does to the main paradigms of Robert's critics.

Chapter 5

Explored Passion and Mind

In Order to trace the operation of a double awareness in Browning's poetry, allowance must at the outset be made for three complicating factors which do not occur in a parallel study of Tennyson. Browning was a much more original artist than the laureate. Whereas Tennyson was content to locate his themes in a familar context, whether literary or relating to comtemporary life, and generally speaking, to present this material in converntional forms, Browning naturally inclined to recondite subject-matter and to experimental methods.

Secondly, Tennyson's habit of mind was introspective, with the result, as we have seen, that the matrices of interest in his poetry are comparatively few and easy to identify. Browning, on the other hand, combined with greater intellectual self-confidence a multiple curiosity about man's external relationships.

Tennyson could never have written as Browning did in the Epilogue to "Pacchiarotto, with Other Poems": "Man's thoughts and loves and hates!/ Earth is my vineyard." Finally, where Tennyson was diffident about private convictions and careful to express them in as uncontroversial a way as possible, Browning, out of enthusiasm for his own highly individualistic beliefs, was unwilling to make concessions to the aptitudes and predilections of his readers.

Browning's most characteristic ideas are traceable to certain psychological assumptions adumbrated in the three substantial poems with which he inaugurated his career. These are: "Pauline" (1833), "Paracelsus" (1835), and "Sordello" (1840; although not published until three years after "Strafford," "Sordello" was begun on the completion of Pauline in 1833.)

These works are in a sense variations on a single theme: the evolution of the creative impulse in artists beset by uncertainty as to the genuineness of their inspiration and the best uses that can be made of their talents. In "Pauline" these problems are formulated in terms of a conflict between reason and instinct. The poem introduces a youthful poet restive under the yoke of received opinion:

How should this earth's life prove my only sphere?
Can I so narrow sense but that in life
Soul still exceeds it?
In their elements
My love outsoars my reason...

To the voice of common sense, recommending subordination of this idealizing tendency to the way of the world, the speaker protests:

There's some vile juggle with my reason here;
I feel I but explain to my own loss
These impulses: they live no less the same.
Liberty! What though I despair? my blood
Rose never at a slave's name proud as now.
0 sympathies, obscured by sophistries!-
Why else have I sought refuge in myself,
But from the woes I saw and could not stay?

As a romantic assertion of the reality of the human emotions, in opposition to the delusory processes of ratiocination, "Pauline" establishes a point of view which dominates all Browning's subsequent thinking. It should be noted, furthermore, that the poet founds his faith in man's instinctual nature on private insights unsusceptible of demonstration by rational means.

So, for example, he maintains that the appeal of Christianity derives from the baffling challenge which Christ offers to philosophic inquiry:

Is it not in my nature to adore,
And e'en for all my reason do I not
Feel him, and thank him, and pray to bim-now?

Can I forego the trust that he loves me?
Do I not feel a love which only ONE . . .
0 thou pale form, so dimly seen, deep-eye!
I have denied thee calmly-do I not
Pant when I read of thy consummate power,
And burn to see thy calm pure truths out-flash
The brightest gleams of earth's philosophy?

"Pauline" contains two additional passages in which the poet calls on his experience of the arts to prove the validity of intuitional experience. The first of these is the well-known evocation of a painting of Andromeda. The second, deriving from music, is still more explicit. The speaker addresses his imagined mistress as follows:

Be still to me
A help to music's mystery which mind fails
To fathom, its solution, no mere clue!
0 reason's pedantry, life's rule prescribed!

The poet's decision, taken immediately hereafter, to shake off self-consciousness is dictated not so much by social awareness as by an intimation of nobler heights of imaginative being than he has yet attained:

I'll look within no more,
I have too trusted my own lawless wants,
Too trusted my vain self, vague intuition-
Draining soul's wine alone in the still night. . .

Once let the artist turn altruist, however, and the question then becomes how he can best exert influence on the minds of others. In his poem devoted to the pseudo-legendary figure of Paracelsus, Browning first attacks the problem of communication, while still insisting on the primacy of the intuitions over the rational intellect. "Paracelsus" is a study of intellectual pride and its humbling.

The philosopher, conscious of his mission to arouse society with "new revealings," places entire confidence in his individual powers, and thereby repudiates both the guidance of tradition and the support of love, as personified by Festus and Michal. Festus repeatedly warns him of the danger of trying to do without human sympathy: "How can that course be safe which from the first/ Produces carelessness to human love?" and again: "But do not cut yourself from human weal!" Paracelsus, however, sets off alone on his wanderings, strong in the conviction that he is sufficient unto himself and that ultimate truth has its seat in the depths of his inner consciousness.

"Paracelsus" is divided into five sections to suggest the stages in the hero's tragic progress. In the second part there begins for Paracelsus the betrayal by the intellect, althouzh he continues to insist that this is the supreme faculy:

God! Thou art mind! Unto the master-mind
Mind should be precious.
Spare my mind alone!
All else I will endure. . .

The lyric poet Aprile now enters the scene to emphasize the protagonist's alienation. Aprile compensates for the weakness of his intellect by a capacity for love denied to Paracelsus. Lacking Festus' humble veneration for humanity, however, he loves unrealistically. For Aprile inhabits a Shelleyean world of make-believe where mankind is an idealized abstraction.

In their isolation both Paracelsus and Aprile are self-infatuated, the one by the life of reason, the other by the life of the imagination. Paracelsus realizes that they are "halves of one dissevered world"; but although, having learned to love Aprile, he has begun to move towards recognition of the need for closer communion with his kind, he is not yet ready to renounce his chosen path. To the dying poet he says:

We wake at length from weary dreams; but both
Have slept in fairy-land: though dark and drear
Appears the world before us, we no less
Wake with our wrists and ankles jewelled still.
I too have sought to KNOW as thou to LOVE -
Excluding love as thou refusedst knowledge.
Still thou hast beauty and I, power.

With the third section disillusionment sets in for Paracelsus. He has found that his teachings are unintelligible to the populace, and scorning the artifices of the demagogue, has taken refuge in aristocratic disdain for his audience. Aprile's example is for the moment lost on him. In his thinking of the dead poet merely as a devotee of art for art's sake, we can perhaps detect Browning's own rejection of that alluring doctrine:

I cannot feed on beauty for the sake
Of beauty only, nor can drink in balm
From lovely objects for their loveliness;
My nature cannot lose her first imprint;
I still must hoard and heap and class all truths
With one ulterior purpose: I must know!
. . . For other men,
Beauty is prodigally strewn around,
And I were happy could I quench as they
This mad and thriveless longing, and content me
With beauty for itself alone...

Festus reappears to suggest that Paracelsus' difficulties are of his own making, the result of a deficiency in the loving wisdom of the heart; but the philosopher reasserts the supremacy of the individual:

'T is in the advance of individual minds
That the slow crowd should ground their expectation
Eventually to follow . . .

Yet he is not so sure of himself as once; and although without much humility, he is beginning to perceive that his failure may be attributable to pride of intellect: Were man all mind-he gains A station little enviable. From God

Down to the lowest spirit ministrant,
Intelligence exists which casts our mind
Into immeasurable shade. No, no:
Love, hope, fear, faith-these make humanity;
These are its sign and note and character,
And these I have lost!

Paracelsus next turns his mental powers to unscrupulous ends, and so betrays himself to the ways of the world. He condescends to magical practices in order to bedazzle his audience. Unwilling to bow to the authority of the magistrates at Basel, he is cast out as a charlatan. Paracelsus thus becomes the first of many compositions in which Browning was to show the enslavement of minds to ambition for material power. The coarsening of Paracelsus' fibre spreads out from the intellect through his whole nature and leads to sensual indulgence.

He falls prey to morbid Satanism: "mind is nothing but disease,/ And natural health is ignorance." In a final despairing effort to hold onto some remnants of self-respect, he makes the gesture of arrogating to himself godlike infallibility:

I am above them like a god, there's no
Hiding the fact: what idle scruples, then,
Were those that ever bade me soften it,
Communicate it gently to the world,
Instead of proving my supremacy,
Taking my natural station o'er their head,
Then owning all the glory was a man's!
— And in my elevation man's would be.

It is only in his old age, a failure and on the point of death, that Paracelsus under Festus' ministrations finally attains to full recognition of his error.

Man in his slow ascent of the evolutionary scale is to be pitied rather than disdained; his groping, but endlessly valiant struggle to rise is the very thing that makes him lovable.

And the superior beings sent to guide the way must possess the faculty of love if they are to fulfill their function. Paracelsus retains to the end his confidence that he is one of those so elected; but the qualities on which he should have relied, as he now realizes, were his "inborn uninstructed impulses,"-not, that is to say, the reasoning mind, but

perception unexpressed,
Uncomprehended by our narrow thought,
But somehow felt and known in every shift
And change in the spirit, — nay, in every pore
Of the body, even ...

This God-given instinct he has perverted through the selfish desire for individual power; yet he cannot refrain from pointing out the temptation to deal with the world in its own terms:

All quackery; all deceit; myself can laugh
The first at it, if you desire; but still
You know the obstacles which taught me tricks
So foreign to my nature — envy and hate,
Blind opposition, brutal prejudice,
Bald ignorance-what wonder if I sunk
To humour men the way they most approved?

And the poem leaves the reader with the ineradicable impression that in Browning's view the way of the original thinker must needs be a lonely one, since devotion to the best interests of humanity inevitably entails incomprehension and active hostility from all those whom one seeks to serve: "We have to live alone to set forth well/ God's praise."

In theme "Sordello" occupies a position midway between "Pauline" and "Paracelsus." The first sections of "Sordello" trace the growth of a poet's mind, the later ones his career in the world.

As had been the case with "Paracelsus," "Sordello" represents an attempt on Browning's part to gain perspective on his own situation through imaginative treatment of an historical figure sufficiently obscure to allow considerable latitude of interpretation. The hero of the poem is obsessed by the problem of making himself heard. The theme of the artist's communicative function, emerging from a welter of imperfectly assimilated material, gives the work what little unity it possesses.

Like the speaker in "Pauline," Sordello is motivated in turn by two impulsions, one turning him inward towards self-contemplation, the other driving him outward to a life of action; and like Paracelsus, his career follows a pattern of alternating advance and retreat, as he assumes and is then dislodged from one position after another "vis-à-vis" society.

In total seclusion from worldly affairs Sordello passes his youth amidst the natural beauties of Goito. His imagination is peopled with ideal beings, and he dreams of emulating Apollo, the poet-god. But such isolation, with its inducements to egocentric complacency, is precarious at best; for we are told that this world of ours by tacit pact is pledged

To laying such a spangled fabric low
Whether by gradual brush or gallant blow.

Sordello's first departure from Goito into a larger sphere of activity comes about under auspicious circumstances. Inspired to spontaneous song, he vanquishes the reigning troubadour, Eglamor, at Palma's Court of Love. Eglamor is an interesting, though somewhat vague figure.

He foreshadows the Pre-Raphaelite ideal of the artist wholly devoted to aesthetic discipline: "Then, how he loved that art!/ The calling making him a man apart/ From men." Like Aprile, however, his preference for fancy over fact is mitigated by a generous capacity for love; he dies acknowledging Sordello his master.

Earlier in the poem Browning had specified two categories of poets. The first includes all those who feel

A need to blend with each external charm,
Bury themselves, the whole heart wide and warm,-
In something not themselves; they would belong
To what they worship. . .

Eglamor clearly belongs to the other category, described as follows:

For there's a class that eagerly looks, too,
On beauty, but, unlike the gentler crew,
Proclaims each new revealment born a twin
With a distinctest consciousness within,
Referring still the quality, now first
Revealed, to their own soul — its instinct nursed
In silence, now remembered better, shown
More thoroughly, but not the less their own. . .

Eglamor, at least, has the virtue of absorption in the technical demands of his craft. Sordello, on the other hand, vainglorious over his easy success, assumes that all he henceforth need do is give unbridled expression to his imagination: "So, range, free soul! — who, by self-consciousness,/ The last drop of all beauty dost express."

At the furthest remove from Eglamor's perfectionism, his sole concern is for popular acclaim- "'t was the song's effect/ He cared for, scarce the song itself." In the outcome he falls between two stools. Lack of worldly experience, coupled with excessive self-confidence, causes him to go astray among abstractions which are meaningless to his audience.

When he attempts to adopt more concrete modes of communication, notably the dramatic, he discovers his temperamental disaffinity to prevailing forms of thought.

The man and the artist split apart:
Weeks, months, years went by,
And lo, Sordello vanished utterly,
Sundered in twain; each spectral part at strife
With each; one jarred against another life;
The Poet thwarting hopelessly the Man,
Who, fooled no longer, free in fancy ran
Here, there, — let slip no opportunities
As pitiful, forsooth, beside the prize
To drop on him some no-time and acquit
His constant faith (the Poet-half's to wit —
That waiving any compromise between
No joy and all joy kept the hunger keen
Beyond most methods) — of incurring scoff
From the Man-portion — not to be put off
With self-reflectings by the Poet's scheme,
Though ne'er so bright. Who sauntered forth in dream,
Dressed anyhow, nor waited mystic' frames,
Immeasurable gifts, astounding claims,
But just his sorry self? — who yet might be
Sorrier for aught he in reality
Achieved, so pinioned Man's the Poet — part,
Fondling, in turn of fancy, verse; the Art
Developing his soul a thousand ways —
Potent, by its assistance, to amaze
The multitude with majesties, convince
Each sort of nature, that the nature's prince
Accosted it. Language, the makeshift, grew
Into a bravest of expedients, too;
Apollo, seemed it now, perverse had thrown
Quiver and bow away, the lyre alone
Sufficed. While, out of dream, his day's work went

To tune a crazy tenzon or sirvent —
So hampered him the Man-part, thrust to judge
Between the bard and the bard's audience, grudge
A minute's toil that missed its due reward!

There ensues a period of withdrawal to Goito and self-renewal at the font which symbolizes the inner sources of Sordello's creative being. As a result of the illumination received during this time, Sordello vows himself to a career of constructive endeavor in the cause of his countrymen suffering under the wars of the Guelphs and the Ghibellines.

As happened to Paracelsus when he aspired the second time, however, Sordello is seduced by a thirst for power.

Finding that Rome is not built in a day, he despairs once more and is ready to exchange his newly assumed mission for the consolations of the imagination. In vain his conscience reprimands him for failure to abide by the choice it dictates:

Only bear in mind,
Ferrara's reached, Goito's left behind:
As you then were, as half yourself, desist!
-The warrior-part of you may, an it list,
Finding real falchions difficult to poise,
Fling them afar and taste the cream of joys
By wielding such in fancy, — what is bard
Of you may spurn the vehicle that marred
Elys so much, and in free fancy glut
His sense, yet write no verses-you have but
To please yourself for law, and once could please
What once appeared yourself, by dreaming these
Rather than doing these, in days gone by.
But all is changed the moment you descry
Mankind as half yourself, — then, fancy's trade
Ends once and always: how may half evade
The other half? men are found half of you.
Out of a thousand helps, just one or two
Can be accomplished presently: but flinch
From these (as from the falchion, raised an inch,
Elys, described a couplet) and make proof
Of fancy,-then, while one half lolls aloof

I' the vines, completing Rome to the tip-top-
See if, for that, your other half will stop
A tear, begin a smile!

Not until after Salinguerra, the ruthlessly practical soldier who acts on instinct, has mocked his feeble vacillations does Sordello come to the recognition that it is the poet's true function to incite his auditors to noble actions:

Thought is the soul of act, and, stage by stage,
Soul is from body still to disengage
As tending to a freedom which rejects
Such help and incorporeally affects
The world, producing deeds but not by deeds,
Swaying, in others, frames itself exceeds,
Assigning them the simpler tasks it used
To patiently perform till Song produced
Acts, by thoughts only, for the mind ...

No sooner has Sordello found the direction in which he must henceforth move, however, than fresh temptations are placed in his way. With the twofold discovery that he is Salinguerra's son and Palma's accepted lover, a career of boundless power opens up for him. In the ensuing conflict between altruism and the will to power, the former wins out, but the price of victory is extinction.

Sordello stamps on Salinguerra's badge of authority and then, emotionally exhausted, dies. Into this somewhat ambiguous denouement Browning steps to confirm the reader's suspicion that Sordello's life is to be viewed as a tragic failure in its twin aspects — both the early immersion in fanciful dreams, the weakness of Pauline's lover, and the later surrender to selfish ambition, Paracelsus' flaw.

Sordello's name is forgotten; his influence, ironically enough, survives to aftertimes in the sole unpremeditated and wholly instinctive utterance of his poetic being, the Elys lyric, as it is sung in fragmentary form by an Italian urchin.

Chapter 6

Paragon and Paregon

There is here a problem of framing, of bordering and delimitation, whose analysis must be very. finely detailed if it wishes to ascertain the effects of fiction.

—Jacques Derrida, "Le facteur de la verite"

If we are to approach a text, it must have an edge.

—Jacques Derrida, "Living On: Border Lines"

The interaction of creativity with interpretation concerned Robert Browning throughout a career in which he made the dramatic monologue converge sound, silence and audition, as well as image and vision. Reading such a poem is like being drawn into it, having to side with its personae, while feeling extraneous or beside the point; more than sympathy or judgment, these alternatives lead readers to self-reflection, to seeing themselves shifting between the centre and the border of some artistic design.

Nevertheless, as many readings of "My Last Duchess" show, "this most dramatically paragonal of all ekphrastic poems" (Heffernan 144) undermines such a simple scheme of moving or fixing readers. This dramatic monologue, arguably Browning's premier work, adds a pictorial, fourth dimension to the usual pattern of speaker and silent auditor in a momentous, reader-monitored situation.

Eyeing the poem's nested utterances, we do not actually see fictitious Fra Pandolf's imaginary portrait of the "last Duchess" (line 1), whose peerless "looks" from inside an iconic "wonder" will supposedly imprint the envoy.

Yet the painted work, surrounded by discourse and history, is invaluable as a touchstone—a paragon— for appraising readers, who "turn" (9, 13), or change, to Browning or his personae.

Our cognition of "My Last Duchess" is parergonal (i.e., framed and framing), like the Duke of Ferrara's intention to finish his wife as a person and as an objet d'art. But also like him, we find art turns on—pivoting, resisting, and starting—interpretive possession, which is what we own that enthralls or inhabits us.

The printed poem is a stable verbal icon, but it becomes metamorphic if we gain the duke's grace, the envoy's hearing, the duchess's fixed glance, and Fra Pandolf's gifted words to draw it out.

Browning learned from his earlier Pauline, Paracelsus, and Sordello to make his poetry less introverted, more collaborative. Although "My Last Duchess" is complete before us, our work supplements Browning's. By removing himself as the centre of attention, the poet allows us to replace him when reading is keen and trim.

That is, strong readers possess a character that puts our work at the cutting edge of language, which nevertheless resists all displays of finishing. Reading, although susceptible to elimination, marks off those openings and surfaces where a poem passes for us or is about us. We achieve this complicity with the poet by seeing through the eyes of characters who shape the dramatic circumstances, while we also register, experience, and cross their limits.

One result of dissolving lines between paragon and parergon, or cynosure and scope, is that we glimpse "truth / Beyond mere imagery on the wall" (The Ring and the Book 12:858-59).

The drama within "My Last Duchess" turns out(ward) to shatter the poem as a mere typographical replica of the "last Duchess" "That's. . . painted on the wall" (1, emphasis added). The duke minds Fra Pandolf's work, however good it may be, less for its potent image than for its (un)canny pretext; Browning's outstanding poem, too, is iconographic, another speaking picture which we heed, while it sizes us up as critical guests.

At the start of their respective careers, a Renaissance aristocrat (whose best art may be showing his art) and a Victorian poet are discovering "That Art remains the one way possible / Of speaking truth, to mouths like [theirs], at least" (The Ring and the Book 12:839-40).

Art "speaking truth" evokes critical dialogue, our wandering looks and unstoppable smiles. Our exposing "My Last Duchess" to interpretive light and its characters to the dust of history transfigures the duke's action when he "puts by / The curtain" covering a work of art. We also are uncovered by having to change how we view ourselves and our stance in relation to an artist and the work of art.

The union of painted image with dramatic utterance induces an almost ghostly experience—convivial, dizzying, transcendent, factitious—for not only the duke's sole guest but also Browning's audience.

The craft of dramatic monologues can be disorienting as we try to reconcile our physical sensations of sound and type, besides our moral-aesthetic attitudes. Julia Wedgwood, for example, in a letter to Browning struggles with The Ring and the Book, particularly the dual representation of the villainous Guido Franceschini, in terms that apply to the structure of "My Last Duchess":

I feel, after finishing the Poem, as if I could not contemplate it without a sort of a squint. Or rather (for you, of all men, ought to have patience with an elaborate simile) it seems to me that a somewhat slight picture has been put into an elaborately carved frame which represents the same subject under a rather different point of view. I look at the Picture and I see a certain incident; I look at the frame and I see the same incident treated in a more ambitious style and with much greater fullness of detail. The result is that one hesitates which to look at.

The text requires from Wedgwood "a sort of a squint" in order to correlate complex dramatic narratives with prime, eidetic events. A similar self-doubt or perceptual double-take occurs when a reader of "My Last Duchess" alternates between a historical "beyond" and a literary corpus.

The lines appear polymorphic, like geometric shapes reversing figure and ground or inside and outside. The last duchess, an eidolon, could not revise herself to please the duke, but from their mismatch (her gaiety with his gravity) Browning makes a poetic paradigm. Fra Pandolf's portrait of her, including the duke's words, reflects how Browning turns us inside out: what adjoins reading to creative work—object and process—is the sensation of discovering a matchless frame that keeps us in trim.

Browning frames the poem in several ways: linking the notice taken of the "Duchess painted on the wall" with the duke's command to "Notice" a bronze statue of"Neptune. . . / Taming a sea-horse"; linking polite questions or requests, "Will't please you sit and look at her?" and "Will't please you rise?"; linking Fra Pandolf and the count's delegate as (dis)qualified speakers; and linking a "now" of aesthetic judgment with a "then" of marital prerogative.

When we understand the point of comparing the less than picture-perfect duchess to Fra Pandolf's rendition of her, we also get the picture of the count's expendable daughter as a framing and framed "object", no longer an illegible figure at the margins of discourse.

The duke's unhappy past with his former mate, however, is never far from the centre of Browning's poem, even when we realise that a future duchess is his "object." A shadowy figure in the duke's self-portrait, the count's daughter is still obscured, a marked woman, in the new foreground; she is already virtually disembodied, compared to the last duchess, who is so attractive that we have to reorient ourselves toward the poem in the few moments left before it ends.

The duke's aristocratic standards cause him to think his last duchess, with "A heart . . . too soon made glad, / Too easily impressed", was undiscriminating, indiscreet, "trifling". The mark against her—as well as on her—is a "spot of joy" that he cannot countenance because it is a synecdoche or token of a vital, yet somehow alien, personality: it was "as if she ranked / [His] gift of a nine-hundred-years-old name / With anybody's gift".

The duchess's inattention to her proud spouse contests his self-image as a paragon. His answer to this paragone (i.e., competition) between their incompatible tastes is to have her "painted on the wall, / Looking as if she were alive" (1-2), epitomizing her pretense.

Thus the art he owns corresponds to her previous artfulness—when "her looks went everywhere", when her evaluations made "all one", and when "Much the same smile" did not favor him. His final gift to her was when he "gave commands," which transformed her "same smile" into "all smiles".

This proves he knows the difference between being common and being absolute. Further, through Fra Pandolf's artistry her passage from curiosity to superiority—often a hermeneutic ideal—illustrates to the legate not only how "she stands", but also how to enforce any duchess's deportment.

In command of drawing the curtain on the duchess, the duke tries to limit her scope to himself and a few privileged others. Browning's comparable mastery of illusion, echo, and intention makes "My Last Duchess" a perceptual challenge which none can read without blinking.

To prove their sharpness is close to matching Browning's, critics need to realise, for example, that the duke's exhibition is not just a working trope: "It's curtains for her." Browning further cites painting and literature as sister arts. Parrhasius bested Zeuxis, famous for a trompel'oeil of grapes, by drawing a curtain.

And Shakespeare's Twelfth Night offers Browning a fit dramatic model when Olivia answers Viola: "Have you any commission from your lord to negotiate with my face? You are now out of your text. But we will draw the curtain and show you the picture" (1.5.218-20).

Browning's best improvising readers have the duchess's joy and roving eyes, whereas the duke's blindness while he covers her type is a "mark," or sign, of high seriousness. Readers with an "approving speech, / Or blush, at least", have the privilege of answering "My Last Duchess" with more than a blank stare, which is the look of critics frustrated by any "sort of trifling". Fra Pandolf's portrait of the duchess exemplifies for the duke her hamartia, being so lively that she "miss[es]" or "exceed[s] the mark" he draws for decorum.

The duke can "call / That piece a wonder, now", because linking his commentary with her verisimilar figure allows him to emblemize her, while continuing to understate his attitudes about her improprieties. He can cut a figure and expose her through an even more reticent medium, yet "he becomes the victim of his own aesthetic sensibility . . forever bound to the portrait through his endless gloss upon it" (Baines 30).

His "call" is performative, not just constative: his speech act makes the "piece" what it is, beyond the artist's humble actions and courteous "stuff". We may be similarly bound to "My Last Duchess," depending on whether what we call it is for or against our trimming gloss.

Like a critic who vainly aims to supplant Browning's artistry, the arrogant, jealous duke appears to be redoing the painter's craft and double-exposing the duchess's "pictured countenance" because he could not stand her egregious disregard for rank.

Thus, he sketches her as a painted woman to make himself an artist manque; his living/dead subject now "stands" on his terms, not hers or Fra Pandolf's. Recalling her coy life-style for the envoy, he can finally claim his own creative privilege because "There she stands / As if alive" (46-47), silent testimony to the visitor of the host's marital, aesthetic, and interpretive command.

The duke, emphatically saying "Fra Pandolf' by design", tries to impress his guest with the artist's credentials; we're thinking "Fra, who?" and perhaps imagining some artistic monstrosity. Yet Browning teases readers familiar with art history. Does the duke lack taste and therefore foolishly overrate unrenowned Pandolf and the portrait, which only our mind's eye sees?

The historical frame of "My Last Duchess" implies that Duke Alfonso II of Ferrara's Este family (distinguished art patrons and collectors) could not be so mistaken about the qualities of the painter and his work? When we study a retitled poem that in a blink of an eye breaks from its hermetic bounds, we find ourselves at an impasse between factual record of Renaissance Ferrara and Browning's imaginative representation of humbug.

When we know that Browning originally called the poem "I. Italy" (1842) and renamed it "My Last Duchess: Ferrara" (1849), is it any wonder his redesign frames literary critique differently? In this new setting, we might wish that the "last Duchess" (emphasis added) has no successor, if the count loves his daughter more than social advancement.

Nevertheless, the actual Duke of Ferrara does get another wife (Barbara of Austria). Like the duke himself, readers find that the "looks" of reality are more upsetting than the way art looks. Thus, given how much Alfonso disliked his mate, we might further conjecture-in order to pass meaning(fully) between life and mime-sis—that his vengeance includes hiring a nobody to paint "such an one", a beau ideal.

Since she disregarded his "favour at her breast" and his "nine-hundred-years-old name", he favors commissioning an artist who finishes her portrait in "a da),". This would "make [the duke's] will / Quite clear" about temper, temporizing and taste.

Our revisionist stance toward the historical reputation of Alfonso II d'Este—framing him as a mere philistine or villain—helps to hone our critical edge so that it is closer to a poet's text, always sharp and already advanced (Derrida, "Living On" 83). Browning structures "My Last Duchess" by deferring information about a prospective marriage that will affect our ability to distinguish the subject, or main work, of the duke's design, from the apparently ornamental, secondary by work.

Such artistic composition illustrates that "[t] he frame. . . becomes not the borderline between the inside and the outside, but precisely what subverts the applicability of the inside/ outside polarity to the act of interpretation" (Johnson 128). Alfonso focuses so narrowly on the portrait and its subject's typical impertinence in the first 47 lines of the monologue that initial readers are unaware of his immediate marital "object": the "self" of another wife, who ought not to test him by comparing his "presence" with "anybody's gift".

His account of the duchess, vis-a-vis Fra Pandolf's painting of her and what we learn of the monologic situation, gives edgy readers the sensation of gazing at dimensional figures and suddenly seeing them reverse positions—centre/ margin, ergon/parergon, master/subordinate, paragon/ delinquent, cynosure/supplement.

Alfonso's parenthetical monologue diverts us from his plans, provided "My Last Duchess" is strange; still it impinges on our consciousness just as the duchess continues to interpose with "looks." The poem, by Browning's design, represents a summational digression or interjection.

As we reread more acutely, we can reshape the monologue—turning it inside out or realigning Alfonso's by-passage with his direction—so that we are almost a match for him. We learn, as the duchess cannot but as the envoy must, that being a paragon requires good form ant] no distractions.

In the duke's pattern—where image is everything—there can be no rivals: for being "such an one," thus violating etiquette, the duchess earns his wrath; he "gave commands; / Then all smiles stopped together".

Browning's wry art makes us smile if we realise that for the nonce an archaism ("an one") phonemically and solecistically represents the duke trying to reduce his blundering, incomparable wife to a "none."

Such a Boeotian rule of the duchess and a recreative contest with Fra Pandolf (who is no Michelangelo, Titian, Veronese, Tintoretto, Moroni, Bronzino, or Bastianino) are spoiled, nonetheless. The framing duke, who by artifice has the power on occasion to draw a curtain over the work of a no one, has been framed poetically as ineffectual and anonymous:

Ironically,. . . the ostensibly male-authorized text of the portrait subverts male authority, effecting a double displacement—a displacement that, itself, displaces. The living Duchess is shifted and relocated onto an icon, becoming a countertext which then deconstructs the Duke's authority to textualize. (Hochberg 80)

Although Alfonso claims to have regained command of his last dnchess, she still has him spellbound. "In effect, Fra Pandolf has been too proficient," says Sanford Pinsker; ". . . the Duke now finds himself in the curious position of having engineered a Pyrrhic victory indeed . . .. [T]he smile-of-Art disturbs the Duke in a manner that does not differ significantly from the smile-of-Fact. . ." (72, 73).

As a ghost of her former self, the duchess will be exorcized from Alfonso's consciousness only when he can replace marital subjects to serve him as objects; then neither one of the duchesses will be "such an one," and their media need not concern him. For him the centre of attention and discourse remains complicated by what he cannot marginalize or frame: the fearless asymmetry of the last duchess.

Browning illustrates here the "contingencies of framing," that is, when "no totalization of the bordering can even occur. The frames are always enframed; and therefore enframed by a given piece of what they contain". Through reprisal against his former wife and rehearsal of the next one, the duke stands to regain his authority.

However, the monologic structure subverts and dovetails all relationships by implicating not only personae but also those of us who "never read . . . . My Last Duchess" without feeling we will remain "strangers" to the poet's angular art, while "'here [we] miss, / Or there exceed the mark'".

Framing his former wife is also a way for the duke to prevent the count's daughter from misprizing him. His absolute rule will allow him to prescribe her behavior, but he depends on the count's emissary to convey his indelicate hints about propriety better than he could verbally respond to the last duchess's miscues.

The envoy is politely "Will't"-ed to replace his host as the object of the duchess's "earnest glance," which still affects one who views Fret Pandolf's "piece" and hears what happens to a vulgar"piece" who resists. Moreover, presumably the delegate's standing with "such an one," with this Renaissance paragon, who experiments with him "as un homme moyen sensual" (Ingersoll, "Perversions" 75-76), includes a protocol of knowing when to be quiet, which he does for as long as Browning permits us to eavesdrop.

The climax of their brief association is the envoy's being verbally enervated in front of a disfigured and muted woman; analysis gets us to talk, however. His reduction to a silent, disembodied textual figure will further erase the last duchess as a remarkable woman with whom he is temporarily joined. Simultaneously, the monologue extricates him from an obscure verbal margin where he has something to say.

With this look-but-don 't-talk attitude, the envoy finds that he is "not the first" to be drawn to what is "painted on the wall"; then he is redrawn, or re-"turned" (9, 13), by the duke's voice to the perspective of "strangers" who can "never read" without assistance from the master's critical voice.

Alfonso uses his troped guest to illustrate how he wants to be treated. The envoy adopts this protocol of reading by conforming his senses to the duke's will, even if this means being diverted visually and aurally for a few minutes from the task of gaining attention for the count's "munificence." Nevertheless, to complete the picture of his "just pretence / . . . for dowry" (50-51), which has been sketched already, Duke Alfonso dismisses the "known munificence" and the unknown female "object" as foregone conclusions; they are not worth his whole attention, which is how he wants any duchess to be. The monologue tests the envoy's eyes and ears to determine his qualifications for cutting a woman down to size.

Meeting the dead, atropic duchess's "earnest glance", which is paradoxically momentary and lingering, the envoy's gaze cuts a bargain between the duke and count, who trade in women's bodies. The envoy is a mute agent of a framing that encloses a "fair" woman, yet also makes her ornament the duke's self-creation.

This next duchess will soon be, like her nixed predecessor, no more than a shade of her "self" in a palace of art where the pattern of femininity is losing its colour. The count's daughter, as a married yet marred woman who minds her "looks" and "approving speech", will know without coaxing that she is "a rarity" (like Clans of Innsbruck's bronze statue of ducal Neptune taming a seahorse) only to the extent she submerges her "self." By means of a final reference to another artifact, the duke serves "notice" again that his having to "tame" another wife will prolong the contest between his supremacy and women's secondary work.

This objet d'art in-Alfonso's possession reinforces the frame around his will and around Browning's poem. Moreover, the illustration of control again points readers beyond the heterocosm of"My Last Duchess" to a locus classicus, Virgil's Aeneid, which shows Neptune as a ruler calming a stormy sea induced by the goddess, Juno.

The fictitious Claus of Innsbruck has an artistic representation "for" the incomparable, innominate duke; for readers, however, Robert Browning allusively recovers a literary, gift more ancient than his speaker's "nine-hundred-years-old name." The duke has something "cast in bronze" that implies closure; but the-verbal arts perplex him because they are less fixed and less exclusive.

His monologue attempts to limit the grounds of discourse. Browning nevertheless realizes that one feature of language's "rarity" is its equivocal might: to "exceed the mark," or not even reach it, even when the lines are set.s Literary analysis too, which is an empowering yet liminal art, is both against us and "for" us in our "Taming".

Unlike the envoy, forced to be a quiet go-between in this porous frontier between two men, two women, and several artists, real and imaginary, readers must find special voices to rate "My Last Duchess." In this dramatic place, where drawing a curtain reveals the effect of a painter's grand "perhaps", silence and critical talk are as precious as any fine art. While looking through Fra Pandolf's craft to the woman beyond it, the envoy also receives lessons in communication.

Her "approving speech" is framed by the laconic duke's monitory words—put in others' mouths—which both violate and elevate their authority. An allegedly immodest woman's silence and a faintly modest man's voice surround this auditor, who has to look a certain way to see "That" which the poem conceals.

However, readers can see that Browning frames the text and many lines pronominally. He also moves Alfonso's "I"'s side-to-side, only twice centering them vis-a-vis speech. The duchess's expressive eyes might account for the envoy's losing his voice, but momentarily he can imagine having the duke's sharp tongue and the duchess's ear:

Even had you skill
In speech—(which I have not)—to make your will
Quite clear to such an one, and say, 'Just this
Or that in you disgusts me; here you miss,
Or there exceed the mark'—and if she let
Herself be lessoned so, nor plainly set
Her wits to yours, forsooth, and made excuse,
—E'en then would be some stooping; and I choose
Never to stoop. (35-43)

Dashes and parenthesis tie a modifying side remark in a double knot. This graphic style typographically offsets the enjambed "skill/In speech," reconstructs the duke's jamb, and centers a severe, upright 'T' that sets the character apart from the surrounding marks. Alfonso's remarkable gloss is skillful yet clumsy, suiting its rhetorical occasion.

To "make [his] will / Quite dear to" this special envoy, "some stooping" may be (par)ergonomically, as well as politically, correct. Browning's craft, in what is rightly called "the phenomenon of a trompe d'oreille" (Berman 67), is less a work of hiding art than an unworking of the virgule that artificially separates verses and women.

The duke is speaking to someone who is "not the first" to inquire about the way the duchess looks, now that she is "painted on the wall"; but to explain her mien could jeopardize his eminence. During the sitting, "Her husband's presence" was not the only "cause" of the duchess's "spot of joy" (14-15, 21). He is still beside himself while recalling how he was a peripheral, third-person figure when the painter's remarks, perhaps inadvertent, drew out the duchess's character. Fra

Pandolf, whose addressee is indeterminate, elicited a facial expression from his true "object"; this obliqueness from an artist, who apparently is no stranger to reading women, constitutes part of the "wonder" that is a painting and a poem. But any discounting, however slight, of his ducal "presence" is enough to trigger resentment in Browning's speaker, for whom this scene typifies his marital troubles. Having admitted his secondariness, the duke has to reestablish his indispensability as a critic.

Because the duchess's "earnest glance"—though now just image-still bothers him, he cannot meet what has become her enduring (not endearing) gaze. Nevertheless, he can focus the envoy's attention on what Fra Pandolf could not see, i.e., a complexion beneath "that pictured countenance." Besides "That piece [being] a wonder, now," what lay behind the eyes of the duchess should be clear.

The duke's "presence" is again paramount, so he stands by (speaking parenthetically) what the envoy could (not) possibly "say" so directly and insultingly to a female superior. The duke's former wife and his current visitor were/are expected as listeners to intuit exactly what "disgusts" someone who is blameless, someone whose "will" and word are acute. Alfonso, briefly granting the envoy the possibility of rhetorical "skill," strips him of it: no one; must rival the duke's command of the last duchess, and anyone "Who'd stoop to blame" her would be undignified.

To be really powerful, like his host, the envoy must transcend candor without "stooping." He will prove himself up to the mark, unlike the duchess, if his being "lessoned" means the proud duke will not have to reframe his "commands" to another duchess.

The poem frames "'ra Pandolf' by design" to tighten the bonding of vision, re-creative speech and audition. The absorbing audiovisual text of "My Last Duchess" traces the images that draw the emissary to "read" a message from "that spot of joy" and to hear it respotted, or reviewed, in Alfonso's words. When those images suddenly stop, as "all smiles stopped together," and when the duke casually mentions the count's daughter as another female "object," language seems renewed, more immediate and effective.

The defensive duke suddenly looks different after speech has drawn him out. Alfonso, rhetorically trim yet needing to "repeat" what he previously "avowed" (48, 52), is confident that the count's "ample warrant" is audible as well as visible. Coincidentally, he himself has finished with Fri Pandolf, who had exacted more from his demure subject by saying, "'Her mantle laps / Over my lady's wrist too much'" (1617), and by delimiting his medium:

'Paint
Must never hope to reproduce the faint
Half-flush that dies along her throat' . . . (17-19)

Like Browning's art, subjected to reading and listening, Fra Pandolf's artistry needs to be (re-)covered by its spectators. Having resurrected his first—but not "last"—mate by uncurtaining her, Alfonso can be seen and heard stopping her looks and smiles again if we imagine him closing the curtain over her image as he replaces her rhetorically and maritally.

Like a snap of his fingers to end the hypnotic spell, the duke's polite inquiry, "Will't please you rise?", lifts the envoy out of a parergonal role as the duchess's subject; having briefly shared her with his host, he returns to being the count's subject and an important accessory to the rule of yet another young, model spouse. In three minutes, while the duke retouches her character, the last duchess becomes a special figure of imagination—ours as well as the envoy's.

When we apprehend the auditor's mediating role, we have to reconnect the speaker's main point (ergon) with what is beside the point (parergon), but the poem itself never confirms that our framing is accurate. As the poem moves from the portrait as object—with a living soul behind it—to the count's daughter as soul-less object, we become almost as involved in the scene as the envoy is.

We can only guess what he has learned about the duke's expectations. Our reading of "that pictured countenance, / The depth and passion of its earnest glance" (7-8), will not conform to his subordinate regard for her masculine regard. In fact, his proximity to the duke and the painted image of the duchess draws, as well as repels, our hermeneutics. His being at the centre and the critical edge of the action is a complicity that all interpreters want to share with the powerful.

Yet our reading, like Fret Pandolf's creativity, "Must never hope to reproduce" the situation exactly. Readers are not posed or sited quite like the çanny envoy. He knows his function well before we are discreet enough to get (into) the picture.

The duke's intentions are more foreign and perplexing to us up to the point—and perhaps even beyond it—when we realise "the mark" he sets for and upon a last or lasting mate. We might hope that the messenger is sensitive enough to warn his "master" later of the duke's destructive megalomania, and that the count's love for his daughter transcends ambition. Nevertheless, we assume the duke will not be disappointed—as well as deluded.

And the sixteenth-century Ferrara outside the nineteenth-century poem confirms our worst expectations. Like the count to whom the envoy will report, we seem superfluous or out of bounds in the interpretive account. Yet we have also been on the duchess's side in "a continuous shifting pattern of oscillation back and forth from looking to being looked at" (Ingersoll, "Lacan" 152).

Browning's peerless ekphrasis commands poetry as speaking picture, painting as mute poetry, and reading as psychoglyph. Through her looks, which paint us into a corner, we glance and gaze to achieve a valid, creative perspective on this dramatic scene. "My Last Duchess" both measures and crosses the boundaries between perceiving subject and perceived object to complement or repeat the way its speaker charms its auditor.

Always knowing his place, the envoy must study his host's revelations (or insinuations) tacitly conversely; readers who are not paragons but nonetheless interpretive contestants must take turns speaking.

Our places in the poem are thus more critical and revocable

than artfully reinscribing social lines on woman-under-erasure or -rubbed-out. We cannot finish reading, or redesigning, such a dramatic monologue without sanction from "The company below", peers who are always hermeneutically framed, and whom we rejoin. It is as foolish to surmise that the duchess "had a form of 'laughing sickness' [and] died of the bubonic plague" in an asylum as to say, "It is surely much more wholesome to accept the text for what it is. . ." (Fleissner 217, 218).

Scholarly authority takes a less "wholesome," a more ducal, approach to textuality by calling, changing, or dropping names. And readers differ and defer because we are as susceptible as the count's envoy to qualifications or "just pretence".

Yet our visual and verbal imaginations depend less than his do on artifact and illocutionary pace. We have a license to redraw and revalue textual boundaries which are sharp yet approachable. To readers "on the dangerous edge of things" that Robert Browning treasures (Bishop Blougram's Apology 395), taming "My Last Duchess" only rarely is better than murdering it.

Chapter 7

With the World As Starting Point

As we have seen, "Pauline," "Paracelsus," and "Sordello" are thematically interrelated by a like conflict; and each leads to the same conclusion: namely, that the artist can only achieve full self-realization through getting into productive communication with the external world. For Browning to embrace this theory, however, was one thing; to illustrate its operation through his own poetry was quite another.

The choice presented to Pauline's lover, Paracelsus, and Sordello is clearly a projection of their creator's own dilemma in the erratic early years of his poetic career. John Stuart Mill's comment on Pauline is well-known: "With considerable poetic powers, the writer seems to me possessed with a more intense and morbid self-consciousness than I ever knew in any sane human being."

This searching criticism made an enormous impression on the youthful Browning, and was perhaps as much as any other single influence instrumental in starting the poet on a succession of technical experiments expressly directed to the formation of a more objective manner.

The attempt to present Paracelsus' spiritual biography in dramatic form was a first step towards externalizing the author's inner perceptions. Fearful, however, that his audience would fail to understand what he was about, and perhaps somewhat suspicious as well of the perfect purity of his artistic motive, the poet took opportunity in the dedication to the original edition to explain the general purpose and method of the poem:

I therefore anticipate his [the reader's] discovery, that it is an attempt, probably more novel than happy, to reverse the method usually adopted by writers whose aim it is to set forth any phenomena of the mind or the passions, by the operation of persons and events; and that, instead of having recourse to an external machinery of incidents to create and evolve the crisis I desire to produce, I have ventured to display somewhat minutely the mood itself in its rise and progress, and have suffered the agency by which it is influenced and determined, to be generally discernible in its effects alone, and subordinate throughout, if not altogether excluded: and this for a reason. I have endeavored to write a poem, not a drama....

In "Sordello," where the mode is narrative rather than dramatic, there is evident, beneath the incrustations of repeated revisions, the author's original intent to employ "an external machinery of incidents to create and evolve the crisis." Yet the principal difficulty which "Sordello" offers the reader is the labyrinthine complexity of the historical events which determine the hero's actions.

In after years, with a better comprehension of where his true talent and interests lay, Browning tended to play down this element in "Sordello" on which he had originally lavished so much care. In dedicating the work to his friend Milsand in 1863, the poet wrote: "The historical decoration was purposely of no more importance than a background requires; and my stress lay on the incidents in the development of a soul: little else is worth study."

Browning met Macready in 1835, and two years later Strafford inaugurated a decade's apprenticeship to the stage. Although Browning's plays were among his earliest productions, while Tennyson did not try his hand at writing for the theatre until the latter part of his life, both men may be said to have turned to dramatic writing out of a desire to reach a wider public.

A distinction should be made, however, between the impulses which led Tennyson and Browning to the drama. The former, secure in his contemporary fame, was looking for new subject-matter of a dignity appropriate to the author of Idylls of the King. Browning, on the other hand, his head crammed with ideas but his reputation all to make, was seeking a manner which would put him into closer correspondence with his age. Even the most superficial consideration of Browning's relationship with Macready indicates how conscientiously the poet was bent on wooing public favor by means of his playwriting efforts. A "Blot in the 'Scutcheon" was announced to the great producer in the following hopeful way:

"The luck of the third adventure" is proverbial. I have written a spick and span new Tragedy (a sort of compromise between my own notion and yours-as I understand it, at least) and will send it to you if you care to be bothered so far. There is "action" in it, drabbing, stabbing, et autres gentillesses,-who knows but the Gods may make me good even yet?

Despite this readiness to compromise, however, Browning was no dramatist for the stage, as anyone who has looked into his plays knows. Of interior or psychological action there is plenty and to spare; but the poet simply could not translate states of mind into the language of external conflict. From the first Macready sensed what was wrong. After rereading Strafford, he wrote in his diary: "I find more grounds for exception than I had anticipated. I had been too much carried away by the truth of character to observe the meanness of plot, and occasional obscurity."

As if in tacit acknowledgment that this play invited such objections, Browning echoed his estimate of "Paracelsus" in the dedication to "Strafford," where he described the drama as "one of Action in Character, rather than Character in Action."

In fact, one cannot escape the conclusion that, real as was his concern to gain an audience for his work, Browning quite early realized that he had no real talent for the theatre, and as a result inclined increasingly to use the dramatic form as a means for working out problems of artistic expression inherent in his own genius. In the choice and development of dramatic themes he exercised greater and greater originality out of seeming indifference to the conventions of theatrical representation; and after the completion of "Colombe's

Birthday" in 1844, he sent a letter to Domett which announced, in effect, his decision no longer to write for production: "I feel myself so much stronger, if flattery not deceive, that I shall stop some things that were meant to follow, and begin again. I really seem to have something fresh to say." The later dramas, furthermore, are strongly characterized by the reemergence of certain themes which were announced in "Pauline," "Paracelsus," and "Sordello." It might even be argued that all of Browning's plays exploit a single situation. A choice confronts the protagonist between two lines of action, one dictated by innate idealism, the other by selfish calculation. The resulting internal conflict supplies the "dramatic" tension of the piece.

Like Sordello, Anael, Djabal's lover in "The Return of the Druses," and Mildred Tresham, the heroine of "A Blot in the 'Scutcheon," both die of emotional exhaustion attributable to the clash between their material and spiritual interests. In "Colombe's Birthday," "Luria," and "A Soul's Tragedy," external action has become almost non-existent, while the speeches of the characters, approximating dramatic monologues, expound with increasing definiteness that master concern in Browning's thinking-the conflict between the wisdom of the heart and the wisdom of the world.

It is too often forgotten that "Bells" and "Pomegranates" included, in addition to the five series devoted entirely to plays, three additional numbers containing dramatic experiments of a very different and much more original kind. These were: "Pippa Passes" (1841), "Dramatic Lyrics" (1842), and "Dramatic Romances and Lyrics "(1845). In explanation of the symbolic title, "Bells and Pomegranates," the poet wrote: "I only meant by that title to indicate an endeavor towards something like an alternation, or mixture, of music with discoursing, sound with sense, poetry with thought."

Towards this blending "Paracelsus" and "Sordello" contributed as much as the plays. The discipline of playwriting sharpened Browning's dramatic sense; but the kinds of dramatic struggle which excited his imagination, as we have seen, were those enacted within the minds of individual characters. In the dramatic lyric and its more sophisticated variation, the dramatic monologue, the poet discovered means for dressing his insights in a guise that would pass muster with a public which had been mystified by "Sordello" and bored by "Strafford."

Although definitely transitional in character, "Pippa Passes" is the first poem which allows us clearly to identify the thematic motifs and technical methods which characterize Browning's mature manner.

The lyric interludes of "Paracelsus" survive in Pippa's songs, but they are now keyed into the story in such a way as to influence its course at climactic moments. Likewise, while the poet still uses dialogue, dramatic effect is largely engendered through tensions antecedent to action.

The subject-matter of the four episodes suggests a striving to fuse the subjective and objective strains in Browning's previous work. A wealth of incident is present by implication; yet the emphasis does not fall directly on the actions of the characters, but rather on the motives out of which action grows.

The psychological analysis of motivation, furthermore, provides Browning with an opportunity for the kind of special pleading at which he was to become so adept. By this means he could endow the creatures of imagination with his own highly individualistic perceptions while seeming to present them as independent beings fully responsible for their own values.

Pippa's refrain, "God's in his heaven-/ All's right with the world!" is often cited as the "reductio ad absurdum" of Victorian optimism. This sentiment, however, is clearly meant to characterize the girl's naïveté and childlike faith, and not the milieu in which she lives.

For Pippa's world is given over to the tyranny of church and state, to corrupt officialdom, to envy and malice and wanton cruelty, to adultery and blackmail and murder. The society which environs the girl from the silk`mills of Asolo makes a mockery of lawful love, patriotism, the familial relationships, and art.

As she wanders the streets on her annual holiday, she brushes shoulders with pimps, prostitutes, debauched students, informers, hired assassins, and parasites of every variety.

Her immunity to worldly degradation lies in her very unworldliness. She is a child of nature, unlettered, inexperienced, guileless, endowed only with a happy disposition, innocence, and the wisdom of her intuitions.

Like Aprile and Eglamor, with whom her kinship is evident, her only means of selfexpression is lyric song. It is through the impact of these songs, so alien to the habits of mind of her auditors, that the theme of the poem comes out. They are heard by "Asolo's Four Happiest Ones" at critical moments in their lives; and they wholly alter the direction of the lives in question by forcing a choice on the hearers.

Pippa's passing awakens the conscience of individuals hitherto enslaved by self-interest, and provokes conduct contrary to the courses of action mapped out by the conscious will. In each case the ultimate decision negates personal inclination and so discredits the materialistic values endorsed by society.

Thus, Ottima and Sebald, having discovered a sense oi guilt, will commit suicide; Jules and Phene will go away together without exacting revenge; Luigi will die in the cause of Italian liberation; and Monsignor will restore her rightful inheritance to Pippa.

Each of the four situations which Pippa influences by her celebration of intuitive feeling hinges on a conflict between individuals and some form of authority. Browning's poems, as we shall see, may be classified into three groups, conforming to the three aspects under which he saw the drama of solitary souls in their strife with the forces of organized society.

One division poses the problem of intellectual assent to established institutions and involves a concept of power: a second poses the problem of emotional assent to conventional morality and involves a concept of love; and third poses the problem of aesthetic assent to artistic traditions and involves a concept of the creative impulse. All three themes occur in

"Pippa Passes," which thus marks out the principal issues with which Browning was henceforth to be concerned.

In the two contrasting panels devoted to the pairs of lovers, Ottima and Sebald and Jules and Phene, Browning advances some of his most characteristic notions about sexual behavior, and in so doing raises issues little in accord with Victorian thinking about such matters.

Confronted by a society which condones loveless marriages, we side with Ottima and Sebald in their splendidly reckless passion, and feel revulsion only after discovering that adultery has led to cold-blooded murder. Pippa's song awakens the lovers to their guilt; but the guilt, be it noted, is for the murder and not for the adultery. And the act of suicide which follows does not seem an additional crime, but rather a confirmation of love's intensity issued in repudiation of society and its usages. Jules is equally insubordinate to accepted norms of social conduct in his reaction to the cruel practical joke perpetrated by his fellow art students.

To have cast off Phene and then avenged his legitimate grievance was obviously the course sanctioned by custom, and the one to which Jules inclined before Pippa's song educed a nobler impulse. In turning from hatred of the students to selfless love for Phene, who shares Pippa's natural innocence, Jules flies directly in the face of convention and thereby attains salvation. His escape to the Greek Isles is the traditional romantic comment on the corrupting ways of the world.

The two concluding episodes present individuals under the shadow of institutionalized authority, in the one case governmental repression represented by the Austrian rule in northern Italy, in the other religious formalism represented by the prestige of the Catholic Church. For Luigi, the champion of liberty, it would be easier to remain with his Chiara in Asolo.

Pippa's song sends him on his mission to Austria, and through averting immediate arrest, reserves him for a patriot's death. It is only on second thought that we realise that in order to establish his point the poet is countenancing political assassination.

Monsignor in the last episode is a preliminary study for a whole family of cynical worldlings who choose the Church as the surest means of satisfying their thirst for power. In listening to Pippa's rhapsody rather than to the insidious arguments of the Intendant, Monsignor abandons the riches which would have smoothed his chosen career.

Finally, Jules' calling as a sculptor gives Browning an opportunity to introduce into "Pippa Passes" some of his theories about the role of the artist. Overly fastidious by temperament and fearful of exposure to the exacting touch of actuality, Jules has made an ivory tower for himself.

Dreaming of ideal beauty, he has fallen into lifeless traditionalism. He describes for Phene a group of statuary on which he has been at work, the central figure of which reflects his concept of himself as the withdrawn and self-immersed votary of art for art's sake:

Quite round, a cluster of mere hands and arms
(Thrust in all senses all ways, from all sides,
Only consenting at the branch's end
They strain toward) serves for frame to a sole face,
The Praiser's in the centre: who with eyes
Sightless, so bend they back to light inside
His brain where visionary forms throng up,
Sings, minding not the palpitating arch
Of hands and arms...

In Phene, however, Jules encounters the higher beauty of living reality which shows up his past work in its true light.

The resulting break with the dead weight of inherited practice is exemplified in Jules' flight from his studio, and in his determination to find a new mode of artistic expression. We learn of the motives responsible for this decision through the letter which Monsignor quotes in the fourth episode:

He never had a clearly conceived Ideal within his brain till to-day.

Yet since his hand could manage a chisel, he has practised expressing other men's Ideals; and, in the very perfection he has attained to, he foresees an ultimate failure: his unconscious hand will pursue its prescribed course of old years, and will reproduce with a fatal expertness the ancient types, let the novel one appear never so palpably to his spirit. There is but one method of escape: confiding the virgin type to as chaste a hand, he will turn painter instead of sculptor, and paint, not carve, its characteristics . . .

Monsignor is sceptical of Jules' success in a career undertaken after so many years of discipleship to a false vision; but his remarks on the artist's change of heart reflect the value which Browning placed on originality, as over against a sterile traditionalism: He may-probably will-fail egregiously; but if there should arise a new painter, will it not be in some-such way, by a poet now, or a musician (spirits who have conceived and perfected an Ideal through some other channel), transferring it to this, and escaping our conventional roads by pure ignorance of them. From "Pippa Passes" to "Dramatic Lyrics" and "Dramatic Romances and Lyrics" is only a short step. In progressing from "Paracelsus" and "Sordello" to plays written expressly for the theatre, Browning had been following a blind alley.

Now he had reversed his direction, and by so doing, had come in sight of his true destination, the dramatic monologue. In the dedication to "Strafford" he had correctly analyzed the bent of his genius; it was to treat "Action in Character, rather than Character in Action." But the murky and self-conscious involutions of "Pauline" had shown that the proper field for such action was not the artist's own character. Through his dramatic experiments Browning had learned to project his insights outward and to give them objective embodiment in imaginary characterizations.

Henceforth he would drop the pretense of external action and confine his attention to the portrayal of individuals under the stress of such interior, psychological conflicts as characterized the play of his own complex and boldly original mind. Seemingly so remote from their creator in time and place and circumstance, these figures would thus become Browning's agents for delivering to his age the messages which be had failed to get across in other ways.

Chapter 8

Authority and The Rebellious Heart

Browning established his eminence among Victorian poets with four volumes published over a period of twenty years in mid-century. Dramatic Lyrics and Dramatic Romances and Lyrics were followed by two additional collections of short poems: Men and Women (1855) and Dramatis Personae (1864). In the ensuing discussion no attempt is made to adhere to the chronological order of these four collections. The fact that for the edition of his poems in 1863 Browning retained the original titles of his first three volumes of short pieces, but completely redistributed their contents, is evidence enough that he did not attach any significance to dates of composition within this body of work.

Whether the form be the lyric, the narrative, or the monologue, the poems in these volumes, as the titles indicate, exhibit a remarkable uniformity of conception in their concentration on the dynamics of behavior. Mindful of the reproof visited on his earlier writing because of its self-conscious quality, the poet rigorously externalized his perceptions under dramatic forms.

The advertisement to the original Dramatic Lyrics in 1842 declares: "Such poems as the following come properly enough, I suppose, under the head of 'Dramatic Pieces;' being, though for the most part Lyric in expression, always Dramatic in principle, and so many utterances of so many imaginary persons, not mine." Henceforth Browning was to exploit all the devices of objectivity at his command in an effort to capture the attention of his age. When he was writing the poems to be gathered in Men and Women, he informed Milsand: "I am writinga first step towards popularity for me-lyrics with more music and painting than before, so as to get people to hear and see."

Yet, a review of the four key works, Dramatic Lyrics, Dramatic Romances and Lyrics, Men and Women, and Dramatis Personae, in the light of what has already been said about his previous work, and especially "Pippa Passes," reveals that like Sordello's reliance on the font at Goito, Browning continued to depend for inspiration on the sources which had fed his imagination from the start.

The dramatic technique, as he employed it, became simply a process of sublimation equivalent in stylistic terms to Tennyson's thematic use of dream, madness, vision, and the quest. By motivating the actors in his dramas with his own ideas and impulses, Browning could speak out with greater originality and boldness than would ever have been possible in his own person.

One wonders how the Victorian middle class with its worship of conformity could have failed to take exception to the poet's outspoken flouting of social conventions. It can only be supposed that approving the apparent regard for morality in his teaching, contemporary readers did not bother to look below the surface to investigate the assumptions on which that morality was founded.

By his constant advocacy of intuitive over rational knowledge, Browning took over the anti-intellectualism of the Romantics and pushed it in the direction of pure primitivism. Along with Carlyle, although much more subtly, Browning endorsed the unconscious as the true wellspring of being.

Pippa is only the first of a long line of innocents, including, to name only a few, the duke's last duchess, the maligned lady of "Count Gismond," Brother Lawrance, the Pied Piper and the resurrected Lazarus of "An Epistle of Karshish." In Browninog's world, the prophets and artists, the lovers and doers of great deeds are never primarily remarkable for intellectual power. Their supremacy is the result of a genius for experiencing life intuitively.

They possess a phenomenal capacity for passionate emotion, combined with a childlike reliance on instinct. These qualities put them in conflict with conventionalized modes of social conduct. Whether it be Fra Lippo, or Rabbi Ben Ezra, or David in "Saul," or the Grammarian, or Childe Roland, Browning's heroes are always the children of their intuitions. In their capacity for instinctive action Browning's heroes are akin to Tennyson's visionaries.

The moments of recognition come to both in the same mysterious and unpredictable ways. Thus, Childe Roland, reaching his journey's end, knows in a blinding flash what is expected of him. Abt Vogler and David improvise their rhapsodies in states of trance-like exaltation. More especially, true love is love at first sight. Such instantaneous perceptions of elective affinity occur, among other poems, in "Count Gismond," "Cristina," "The Statue and the Bust," "Evelyn Hope."

His belief that the intuitions operate through the instrumentality of the emotions rather than the intellect led Browning to a frank celebration of man's physical nature, very foreign to Victorian reticence in such matters. Remembering the Prior's pretty niece, Fra Lippo says: "If you get simple beauty and nought else,/ You get about the best thing God invents." Such an admission is unthinkable in Tennyson, for whom the essential philosophic problem was to league mind and spirit into effective opposition against the bodily appetites. To Browning, on the other hand, flesh and the spirit seemed natural allies against the insidious distortions of the intellect.

So Fra Lippo in his defence of the street-urchin's apprenticeship to life exclaims: "Why, soul and sense of him grow sharp alike." Browning's constant assertion of the soul's interrelationship with the body on an instinctual plane permits him to make claims for the latter which would not otherwise have been admissible. Indeed, two of the most forthright statements that fleshly and spiritual well-being are bound up together come from the mouths of holy men. The Apostle John in "A Death in the Desert" says:

But see the double way wherein we are led,
How the soul learns diversely from the flesh!
With flesh, that hath so little time to stay,
And yields mere basement for the soul's emprise,
Expect prompt teaching.

And in the words of Rabbi Ben Ezra:

Let us not always say
"Spite of this flesh to-day
"I strove, made head, gained ground upon the whole!"
As the bird wings and sings,
Let us cry "All good things
"Are ours, nor soul helps flesh more, now, than flesh helps soul!"

The vitalism inherent in Browning's emphasis on man's intuitive as opposed to his ratiocinative faculties further explains the poet's acceptance of the real and demonstrable, and, conversely his distrust of make-believe. The characters in his poems whom we are asked to admire are all exceptionally clear-sighted in their confrontation of actuality.

They see through the false shows at which society connives, preferring to meet life on its own terms rather than to indulge in fanciful self-delusion. Although Browning's lovers are usually unhappy, there is never any question of escape into a Tennysonian dream world. In his hopeless predicament the lover of "In a Gondola" three times falls to imagining ideal situations which would allow his mistress and himself to be together, and as often rejects the wish for the fact:

Rescue me thou, the only real!
And scare away this mad ideal
That came, nor motions to depart!
Thanks! Now, stay ever as thou art!

Finally, worldly criteria for success lose their validity in Browning's poetry. The poet's so-called philosophy of imperfection, with its lesson that "a man's reach should exceed his grasp," has anti-social implications. This belief holds that an individual's first and highest obligation is to fulfill his own being, regardless of consequences. A lifetime of devotion to settling ""Hoti"'s business," properly basing "Oun," and providing "us the doctrine of the enclitic De" entitles the grammarian to a final resting-place on the heights. The lover of In a Gondola makes a Romeo-like death in the fullness of his passion:

The Three, I do not scorn
To death, because they never lived: but I
Have lived indeed, and so- (yet one more kiss) -can die!

And Childe Roland's ultimate intuition is that success in his quest means just to die bravely. Once the intuitional psychology at the heart of Browning's thinking is fully understood, all the major thematic concerns in his poetry become meaningful as deriving therefrom. Among Victorian poets he is the great champion of individualism. If self-realization is the purpose of life, then it follows that any agency which thwarts that process is inimical to the best interests of human nature.

And since formalized systems of thought operating through social institutions have always tended to repress freedom of belief and action, Prownings most characteristic poems have to do with the conflict-between the individual and his environment. There is a wisdom of the mind and a wisdom of the heart; and the two are always at odds, since the one teaches compliance with the ways of the world while the other inculcates non-conformity. Thus, where his political and religious convictions or his beliefs about love and art are concerned, each man must make a choice between intellectual subservience to customary values and emancipation from all such restrictions.

In insisting on the integrity of the individual soul, Browning allies himself on one side with the Romantic poets, and on the other with the Pre-Raphaelites. He differs from both, however, in his concept of the artist's responsibilities. Whereas Byron delivered frontal assaults on contemporary manners and morals and Rossetti inclined to ignore his milieu, Browning adopted an oblique approach to his age. By dramatizing individual case histories, he stepped before his readers in such a variety of poetic guises that it was impossible to identify him with any single role.

Furthermore, since he made his attacks piecemeal through anatomizing characters each of whom embodied but a single aspect of contemporary thought, he could be sure of enlisting on his side all those who did not share this particular foible, and so of forestalling unified opposition.

It is only when the widely diversified types in Browning's catalogue are grouped according to family resemblance that one begins to comprehend the scope and consistency of the poet's opposition to existing values, and hence the extent of his alienation from Victorian society.

One such grouping, it has been suggested, would include all those characters whose ways of life are conditioned by some clearly defined set of conventions. Superficially dissimilar though they are, "My Last Duchess" and "Soliloquy of the Spanish Cloister" present versions of a single conflict. Just as the duke in the former is motivated in all he does by punctilious pride of rank, so the hypocritical friar who soliloquizes in the second poem appeals to the minutiae of religious observance.

And just as the dead duchess in her childlike response to all innocent pleasures unknowingly made a mockery of her husband's ceremoniousness, so Brother Lawrence's every spontaneous action criticizes religious formalism. In both poems the central irony grows out of the fact that the speaker damns hiimself in endeavouring to cast discredit on his unsuspecting adversary.

So, in poem after poem representing every kind of career, the protagonist must make his decision between the practical inducements to worldly success and lonely integrity of spirit. The Lost Leader, who sold out "just for a handful of silver ... just for a riband to stick in his coat," stands in telling contrast to the Italian in England who, even in exile, remains loyal to the patriot's dream. For the grammarian, gifted above his fellows, the search for knowledge means sacrifice of all that would otherwise have been his due:

He knew the signal, and stepped on with pride

Over men's pity;
Left play for work, and grappled with the world
Bent on escaping...

Childe Roland's thoughts are saddened by memories of his lost companions, Cuthbert and Giles, who, presumably unable to sustain the rigors of the quest, fell away, seduced by the world's allurements. All the grotesque properties of this poem-the "hateful cripple," the "stiff blind horse, his every bone astare," the engine of torture, the "great black bird, Apollyon's bosom-friend"-are marshalled as if to epitomize the malice of society against the dedicated ones who step aside from the trodden path.

Browning's most forcible condemnations of rationalism, however, come in those poems which deal with the problems of religious belief. In "Christmas-Eve" and "Easter-Day," published in the same year as "In Memoriam," the poet had worked out the grounds of his own highly individualistic faith. It sprang from a purely intuitive conviction of the necessity for a loving God.

"Saul" and "Rabbi Ben Ezra" give full expression to this religious optimism; but the modern reader may well take greater interest in those works which dramatize alternative positions and show the poet dealing with the seeptical tendencies in contemporary thought. Among the best things to be found in Men and Women and Dramatis Personae is a series of monologues surveying the principal intellectual traditions which have militated against the Christian revelation.

A uniform tone of nostalgia pervades "An Epistle, containing the Strange Medical Experience of Karshish, the Arab Physician; Cleon; and Caliban upon Setebos; or, Natural Theology in the Island." The speaker in each poem, instinctively realizing the spiritual limitations of the system of thought to which he is committed, is driven against his will to postulate a Christian deity.

Yet wistful longing never actualizes itself in terms of faith, because it is smothered under the weight of inherited prejudice. Karshish stands for the scientific mentality wholly at a loss to cope with the mystery of Lazarus' resurrection. Cleon, living in the end of the Hellenistic era, finds such meager consolation as he can in the synthesizing temper of a decadent culture. In the superficial view Caliban appears to belong among Browning's primitives; actually he is man materialized to the point where he can only construct God in his own capricious and spiteful image.

The historical or literary guise under which these issues are presented suggests the devious operation of Browning's critical intent. The poet was not really interested in the historical process, as Carlyle or Ruskin tried to be; nor did he have Tennyson's genius for reanimating myth.

Karshish, Cleon, and Caliban are representative Victorians in fancy dress. As time passed, Browning inclined more and more to put aside the cloak of historical remoteness and to address himself to the psychoanalysis of contemporary types. "Bishop Blougram's Apology" and "Mr. Sludge," ""The Medium,"" for example, bring the charge of spiritual sterility directly home to Victorian society.

"Bishop Blougram's Apology" is an early example of the special pleading, the skillful conduct of casuistic argument, which bewildered so many of Browning's readers.

The difficulty, of course, is that Blougram is a sort of devil's advocate who appropriates typical Browningesque doctrines and converts them to his own ends. In the words of his creator: "He said true things, but called them by wrong names." The whole tenor of the Bishop's plea points to the conclusion that worldly self-interest is identical with spiritual well-being. In demonstrating this line of reasoning, Blougram boldly enlists theories which have a diametrically opposed significance in Browning's own thinking.

Thus, he says: "My business is not to remake myself,/ But to make the absolute best of what God made"; and again:

Let us concede (gratuitously though)
Next life relieves the soul of body, yields
Pure spiritual enjoyment: well, my friend,
Why lose this life i' the meantime, since its use
May be to make the next life more intense?

Only gradually do we recognize the extent of the clever Bishop's compromise with the existing order. In making choice of a way of life, he has consulted only his physical comfort, out of regard for which he has become the servant of institutionalized religion. He has, in other words, allowed himself to be corrupted by the self-deluding operations of his own intellect.

The key to Browning's meaning in the more abstruse dramatic monologues may nearly always be discovered in the culminating action. In this case Gigadibs instinctively revolts against Blougram's intellectual gymnastics, and turning his back on England, take up a Carlylean life of unthinking action as a colonist.

"Mr. Sludge," ""The Medium"" follows a similar pattern. Browning, of course, had no use for mediums, seeing in their vogue clear evidence of the frivolous sensation-seeking of a society that had lost its spiritual bearings. Nevertheless, until the last extraordinary diatribe which reveals Sludge as the unregenerate charlatan he is, the poet allows his protagonist to make out the best possible case for himself. Ironically, despite the fact that Sludge has been caught red-handed at his sham practices, he has relied on trickery for so long that he is partially self-duped:

I tell you, sir, in one sense, I believe
Nothing at all, — that everybody can,
Will, and does cheat: but in another sense
I'm ready to believe my very self —
That every cheat's inspired, and every lie
Quick with a germ of truth.

More damaging, however, as a concealed expression of Browning's own sense of the price which society pays for trifling with its genuine spiritual impulses, is Sludge's mocking vindication of himself. In a world where the prizes go to those who live by their wits, Sludgehood is a normal phenomenon:

Or, finally,
Why should I set so fine a gloss on things?
What need I care? I cheat in self-defence,
And there's my answer to a world of cheats!

Cheat? To be sure, sir! What's the world worth else?

Browning's intuitionism announces itself most ardently when he writes about love, this being a subject which he handles with greater candor and penetration than any other poet of the early and mid-Victorian periods. It is not hard to understand why he should have thought the experience of love so important.

Through the emotions which it releases man reaches heights of intensity, both physical and spiritual, such as are achievable in no other way. Romantic love, however, is little subject to discipline; and the Victorians in their regard for social stability endeavored to safeguard themselves against its disruptive power behind an elaborate system of conventions. A double standard of conduct was in force for the sexes, and the family stood as the central support of the entire social fabric.

To the authority of these ideals Tennyson's poetry bears constant testimony. Browning, on the other hand, challenges the sexual morality of the Victorians at nearly every point. His interest is in the fulfillment of passion, rather than in the preservation of domestic proprieties. In no way are his convictions less conformable to accepted theories than in his refusal to recognize any basis for social inequality between men and women.

His adoration of Elizabeth Barrett no doubt explains a good deal in this connection; but while Browning yielded to no other Victorian in his idealization of womanhood, his thinking had very little in common with the contemporary concept of the womanly woman. Only Meredith's heroines challenge Browning's in the qualities of fortitude, loyalty, idealism, intelligence, and insight.

The Euripides of "The Last Adventure of Balaustion" is speaking for his creator when he says: "Mere puppets once, I now make womankind,/ For thinking, saying, doing, match the male." Browning, like Meredith, finds that the woman is usually right. With a few exceptions, his love lyrics fall into two classes. In the first the speaker is a man who has been rejected and who humbly accepts responsibility for failure, attributing it to some inadequacy in his own nature. In the second it is the woman who has been cast off. She too is humble; but we are made to feel that she suffers not because of any innate unworthiness, but rather because of some flaw in her lover.

The central problem in Browning's love poetry is invariably one of communication between the sexes. The intangible influences which encourage or destroy intimacy between men and women elicit all his skill in psychological analysis; for love exists in and through human intuitions. Reference has already been made to the poet's belief that destined lovers recognize each other on first sight.

But these moments of full and perfect communion are precarious; and, save for the most exceptional cases, the initial harmony does not survive social pressures or the importunities of individual temperament. It is rare in Browning's work to find such a poem as "By the Fire-Side," in which the lovers have so come to exist in each other that one of them can say:

When, if I think but deep enough,
You are wont to answer, prompt as rhyme;
And you, too, find without rebuff
Response your soul seeks many a time
Piercing its fine flesh-stuff.

More commonly the good moment passes, as in "Two in the Campagna," where we watch it slip away despite the lovers' longing to prolong their felicity; or "The Last Ride Together," in which the speaker strives desperately to eternalize his fleeting togetherness with the woman he loves.

Ideal love is for Browning the consummation of an intuitive process by which the lovers transcend the barriers of their separate individualities and achieve spiritual union. Whenever this happens, there results the most exquisite and productive form of communication possible between human beings.

The very possibility of a love like this excites the heroine of "The Flight of the Duchess" to say:

If any two creatures grew into one,

They would do more than the world has done:
Though each apart were never so weak,
Ye vainly through the world should seek
For the knowledge and the might
Which in such union grew their right...

Browning's men and women, then, are always seeking to pierce the barrier which, in his favourite metaphor, separates two isolated souls reaching towards each other. The lover of "In a Gondola" pleads with his mistress:

Do, break down the partition-wall
'Twixt us, the daylight world beholds
Curtained in dusk and splendid folds!
What's left but — all of me to take?

And in "By the Fire-Side" Browning, speaking for once in his own person, describes the loss of personal identity under love's mysterious spell:

If two lives join, there is oft a scar,
They are one and one, with a shadowy third;
One near one is too far.
A moment after, and hands unseen
Were hanging night around us fast;
But we knew that a bar was broken between
Life and life: we were mixed at last
In spite of the mortal screen.

As one would expect from what has already been said, Browning holds that undue reliance on the intellect with its ulterior motivations makes for failure in affairs of the heart. The feminine nature is wiser than the masculine in its instinctive response to emotional impulse.

In a number of poems love is destroyed through the man's determination to establish his mental superiority over the woman. This is the theme of Mesmerism, for example, as well as of "A Woman's Last Word" in which the woman soliloquizes:

What so false as truth is,
False to thee?
Where the serpent's tooth is
Shun the tree —

Since in the poet's thinking the intellectual faculties are self-corrupting and prone to infection by the uses of the world, another group of poems, written from the female point of view, lays blame for the man's infidelity on the temptations held out by society.

Examples in this vein are "Any Wife to Any Husband," and the group of highly sophisticated lyrics, "James Lee's Wife." The comparatively early "Cristina" departs from the usual pattern of Browning's love poems after he had come to know Elizabeth Barrett. For here it is the woman who is found wanting to the moment of recognition when "mine and her souls rushed together":

Oh, observe! Of course, next moment,
The world's honours, in derision,
Trampled out the light for ever:
Never fear but there's provision
Of the devil's to quench knowledge
Lest we walk the earth in rapture!
— Making those who catch God's secret
Just so much more prize their capture!

Browning's conviction that the passionate intensity of romantic love is incompatible with conventionalized social morality leads him to glorify the one at the expense of the other. That perennial theme, the world well lost for love, is so appealing that Victorian readers in their sentimentality were apparently willing to overlook its frequent anti-social corollary in Browning's poetry, where the decision to give all for love more often than not involves some course of action at variance with established codes of conduct.

Too extreme, perhaps, is the example of "Porphyria's Lover" where the demented narrator has committed murder and in this way made the final choice for a mistress

Too weak, for all her heart's endeavour,
To set its struggling passion free
From pride, and vainer ties dissever,
And give herself to me for ever.

In "The Flight of the Duchess," however, we are compelled to sympathize with the duchess in her flight from the staidly formalistic home of her husband to join the gypsies; and the prevaricating speaker in "Too Late" seems most manly when he reconstructs the lost opportunity to take his beloved away from her husband, by force if necessary.

"In a Gondola" presents a more fatal but equally persuasive picture of adultery as the solution to loveless marriage. And the inescapable implication of "Respectability" is that the illicit affair there described has gained its intensity and seriousness from being carried on outside the pale of social conventions:

Dear, had the world in its caprice
Deigned to proclaim "I know you both,
"Have recognized your plighted troth,
"Am sponsor for you: live in peace!"
How many precious months and years
Of youth had passed, that speed so fast,
Before we found it out at last,
The world, and what it fears?
How much of priceless life were spent
With men that every virtue decks,
And women models of their sex,
Society's true ornament, —
Ere we dared wander, nights like this,
Thro'wind and rain, and watch the Seine,
And feel the Boulevard break again
To warmth and light and bliss?
I know! the world proscribes not love;
Allows my finger to caress
Your lips'contour and downiness,
Provided it supply a glove.
The world's good word! —

"In a Balcony" and "The Glove" present in unequivocal terms the conflict between the wisdom of the intuitions and the usages of society. The theme of "In a Balcony" is conveyed in Norbert's reference to the "instincts of the heart that teach the head." The Queen, a marble figure of authority, comes, through passion for her minister of state, to recognize the hollowness of worldly power.

Of the reality of love, on the contrary, she learns:

'T is as different from dreams,
From the mind's cold calm estimate of bliss,
As these stone statues from the flesh and blood.

Meanwhile, Constance, the Queen's protegée, who resembles the speaker in "Respectability" in her fear of the world's callous incomprehension, would prefer that her liaison with Norbert remain clandestine. In effect, she is matching wits against society out of a desire to secure her lover to herself. When Norbert wants to make an open declaration of their attachment, she replies:

A year of this compression's ecstasy
All goes for nothing! You would give this up
For the old way, the open way, the world's,
His way who beats, and his who sells his wife!
What tempts you?-their notorious happiness
Makes you ashamed of ours?

In the end Constance prevails on Norbert to make his request in a manner so ambiguous that the Queen misunderstands his intention and believes that her own love is returned.

Only when Constance's subterfuges have ruined her hopes does she learn the error of playing the world's game in the world's way. Then finally she lets her heart speak out without restraint. She is willing to sacrifice her happiness to Norbert's career, but at the same time she will stop treating love as though it were a marketable commodity:

I know the thriftier way
Of giving-haply,'t is the wiser way.
Meaning to give a treasure, I might dole
Coin after coin out (each, as that were all,
With a new largess still at each despair)
And force you keep in sight the deed, preserve
Exhaustless till the end my part and yours,
My giving and your taking; both our joys
Dying together. Is it the wiser way?
I choose the simpler; I give all at once.
Know what you have to trust to, trade upon!

Use it, abuse it, — anything but think
Hereafter, "Had I known she loved me so,
And what my means, I might have thriven with it."
This is your means. I give you all myself,

The social satire in "The Glove" results from a seeming paradox in the lady's behavior. Her motive for casting the glove into the lion-pit seems purely capricious; and the reader's first inclination is to side with King Francis' court in its condemnation of the lady and approval of De Lorge when he flings the glove back in her face after its retrieval. On reconsideration, however, we perceive that our initial judgment was conditioned by a code of etiquette, rather than by any real concern for the heroine's situation.

By trifling with convention in an apparently irresponsible way, she has shown up the ingrained conventionality of her admirer whose bravery, like his subsequent rudeness, was displayed not for the lady's sake, but solely to win popular approval.

The dénouement reveals the poet's meaning. The lady, followed by the youth who alone comprehends her action, departs from the artificial life of the court, while De Lorge remains to marry a lady-in-waiting and to see her become the king's mistress, while he is relegated to the position of glove-bearer.

If, for Browning, true love necessitates total disregard of the ways of the world, then it follows that self-interest is love's greatest enemy. A long succession of poems, concerned with individuals for whom the voice of society drowns out that of passion, dramatizes, on the negative side, the poet's sense that no worldly gain is ever achieved without spiritual loss.

The disillusioned lover of "Dis Aliter Visum; or, Le Byron de nos Jours" recalls in bitterness of heart how he let opportunity slip through his fingers from cynical disbelief that the good moment could be prolonged:

She might take me as I take her.
Perfect the hour would pass, alas!
Climb high, love high, what matter? Still,
Feet, feelings, must descend the hill:

An hour's perfection can't recur.
So, instead, he has elected the tamer consolation of a career:
What? All I am, was, and might be,
All, books taught, art brought, life's whole strife,
Painful results since precious, just
Were fitly exchanged, in wise disgust,
For two checks freshened by youth and sea?

But the moment, once gone past, does not return; and in the resolution we learn that each has made a wretched marriage, he with a young ballet-dancer, she with a too-old whistplayer.

Artistic ambition is the force which keeps the lovers of "Youth and Art" apart; but through their failure to perceive the all-important connection between art and life, the former has betrayed them to triviality. The girl, who would surpass Grisi, is now queen at "bals-paré"; and the sculptor, aspiring to replace Gibson, has had to be content with the dubious distinction of membership in the Royal Academy.

Browning's most provocative examination of failure in love as the penalty of faint-hearted conformity to social conventions occurs in "The Statue and the Bust." The duke first beheld the lady on the day of her wedding to another man, and at once their souls "rushed together." Neither is restrained by moral scruples; yet they postpone the consummation of their love.

Each is content with the daily encounter when the duke rides under the window where his beloved sits like another Lady of Shalott, but more remote from reality in her too-patient waiting.

So the passing of time and the inconsequential demands of everyday existence imperceptibly dull the edge of resolve, although the lovers continue to delude themselves with the belief that such steadfastness as theirs must eventually be rewarded. Meanwhile, it is better not to provoke a scandal:

And still, as love's brief morning wore,
With a gentle start, half smile, half sigh,
They found love not as it seemed before.
They thought it would work infallibly,

But not in despite of heaven and earth:
The rose would blow when the storm passed by.
Meantime they could profit in winter's dearth
By store of fruits that supplant the rose:
The world and its ways have a certain worth:
And to press a point while these oppose
Were a simple policy; better wait:
We lose no friends and we gain no foes.

When it is too late, they awaken to the realization that they have wasted their lives in make-believe:

And both perceived they had dreamed a dream;
Which hovered as dreams do, still above:
But who can take a dream for a truth?
Oh, hide our eyes from the next remove!

In the end the lovers call in art to eternalize their devotion; but the statue and the bust mock rather than glorify the impulse which brings them into being. Fixed in their apartness, they are as futile and as static as the couple they commemorate. Art has been made a substitute for, not a confirmation of life. That there might be no mistaking his meaning, Browning attached a coda to the poem.

In Hamlet's phrase, "The readiness is all." Virtue is not in the goal, but in the passionate intensity of striving:

Do your best, whether winning or losing it,
If you choose to play! — is my principle.
Let a man contend to the uttermost
For his life's set prize, be it what it will!
The counter our lovers staked was lost
As surely as if it were lawful coin:
And the sin I impute to each frustrate ghost
Is — the unlit lamp and the ungirt loin,
Though the end in sight was a vice, I say.

If we turn now to Browning's aesthetics, it is immediately apparent from such poems as "Youth and Art" and "The Statue and the Bust" that for this poet art could never supplant life.

No position is more consistently maintained throughout his writing than the one deriving from the assumption that all enduring artistic expression is incidental to the experience which inspires it. Poems otherwise so different as "The Last Ride Together, In a Balcony, Cleon, Old Pictures in Florence, "Transcendentalism: A Poem in Twelve Books," James Lee's Wife," and "One Word More" reiterate the author's vitalism.

Art exists simply as one form of creative endeavor to educe life's meaning. The test of an artist's genius lies in his ability to move his audience to action. "The Pied Piper," "Fra Lippo Lippi," and the David of "Saul" have this faculty in common.

The rats and child‸en of Hamelin Town jubilantly follow wherever the piper's music leads. Fra Lippo is going to have to repaint his fresco of St. Laurence at Prato since the faithful are obliterating its details in their devout rage. The mounting ecstasy of David's songs lifts from Saul's spirit the gloom which has incapacitated him.

On first glance, Browning's artistic theories seem to accord fully with his age in its endorsement of the Ruskinian arguments that the highest art results from the perception of moral truth and promotes virtuous conduct. The poet's application of these propositions, however, is again suggestive of a double awareness.

Just as the religious or political man must take a stand with regard to institutionalism and the lover with regard to conventional morality, so the artist is threatened by the tyranny of tradition. As it impinges on the life of the imagination, traditionalism has a dual authority.

Its influence may be largely intellectual, regimenting instinct to a lifeless formalism. This way leads to art for art's sake. Or, in its more popular aspect, tradition may inform the artist's desire to communicate and so make of him a virtuoso. Whether he inhabit an ivory tower or the market place, the artist who subordinates his native talent to traditional modes has, in Browning's opinion, betrayed his birthright.

The nameless painter of "Pictor Ignotus," like Aprile and Eglamor, has sought refuge from the harsh importunities of the world in the recesses of his inner being. As one naturally inquisitive, to scan

The licence and the limit, space and bound,
Allowed to truth made visible in man,

He is all too conscious of the loss in vitality to his painting consequent on denial of the sensory world. He looks outward and sadly asks: "0 human faces, hath it spilt, my cup?" Self-withdrawal, we learn, has not taken place out of temperamental inability to respond to external stimuli, but rather because the painter shrinks from the callously imperceptive way that would-be connoisseurs deal with artists and their work.

Yet within the privacy of his individual consciousness he discovers no impulse towards original creation, but only the pale inspiration of inherited tradition. The sole consolation left him after producing unending variations on stock religious themes is that he has at least dictated the terms of his defeat:

If at whiles
My heart sinks, as monotonous I paint
These endless cloisters and eternal aisles
With the same series, Virgin, Babe and Saint,
With the same cold calm beautiful regard, —
At least no merchant traffics in my heart;
The sanctuary's gloom at least shall ward
Vain tongues from where my pictures stand apart:
Only prayer breaks the silence of the shrine
While, blackening in the daily candle-smoke,
They moulder on the damp wall's travertine,
'Mid echoes the light footstep never woke.
So, die my pictures! surely, gently die!
0 youth, men praise so,-holds their praise its worth?
Blown harshly, keeps the trump its golden cry?
Tastes sweet the water with such specks of earth?

The reasons for the failure of Andrea del Sarto are at once more complex and more symptomatic of the iconoclastic bias which carries over into Browning's aesthetic thinking.

Where the speaker in "Pictor Ignotus" is frightened of the world's rough handling, Andrea has shamelessly courted popularity. The unknown painter's talent is exercised for purely private ends; Andrea paints to make money, allowing his choice of subjects to be determined by the market. He panders to the type of material-minded collector that Browning describes in "My Last Duchess" and "The Bishop Orders his Tomb at St. Praxed's Church."

The Pictor Ignotus follows in the tradition of the Primitives who stressed soul at the expense of body; Andrea is no less slave to a realistic tradition which ignores spiritual overtones in its care for anatomic fidelity. Reluctant to acknowledge where he has gone wrong, Andrea, like the unknown painter, hypocritically pretends to exist in the realm of his imaginings:

I, painting from myself to myself,
Know what I do, am unmoved by men's blame
Or their praise either.

Later on he declares: "Beside, incentives come from the soul's self;/ The rest avail not." But the hypocrisy of this statement, when applied to his own work, is evident even to Andrea. The error lies not in his hand with its matchless skill, but in the soul which directs that hand. Preferring any compromise to the loss of his worthless wife, the painter has silenced the admonitions of his spiritual nature.

Thinking of the gigantic, though flawed genius of Michelangelo and Leonardo and Raphael, he ejaculates: "The sudden blood of these men!" The recognition that he can put over against their achievements only a certain cold proficiency wrings from him the lament: "But all the play, the insight and the stretch-/ Out of me, out of me!" No sooner does he undertake to correct a clumsy line in a drawing by Raphael than the chalk falls from his fingers: "Ay! but the soul! he's Rafael! rub it out!"

Andrea's virtuosity, we see, is simply a skill acquired through patient mastery of others' techniques, handed down in the schools and now corrupted for venal ends. It is his unforgivable fault to be faultless: "Well, less is more, Lucrezia: I am judged."

In "An Essay on Shelley," written in 1852 to preface a spurious collection of that poet's letters, Browning distinguished between two kinds of objective poet or "fashioner." Concerning the creative impulse of the first kind, the question to be asked is: "Did a soul's delight in its own extended sphere of vision set it, for the gratification of an insuppressible power, on labour, as other men are set on rest?" For the second class, the question is rephrased as follows: "Or did a sense of duty or of love lead it to communicate its own sensations to mankind?

Did an irresistible sympathy with men compel it to bring down and suit its own provision of knowledge and beauty to their narrow scope?" "Pictor Ignotus" and "Andrea del Sarto" seem to exemplify the corrupt extremes of these two types. The unknown painter has become the morbidly self-conscious victim of his "soul's delight in its own extended sphere of vision," while Andrea in his desire to communicate has sacrificed originality and compelled his talent "to bring down and suit its own provision of knowledge and beauty" to the "narrow scope" of a vulgar audience.

"An Essay on Shelley," however, goes on to propose another kind of poet whose response to experience is primarily subjective. This is the seer, described by Browning as follows:

He, gifted like the objective poet with the fuller perception of nature and man, is impelled to embody the thing he perceives not so much with reference to the many below as to the one above him, the supreme Intelligence which apprehends all things in their absolute truth, — an ultimate view ever aspired to, if but partially attained, by the poet's own soul. . . . Not with the combination of humanity in action, but with the primal elements of humanity, he has to do; and he digs where he stands, — preferring to seek them in his own soul as the nearest reflex of the absolute Mind, according to the intuitions of which he desires to perceive and speak. . . . He is rather a seer, accordingly, than a fashioner, and what he produces will be less a work than an effluence.

Although in his Shelley essay Browning declined to favor either the objective or the subject artist at the expense of the other, the general tone of his remarks strongly suggests that in his concept of the seer he was proposing a higher orientation for the poetic impulse than would result from conforming to the demands either of the individual ego or of society at large.

And certainly in Browning's own poetry devoted to the arts and their practice it is the seer who emerges as the supreme type of artist, embodying in transmuted form the two aspects of the fashioner and merging them under the authority of a transcendent vision adequate to the opposing impulses which inhere in a double awareness.

Although "Christmas-Eve and Easter-Day" is largely a defence of Browning's particular brand of Christianity, the philosophic implications of religion and art were so closely allied in his thinking that the poem is also a declaration of his aesthetic creed. "Christmas-Eve" considers among other things the discrepancy between the ideal and the actual in this life-all that is signified by Abt Vogler's statement: "On earth the broken arcs; in heaven, a perfect round."

The ideal, as it exists in God, is unattainable on earth; but this knowledge does not exonerate humanity from attempting the impossible; for in the effort lies the hope of spiritual salvation.

Hence Andrea del Sarto's saddened perception: "Ah, but a man's reach should exceed his grasp,/ Or what's a heaven for?" The artist, endowed with special intuitions, is better equipped than other men to apprehend the spirit world. His senses are more keenly responsive to beauty and his mind probes deeper into the laws of cause and effect; but the faculty on which before all others he relies is imaginative insight. Possession of this attribute to an unequalled degree made Shakespeare a poet apart.

But, as Browning proceeds to expound in "Easter-Day," the artist's unique gifts impose on him the highest possible responsibility. Perceiving the divine plan, he must place his genius at God's disposal.

Thus, although the creative impulse has its source within the individual consciousness, its operation must not be expended on self-expression, but rather on elucidation of the heavenly will. It is on these grounds that Browning takes issue witb art for art's sake. Whereas the deluded devotee of this doctrine endeavors to meet self-imposed standards of perfection, the true artist hears a more imperious voice speaking through his intuitions. While humbly aware that the human imagination is at best a distorting medium, he nevertheless tries, as much as possible, to keep his message uncontaminated by the vanity of artifice.

So the apocalyptic presence in Easter-Day admonishes the desperate poet who places reliance in his own earth-bound powers:

"And so much worse thy latter quest,"
(Added the voice,) "that even on earth —
Whenever, in man's soul, had birth
Those intuitions, grasps of guess,
Which pull the more into the less,
Making the finite comprehend
Infinity, — the bard would spend
Such praise alone, upon his craft,
As, when wind-lyres obey the waft,
Goes to the craftsman who arranged
The seven strings, changed them and rechanged
Knowing it was the South that harped.
He felt his song, in singing, warped;
Distinguished his and God's part: whence
A world of spirit as of sense
Was plain to him, yet not too plain,
Which he could traverse, not remain
A guest in: — else were permanent
Heaven on earth its gleams were meant
To sting with hunger for full light,
Made visible in verse, despite
The veiling weakness, — truth by means
Of fable, showing while it screens, —
Since highest truth, man e'er supplied,
Was ever fable on outside.
Such gleams made bright the earth an age;
Now the whole sun's his heritage!
Take up thy world, it is allowed,
Thou who hast entered in the cloud!"

Browning's belief that the creative instinct can only function at its highest potential under divine inspiration is the counterpart of Tennyson's reliance on vision. It follows, then, that the poet-seer must acknowledge the sanction under which he fulfills his mission, and that, in Browning's own words, he will be "impelled to embody the thing he perceives not so much with reference to the many below, as to the one above him, the supreme Intelligence which apprehends all things in their absolute truth."

"How It Strikes a Contemporary" exemplifies this concept of the artist in his capacity as God's "recording chief-inquisitor."

The protagonist of the poem is a solitary figure, alert to every incident in the life around him, yet mysteriously alien to his environment, his whole loyalty absorbed by the "King" to whom he writes his nightly missive. Of the poet-seer Browning also says that his writing will "be less a work than an effluence." "Saul" and "Abt Vogler" illustrate the true nature of artistic inspiration.

David in the former poem, at the approach of the final ecstatic vision of Christ, flings away the harp which has formalized his earlier utterances: "Then truth came upon me. No harp more-no song more!" And in contrast to the musician who labors over the mannered fugues of Hugues of Saxe-Gotha, Abt Vogler is a master of extemporization. Vogler, furthermore, is playing in an empty church solely for his own pleasure when the inspiration descends.

His mystic communion with God is thus achieved as a private revelation. And although his improvisations can never be recaptured on earth, he is consoled by the knowledge that they have reached the One to whom they were addressed:

All we have willed or hoped or dreamed of good shall exist;

Not its semblance, but itself; no beauty, nor good, nor power
Whose voice has gone forth, but each survives for the melodist
When eternity affirms the conception of an hour.
The high that proved too high, the heroic for earth too hard,
The passion that left the ground to lose itself in the sky,
Are music sent up to God by the lover and the bard;
Enough that he heard it once: we shall hear it by-and-by.

But Abt Vogler remains something of an exception in Browning's gallery of artists. Even the seer's field of activity is this world and the life which he shares with other men. God is manifest through his handiwork, and all that mortals can know of his being comes in rightly interpretating the phenomena which condition earthly existence.

It is on these phenomena that the imagination must exercise itself, avoiding all willful delusions prompted by the intellect. Any work of the imagination which fails to take cognizance of the facts of human experience is necessarily for Browning either false or imperfect.

Thus, in "Old Pictures in Florence" he chooses Christian in preference to Greek art because of the classic artist's unrealistic refusal to "paint man man." Similarly, the speaker in the eighth lyric of "James Lee's Wife" has learned from Leonardo that there is more true beauty in the workworn hand of a peasant than in any academic dream of perfection that "lived long ago or was never born."

And in ""Transcendentalism: A Poem in Twelve Books"" the youthful poet gets severely scolded for letting his vision of actuality become obscured by metaphysical theories: "So come, the harp back to your heart again!/ You are a poem, though your poem's naught."

The greatest artists are those whose senses and intuitions work together in harmonious unison. The great enemy of man's intuitional nature, as we have seen, is the intellect; and in artistic enterprises the intellect's weapon of attack against the freshness and immediacy of sensory impressions is tradition.

Therefore, the artists whom Browning holds up for admiration are, like his lovers and men of action, noncomformists, rebels, and individualists on instinct. The fullest expression of the poet's aesthetic philosophy is to be found in "Fra Lippo Lippi." The circumstances under which we encounter Fra Lippo are significant in themselves; for he has just been apprehended as a potential law-breaker.

We learn that he has fled the confinement of his patron's house because it is carnival time and he is unable to resist the lure of the streets. The irrepressible gaiety of life is implicit in the jigging refrain that keeps running through the painter's mind:

"Flower o' the broom,
Take away love, and our earth is a tomb!"

With this preparation, it is not surprising to find that Fra Lippo has rejected the institutional repression of the Church, and especially that he has thrown over traditional forms of ecclesiastical art as exemplified in the work of such artists as Fra Angelico and Lorenzo Monaco. Fra Lippo is one of Browning's incorruptible innocents.

He paints by instinct; and what he paints is the world of his perceptions, not an intellectualized abstraction of it: "The world and life's too big to pass for a dream." But underlying the intensity of his response to human experience is the innate perception of a higher reality made manifest, if at all, through the appearances of this world.

The artist cannot do better than reproduce with as great fidelity as possible his individual sense of the observed fact; in so doing he records his own gratitude for the privilege of living, and in the process opens the eyes of others to the meaning of life:

However, you're my man, you've seen the world
— The beauty and the wonder and the power,
The shapes of things, their colours, lights and shades,
Changes, surprises, — and God made it all!
— For what? Do you feel thankful, ay or no,
For this fair town's face, yonder river's line,
The mountain round it and the sky above,
Much more the figures of man, woman, child,
These are the frame to? What's it all about?
To be passed over, despised? or dwelt upon,
Wondered at? oh, this last of course! — you say.
But why not do as well as say, — paint these
Just as they are, careless what comes of it?
God's works — paint any one, and count it crime
To let a truth slip. Don't object, "His works
"Are here already; nature is complete:

"Suppose you reproduce her — (which you can't)
"There's no advantage! you must beat her, then."
For, don't you mark? we're made so that we love
First when we see them painted, things we have passed
Perhaps a hundred times nor cared to see;
And so they are better, painted — better to us,
Which is the same thing. Art was given for that;
God uses us to help each other so,
Lending our minds out. Have you noticed, now,
Your cullion's hanging face? A bit of chalk,
And trust me but you should, though! How much more,
If I drew higher things with the same truth!
That were to take the Prior's pulpit — place,
Interpret God to all of you! Oh, oh,
It makes me mad to see what men shall do
And we in our graves! This world's no blot for us,
Nor blank; it means intensely, and means good:
To find its meaning is my meat and drink.

In the appeal which his paintings make to the emotions of an unsophisticated populace Fra Lippo finds the ultimate vindication of his artistic theories. But while Browning believed that great art would always communicate so long as the sensibilities of its audience had not been deadened by tradition or materialized by social pressures, the half-hearted reception of his own early work inclined him to emphasize the creator's individual integrity rather than his influence.

After "Sordello," worldly prestige is never invoked as a consideration relevant to artistic success. Almost invariably, the artists in his poetry are somewhat alien figures, either neglected or misprized by the society in which they live.

Even Fra Lippo shows a defensive attitude in challenging the tradition-ridden prejudices of his age. In "A Toccata of Galuppi's" the composer plays his premonitory compositions to an unheeding audience. "Memorabilia" and "Popularity" have a like theme in the disheartening failure of Shelley and Keats to make an impression on their generation.

And in "One Word More" Browning, speaking out of his own experience, refers to the intolerable burden of misunderstanding to which the modern poet is subject when once he has assumed the prophet's role:

Wherefore? Heaven's gift takes earth's abatement!
He who smites the rock and spreads the water,
Bidding drink and live a crowd beneath him,
Even he, the minute makes immortal,
Proves, perchance, but mortal in the minute,
Desecrates, belike, the deed in doing.
While he smites, how can he but remember,
So he smote before, in such a peril,
When they stood and mocked-"Shall smiting help us?"
When they drank and sneered-"A stroke is easy!"
When they wiped their mouths and went their journey,
Throwing him for thanks — "But drought was pleasant."
Thus old memories mar the actual triumph;
Thus the doing savours of disrelish;
Thus achievement lacks a gracious somewhat;
O'er — importuned brows becloud the mandate,
Carelessness or consciousness, the gesture.
For he bears an ancient wrong about him,
Sees and knows again those phalanxed faces,
Hears, yet one time more, the 'customed prelude —
"How shouldst thou, of all men, smite and save us?"
Guesses what is like to prove the sequel —
"Egypt's flesh-pots-nay, the drought was better."
Oh, the crowd must have emphatic warrant!
Theirs, the Sinai-forehead's cloven brilliance,
Right-arm's rod-sweep, tongue's imperial fiat.
Never dares the man put off the prophet.

Browning's masterwork, The Ring and the Book, like Tennyson's Idylls of the King, draws together the principal strands in its author's thinking and integrates them within a single grand design. Where Tennyson turned to legend, Browning characteristically found his theme in the court records of an old criminal trial.

The case history of Count Guido Franceschini's murder of his wife, Pompilia, not only raised psychological problems which challenged the author's analytic habits of mind, but also offered a type of situation which could be counted on to hold the attention of an audience schooled to melodrama.

The details of the affair were certainly sensational. Yet for all its violence and sordid malignancy, the case invited moralistic interpretation, since it involved within a religious framework all the familial relationshipsfilial piety, connubial faith, mother-love.

And, indeed, " The Ring and the Book has continued to be cited as the final summation of those strenuous qualities of optimism and moral fervor which, according to the received notion, made Browning a representative Victorian.

If The Ring and the Book is reexamined in the light of what has been said in the foregoing pages, however, it may appear that this treatment of the conflict between good and evil in terms of domestic tragedy dramatizes certain concepts not altogether congenial to the age in which it was written. As is also true of Idylls of the King, The Ring and the Book needs to be approached on more than one level if its theme is to become fully evident.

The reader who bothers to look below surface meanings finds opening up unexpected perspectives into the author's mind. For The Ring and the Book not only presents a full-scale vindication of Browning's intuitional psychology, it also embodies the author's moral and aesthetic philosophy.

Pompilia is the central figure among Browning's heroines. In common with Pippa she possesses the wisdom of the heart in its purest form.

She is illiterate, and by heredity and environment the victim of every mischance. Her only defence against the world is the primitive faith which finds expression in natural goodness and a boundless capacity for love; but these qualities stand by her through all her fearful trials. Browning would persuade us that a corrupt social order is solely responsible for Pompilia's misfortunes.

The initial injustice is traced back to the circumstances of her birth as the by-product of a prostitute's struggle for survival.

At successive periods she is victimized by Violante's

snobbery, by Guido's greed, and by the rigid authoritarianism of church and state. She submits to the tyranny of each, because in her naÏveté she has accepted the world's assurance that parents, husbands, and social institutions have a care for the best interests of the individuals placed in their charge. In so doing she goes against her intuitions which tell her that she is at the mercy of hostile forces; and her ultimate revolt, when it comes, is an instinctive one motivated by a frantic determination to give her son the freedom she has never enjoyed.

Perhaps the most skillful stroke in Browning's portrayal of Pompilia is the way he suggests her intuitive reaction against the falsity of the social conventions under which she suffers. The girl's imagination operates through symbols, the significance of which is never explicit to her, although she feels and acts under their emotional drive.

No other character in the poem has anything like her insights. Thus, for example, the memory of the church where she was married brings to her mind the marble lion in the street outside: "With half his body rushing from the wall,/ Eating the figure of a prostrate man." As a child she had always borne her offering to the poor Virgin that I used to know

At our street-corner in a lonely niche, —
The babe, that sat upon her knees, broke of...

Thoughts of Caponsacchi and St. George go hand in hand because she had once seen the saint's exploit depicted in a tapestry. Her decision to flee from Guido's bondage, taken in the first blinding apprehension of pregnancy, is dramatized through a passage in which Pompilia unknowingly recreates the scene of the Annunciation as she must have known it from a hundred Renaissance paintings.

Pompilia is the only character in The Ring and the Book whose actions are never (save for her escape from Arezzo) calculated in advance. Even the Pope and Caponsacchi pause to estimate the probable consequences of their conduct. Guido, of course, is all materialized body, as Pompilia is all etherealized spirit. He is the darkness to her light, the hate to her love, the craft to her guilelessness. [An interesting and important study might be made of light effects in Browning's work. The poet constantly calls on the painter's eye in composing his scenes.

See the chapter on Gerard de Lairesse in W. C. DeVane's Browning's Parleyings; "The Autobiography of a Mind."] But all possible variants of their difference may be subsumed under the one enormous antithesis between conscious intellect and unconscious intuition. As we shall see, the evil in Guido does not derive from mere conformity with the ways of the world; its power is deeper and more enigmatic.

Like Iago, Guido deliberately exploits social usages which have no real meaning for him. He is the completely rational man; and by showing the lengths to which rationality, undirected by any altruistic motive, can go, Browning immeasurably strengthens his case against over-intellectualism. For Guido is incapable of any decisive action which has not first gone sour through delay.

The campaign of spite incidental to getting rid of Pietro and Violante, the slow, relentless persecution of Pompilia, the involved maneuvers to entrap Caponsacchi in the plot are all characteristic of a man who has never been able to bring any undertaking to a conclusive issue, who has mismanaged his patrimony, trifled with religious orders, frittered away years of sycophantic time-serving in Rome.

No court, Browning hints, would have convicted him had he murdered Pompilia and Caponsacchi in hot blood when he caught up with them at Castelnuovo. The stupid oversight as a result of which the assassins are apprehended before they can make good their escape is, we feel, a fittingly ironic commentary on Guido's want of imagination.

Pompilia, Caponsacchi, and the Pope share a lonely eminence, environed on every side by the outraged forces of social prejudice. Of the ten books which bear directly on the poem's action, four ("Giuseppe Caponsacchi," "Pompilia," "The Pope," and "Guido") are most helpful in illuminating the truth as Browning perceived it.

The other books call in for purposes of contrast a variety of conventionalized views of the affair. Since the persons who give their versions are, in fact, types representative of standard societal attitudes, the crime is made to take on far-reaching implications. Ultimately the problem expands to include the nature of the individual's responsibilities to the institutions on which any social order is based.

The three introductory monologues present the gossip about Guido's crime current in Roman society. The speaker in "Half-Rome" is a jealous husband who has reason to suspect a rival. He naturally takes Guido's side, and in so doing distorts the facts to reflect his own spiritual meanness. "The Other Half-Rome" comes to Pompilia's defence in a no less biased way.

Here the narrator is a sentimentalist of the kind to be titillated by a "crime passionel." Taking for granted an adulterous passion between Pompilia and Caponsacchi, he endows their intrigue with all the elements of cloak-and-dagger romance played by stock characters.

"Tertium Quid" adds cynical commentary from the mouth of a total worldling. The speaker is wholly detached, interested only in displaying his wit to a fashionable audience. He refuses to commit himself to any moral judgment, but rather makes a malicious game of sorting over all conceivable motives for the murder.

The civilized man, he would have us understand, is a relativist who knows that right and wrong are never absolute, since they depend on the particular circumstances of a given situation. In these three books Browning is showing, in effect, that society is too much dominated by its own selfish interests ever to be able to adjudicate the actions of its individual members.

The books devoted to the arguments of the lawyers broaden Browning's social satire to include the institution of law which pretends to hold the scales of justice. Here the anti-social implications are still more prominent, for the two attorneys make a travesty of legal procedure. Hyacinthus resolves in his defence of Guido to uphold his client's conduct on the score of wounded honor.

The trial, offering at best an opportunity to exercise his

talent for casuistry, seems rather a joke to him. While he prepares his brief, the concerns really uppermost in his mind are his small son, the purity of his Latin, malice against his rival, and the joys of the table. His celebration of natural man's reliance on instinct, although applied to Guido, is in actuality a vindication of Pompilia and Caponsacchi.

In his self-admiring speech, Bottinius, the state prosecutor, juggles with logic and parades all the tricks of the rhetorician. His repeated insinuations of Pompilia's wantonness would be more appropriate in Guido's support.

We are not surprised to learn in the last book that Bottinius has made a "volte-face" and is now getting ready to defame the girl's reputation, partly as a means of depriving her son of his inheritance, but more to assert the law's authority in an unjust cause.

In these two books, then, it is Browning's intent to show that the machinery of social justice is as prejudiced as public opinion, and no more capable of distinguishing between right and wrong.

At the summit of the social hierarchy stand church and state; and in The Ring and the Book Browning's severest strictures are reserved for these ultimate seats of authority. The governor of Arezzo, concerned only to guarantee property and rank, delivers Pompilia back into her husband's hands when she throws herself on his mercy.

And the central government in Florence condemns Pompilia in "absentia" and would unhesitatingly have exonerated Guido and his companions had they succeeded in escaping from papal territory. Even darker is Browning's portrayal of ecclesiastical administration in its abandonment to material self-interest.

The archbishop to whom Pompilia despairingly appeals is the religious counterpart of the governor, and equally ready to sacrifice the individual to the system. Of him Pompilia says: "My heart died out at the Archbishop's smile;/ — It seemed so stale and worn a way o' the world."

Even the Augustinian friar, although moved to pity by Pompilia's plight, is afraid to jeopardize his career by any overt action in her behalf. Caponsacchi's scornful comment on him is significant: "He fears God, why then needs he fear the world?"

It is through the characters of Guido and the Pope, however, that Browning most fully develops the anti-social implications of his theme in The Ring and the Book.

Although poles apart in other respects, the two are alike in three ways: both are thinkers rather than doers; both seek a rational basis for intuitive perceptions; and both are intellectually emancipated from social conventions.

In his first monologue Guido cleverly exploits every vulgar prejudice that has found voice in the three preceding books. The inference is inescapable: if Guido's actions are to be judged by worldly standards, then he is innocent. Notice, for example, how shrewdly he translates the Marital relationship into terms calculated to discomfit his inquisitors:

Am I to teach my lords what marriage means,
What God ordains thereby and man fulfils
Who, docile to the dictate, treads the house?
My lords have chosen the happier part with Paul
And neither marry nor burn, — yet priestliness
Can find a parallel to the marriage-bond
In its own blessed special ordinance
Whereof indeed was marriage made the type:
The Church may show her insubordinate,
As marriage her refractory. How of the Monk
Who finds the claustral regimen too sharp
After the first month's essay? What's the mode
With the Deacon who supports indifferently
The rod o' the Bishop when he tastes its smart
Full four weeks? Do you straightway slacken hold
Of the innocents, the all-unwary ones
Who, eager to profess, mistook their mind?
Remit a fast-day's rigor to the Monk,
Who fancied Francis'manna meant roast quails, —
Concede the Deacon sweet society,
He never thought the Levite-rule renounced, —
Or rather prescribe short chain and sharp scourge

Corrective of such peccant humors? This —
I take to be the Church's mode, and mine.

It is only in his second monologue that Guido, now shorn of hope, declares himself in his true colors and lets it be seen that he is in his way as little conformable to traditional codes of behavior as Pompilia. Perhaps part of the fascination which Browning found in the workings of the criminal mentality was their very oppugnancy to the hollow formalities of social intercourse.

In any event, Guido in his farewell appearance arouses moral indignation of a kind hardly to be satisfied by the edict of any earthly tribunal. The reader is appalled to realise that this world should after all provide so fair a field for the exercise of man's infernal potentialities.

Just as, on the one side, Guido for all his intelligence possesses only the most rudimentary kind of social conscience, so, on the other, the Pope in his spirituality has passed through and beyond the limitations of convention. Thus, while the two characters stand apart from society, they look on it from opposite extremes.

Guido makes capital of institutions; the Pope, deriving his authority from the greatest of all institutions, seeks the living reality within the outer shell. Guido treats the world as his friend, in order further to corrupt it to his own ends; the Pope repudiates the world, fearing its powers of corruption over himself.

The Pope voices Browning's conviction that men are to be judged not by their actions, but by the motives which generate those actions:

For I am 'ware it is the seed of act,
God holds appraising in his hollow palm,
Not act grown great thence on the world below,
Leafage and branchage, vulgar eyes admire.

The world, of course, values only appearances. Therefore, it is vain to try to make of society an agency for the moral discipline of its members: "What does the world, told truth, but lie the more?"

Still, the world has its use as a spiritual point of reference;

the degree of opposition or submission to its dictates is the measure of the soul's state of grace. Thus, the Pope, fully sensible of human fallibility, does not at first trust his intuitions in apportioning guilt to those who have had a hand in Pompilia's death, but brings their conduct to the bar of Christian justice.

When viewed in this light, Guido and his associates are seen to have misused their worldly privileges and thereby to have strengthened the existing powers of evil. Thanks to Guido's example, intrinsically noble ideals of conduct have been further degraded:

Honor and faith, — a lie and a disguise,
Probably for all livers in this world,
Certainly for himself!

As the Pope passes in review the characters who have persecuted Pompilia, he finds each guilty of a vice indicative of its possessor's rejection of spiritual salvation for material ends. Guido is perhaps the exception here, since his inborn capacity for hatred would have put him outside the pale of humanity under any circumstances.

But all of the others bear the world's stigma in some characteristic form: ambition for Paul, lust for Girolamo, greed for the hired assassins, power for the archbishop. Social institutions, the Pope sorrowfully concludes, simply consolidate the selfish interests of the individuals on whom they depend:

Since all flesh is weak,
Bind weaknesses together, we get strength:
The individual weighed, found wanting, try
Some institution, honest artifice
Whereby the units grow compact and firm!
Each props the other, and so stand is made
For our embodied cowards that grow brave.

It is small wonder, then, that the Pope, now in his extreme old age and worn out in the search for truth, yearns for a better world where knowledge will be simply a matter of intuitive perception:

We men, in our degree, may know

There, simply, instantaneously, as here
After long time and amid many lies,
Whatever we dare think we know indeed...

At the end of his life the Pope's sympathy goes out to those in whom instinct and act are as one. For in unhesitating response to emotional impulse, as over against the devious processes of the intellect, he recognizes the token of God's immanence in human affairs.

Caponsacchi is exonerated in the Pope's eyes because he acted "at an instinct of the natural man," and so revealed himself a true exemplar of "the chivalry/ That dares the right and disregards alike/ The yea and nay o' the world." It is Pompilia, however, who fully confirms the Pope's faith.

In the naked simplicity of her feelings, in her yielding to the promptings of primitive instinct, he perceives the operation of a moral sense about which civilized society knows nothing. Her decision to fly from Guido bore witness to a higher fidelity than is due to conventional canons of behavior:

But, brave,
Thou at first prompting of what I call God,
And fools call Nature, didst hear, comprehend,
Accept the obligation laid on thee,
Mother elect, to save the unborn child . . .

Under the shadow of death the Pope pins his faith to a loving God, as revealed not through the intellectual traditions of the Church, but through the intuitions of an innocent victim of the Church's authority:

First of the first,
Such I pronounce Pompilia, then as now
Perfect in whiteness: stoop thou down, my child,
Give one good moment to the poor old Pope
Heart-sick at having all his world to blame —
Let me look at thee in the flesh as erst,
Let me enjoy the old clean linen garb,
Not the new splendid vesture! Armed and crowned,
Would Michael, yonder, be, nor crowned nor armed,
The less pre-eminent angel? Everywhere
I see in the world the intellect of man,

That sword, the energy his subtle spear,
The knowledge which defends him like a shield —
Everywhere; but they make not up, I think,
The marvel of a soul like thine, earth's flower
She holds up to the softened gaze of God!
It was not given Pompilia to know much,
Speak much, to write a book, to move mankind,
Be memorized by who records my time.
Yet if in purity and patience, if
In faith held fast despite the plucking fiend,
Safe like the signet-stone with the new name
That saints are known by, — if in right returned
For wrong, most pardon for worst injury,
If there be any virtue, and praise,
Then will this woman-child have proved — who knows?
Just the one prize vouchsafed unworthy me,
Seven years a gardener of the untoward ground
I till, — this earth, my sweat and blood manure
All the long day that barrenly grows dusk:
At least one blossom makes me proud at eve
Born 'mid the briers of my enclosure!

Interest in the Pope's monologue as a lofty exposition of Browning's own philosophic optimism has tended to obscure the dramatic relevance of the grounds on which the old man finally judges Guido. After he has reached the end of his metaphysical speculations, a new voice is heard, advocating mercy. This is "the spirit of culture," ironically described as

a new tribunal now
Higher than God's — the educated man's!
Nice sense of honor in the human breast
Supersedes here the old coarse oracle...

Disguised in the Mephistophelean guise of cool and lucid reasonableness, worldly interest summons all its inducements in a final endeavor to undermine the Pope's confidence in the validity of his position. The assault comes from every side, and the logical inconsistency of many of the arguments is concealed by the cogency of their appeal to human weakness. Since Guido has taken minor orders, his acquittal is essential to preservation of the Church's prestige. To condemn him would look like an attempt to cover up Caponsacchi's guilt, a blunder calculated to play straight into the hands of the Molinists.

In tune with the absolutist drift of the times, intervention in Guido's behalf offers a fitting opportunity for the arbitrary assertion of papal power.

The death of the criminals would jeopardize the very compacts which knit society together: the wife's obedience to her husband, the servant's fealty to his master. And so on. "Mercy is safe and graceful," says the voice of the world. And because the safe thing and the graceful thing spell damnation, the Pope in a final gesture of repudiation seizes pen and signs Guido's death-warrant:

Enough, for I may die this very night:
And how should I dare die, this man let live?

Pompilia completes the Pope as a speculative man, and in the same way she completes Caponsacchi as a man of action. In both cases she accomplishes this by releasing their intuitive being from the shackles of tradition and convention.

On the evidence, there can be no doubt that Pompilia and Caponsacchi in Browning's conception loved each other. Their moment of recognition demonstrates the poet's doctrine of elective affinity. Guido's forged correspondence had prepared each to take the cheapest view of the other; but at the first meeting of their eyes and without the need for a spoken word, the two penetrate the deception.

A flash of insight tells Caponsacchi that Pompilia could not possibly have written those "billets-doux":

. . . oh! I gave a passing glance
To a certain ugly cloud-shape, goblin-shred
Of hell-smoke hurrying past the splendid moon
Out now to tolerate no darkness more,
And saw right through the thing that tried to pass
For truth and solid, not an empty lie . . .

And Pompilia with equal certainty has taken measure of the priest:

But now, that you stand and I see your face,

Though you have never uttered word yet, — well, I know,
Here too has been dream-work, delusion too,
And that at no time, you with the eyes here,
Ever intended to do wrong by me . . .

After this, the confederacy of Pompilia and Caponsacchi against the world is a foregone conclusion. In her time of need Caponsaccbi without a moment's hesitation brushes aside the proprieties, unmindful that his conduct in arranging Pompilia's escape is on the face of it a betrayal of his priestly function and of her wifely duties. At Castelnuovo it is not only Guido but all society with its outraged prejudices which comes between them.

Thinking of Caponsacch's rustication at Civita, Pompilia cries: "do I once doubt/ The world again is holding us apart?" But although separated, each finds through the other courage to face his solitary fate. Henceforth the priest will go about his duties sustained by dreams of what might have been:

I do but play with an imagined life
Of who, unfettered by a vow, unblessed
By the higher call, — since you will have it so, —
Leads it companioned by the woman there.

And the dying Pompilia finds solace in the hope of meeting Caponsacchi in heaven, there to be joined with him in everlasting union.

The anti-social bias that is inseparable from Browning's ideal of romantic love emerges through the evolution of Caponsacchi's character after be has come under Pompilia's influence. Before this his career in the Church had promised well on the basis of accomplishments anything but spiritual. "The young frank personable priest" bad declared himself "earth's clear-accepted servitor." The Church had need for such sparkling young aristocrats in its fashionable forefront; and as long as he wore his vestments with dash and elegance, his superiors were ready to overlook the peccadilloes incidental to the rôle.

When Caponsacchi exchanges play-acting for the real thing, however, when the mistress becomes the runaway wife of a nobleman in minor orders, when the hand accustomed to twanging a lute and inditing a sonnet grips a sword, the situation takes on a very different complexion. To Pompilia's eyes Caponsacchi may seem the reembodiment of St. George, but the Renaissance Church found saintliness an inconvenient concept.

When called on by his examiners to explain his motive in befriending Pompilia, Caponsacchi champions the superiority of intuition over reason in as forthright a manner as the Pope:

"Thought?" nay, Sirs, what shall follow was not thought:

I have thought sometimes, and thought long and hard.
I have stood before, gone round a serious thing,
Tasked my whole mind to touch and clasp it close,
As I stretch forth my arm to touch this bar.
God and man, and what duty I owe both, —
I dare to say I have confronted these
In thought: but no such faculty helped here.
I put forth no thought,-powerless, all that night
I paced the city: it was the first Spring.
By the invasion I lay passive to,
In rushed new things, the old were rapt away;
Alike abolished-the imprisonment
Of the outside air, the inside weight o' the world
That pulled me down. Death meant, to spurn the ground,
Soar to the sky,-die well and you do that.
The very immolation made the bliss;
Death was the heart of life, and all the harm
My folly had crouched to avoid, now proved a veil
Hiding all gain my wisdom strove to grasp:
As if the intense centre of the flame
Should turn a heaven to that devoted fly
Which hitherto, sophist alike and sage,
Saint Thomas with his sobre gray goose-quill,
And sinner Plato by Cephisian reed,
Would fain, pretending just the insect's good,
Whisk off, drive back, consign to shade again.
Into another state, under new rule
I knew myself was passing swift and sure . . .

The "new rule" which the priest has accepted is, of course, that of man's instinctual nature. From Pompilia he has learned the heart's wisdom; and Browning wants us to realise that, having experienced the compulsion of love, he is at last qualified to do God's work. "Priests," says Caponsacchi, "should study passion; how else cure mankind,/ Who come for help in passionate extremes?"

Whatever future awaits him in the way of ecclesiastical preferment, we may be sure that, awakened by Pompilia, he will never again subscribe to the comfortable forms of worldly religion. He conducts his defence in a spirit of fierce and belligerent individualism.

The responsibility for Pompilia's tragic death he attributes directly to the organized forces of justice, which in their regard for the word rather than the spirit have disastrously bungled their God-given function. His furious indictment of officialdom for its blindness to truth evokes by inference Browning's own antipathy to social institutions:

But you were law and gospel, — would one please
Stand back, allow your faculty elbow-room?
You blind guides who must needs lead eyes that see!
Fools, alike ignorant of man and God!

The first and last books of The Ring and the Book discuss the circumstances under which the poem came to be written and the manner of its writing. Here Browning reveals with unusual explicitness his aesthetic theories. There is first the belief that the artist carries on his work under the express sanction of God. Thus, we are told "a Hand,/ Always above my shoulder" one day pointed out amid the bric-à-brac of a Florentine street-mart the Old Yellow Book in which the poet found his subject.

The literal accuracy of the "ring" metaphor has been questioned, but the meaning which Browning meant to convey through its use is clear enough. The truth about Guido's murder of Pompilia reposed in the legal documents containing the details of the case, but was only to be deduced through interpretation of the material by a mind endowed with imaginative insight. Describing how he ultimately penetrated the raw facts to the heart of their significance, the poet says:

I fused my live soul and that inert stuff,
Before attempting smithcraft,

with the result that "the life in me abolished the death of things." The inference here is unmistakable. The artist's attitude towards his subject-matter is highly subjective, depending on the private vision which the imagination sheds on the facts with which it works. Browning makes lofty claims for the inner urge from which the creative act originates:

Yet by a special gift, an art of arts,
More insight and more outsight and much more
> *Will to use both of these than boast my mates,*
I can detach from me, commission forth
Half of my soul. . .

At the same time he scrupulously traces the artist's special insights, not to any centre of self-sufficiency in the individual being, but rather to the Creator of all being.

Man is, properly speaking, incapable of creation; at best, he seeks to imitate the creative process as it occurs in God's mind, In so doing, he fulfills the supreme law of life — the aspiration to comprehend, however imperfectly, the divine purpose:

I find first
Writ down for very A B C of fact,
"In the beginning God made heaven and earth;"
From which, no matter with what lisp, I spell
And speak you out a consequence — that man,
Man, — as befits the made, the inferior thing, —
Purposed, since made, to grow, not make in turn,
Yet forced to try and make, else fail to grow, —
Formed to rise, reach at, if not grasp and gain
The good beyond him,-which attempt is growth, —
Repeats God's process in man's due degree,
Attaining man's proportionate result, —
Creates, no, but resuscitates, perhaps.
Inalienable, the arch-prerogative
Which turns thought, act-conceives, expresses too!

Thus it is that Browning can call his poem his "due to God," since the artist's primary responsibility must be to the source of his inspiration.

As interpreter of God's will to humanity, however, the artist has a secondary responsibility to society. Near the end of the first book Browning addresses his Victorian readers as follows:

Such, British Public, ye who like me not,
(God love you!) — whom I yet have labored for,
Perchance more careful whoso runs may read
Than erst when all, it seemed, could read who ran,
Perchance more careless whoso reads may praise
Than late when he who praised and read and wrote
Was apt to find himself the selfsame me,
Such labour had such issue, so I wrought
This arc, by furtherance of such alloy,
And so, by one spirt, take away its trace
Till, justifiably golden, rounds my ring.

This is an important confession of the change that had taken place in the poet's concept of his relationship to his audience. He admits the importance to the artist of the communicative faculty. Having in his early work misestimated the capabilities of his readers, he has subsequently made a sincere attempt to capture their attention through writing more intelligibly.

On the other hand, he categorically denies that he has courted a wider circle of readers out of any desire for popularity. He is willing to adapt his manner to the world's capacity, but his matter is in higher keeping.

With the body of the poem behind, Browning goes on in the concluding lines to develop the theory which he had previously sketched in "Fra Lippo Lippi." First he suggests that the true theme of The Ring and the Book is

This ιesson, that our human speech is naught,
Our human testimony false, our fame
And human estimation words and wind.

But since it ought to be obvious that ultimate truth is only apprehensible by intuitive means, "Why," he continues, "take the artistic way to prove so much?" The answer follows at once:

Because, it is the glory and the good of Art,
That Art remains the one way possible
Of speaking truth, to mouths like mine at least.

The elaboration of the meaning contained in these lines leads the poet to acknowledge the double awareness as a condition of artistic expression.

The creative impulse, originating as imaginative insight in the individual consciousness, imposes on the artist the obligation to find suitable forms for its embodiment, since the process of arousing men's deeper responses begins in an appeal to their superficial sympathies. The artist mediates between God and humanity; and his art, if truly inspired, in giving pleasure becomes at the same time a means of grace:

But Art, — where man nowise speaks to men,
Only to mankind, — Art may tell a truth
Obliquely, do the thing shall breed the thought,
Nor wrong the thought, missing the mediate word.
So may you paint your picture, twice show truth,
Beyond mere imagery on the wall,
So, note by note, bring music from your mind,
Deeper than ever een Beethoven dived, —
So write a book shall mean beyond the facts,
Suffice the eye and save the soul beside.

Chapter 9

The Victorian Long Poem

In Memoriam, The Idylls of the King, Aurora Leigh, and The Ring and the Book all represent major Victorian attempts to explain the ways of God to man in long poetic forms. Their themes, definition of the role of the poet, and their redefinition of major literary forms make them nineteenth-century versions of Milton's great epic that try to serve as viable contemporary versions or replacements for the epic.

By proposing a woman — and a woman author at that — as the protagonist of Aurora Leigh, Barrett Browning offers the most obviously radical redefinition of the hero of these four works; but Tennyson, who wishs to retain Arthur as traditional hero, makes an equal challenge to the convention of literary heroism: Arthur exists only as an absence at the heart of The Idylls of the King, for the blameless king himself rarely acts, since most of the individual idylls are about his influence upon others.

The Ring and the Book, which divides the role of hero among a priest who fails his rescue mission, an innocent young girl who is the daughter of a prostitute, an aging pope, and the poet himself, also makes clear that the older epic or romance hero is irrelevant to modern literature. In Memoriam, which appeared the same year as Wordsworth's Prelude, makes an epic of the poet's own experiences, creating the Victorian version of what Keats had called the egotistical sublime.

All four works self-consciously employ devices of epic and romance, including invocations, mythic allusion, and the test of the hero from the medieval romance and the elevation of the hero or aristea from epic. Two of them also make central to their plots the mysterious birth of a major character — Pompilia in Browning's poem and King Arthur in Tennyson's. All the poems also have antagonists who appear to be incarnate evil.

Finally, although In Memoriam and Aurora Leigh have contemporary settings, both The Ring and the Book and The Idylls of the King take place in a distant if Victorianized past. Both Tennyson and Browning, in other words, use the past as a literary laboratory that allows them to discuss contemporary issues and problems while preserving an aesthetic distance. All three works by Tennyson and Browning also employ prologues, epilogues, and framing sections that isolate the work's interior from the contemporary world.

These partial imitations of Miltonic epic challenge the form more than they follow it, for all four reject epic narrative as inappropriate to a modern age. In Aurora Leigh Barrett Browning transfers the subject and method of the Victorian woman's novel to the long poem, and all three of the other poems attempt to construct a long form out of fragments, much as do Dante Rossetti in The House of Life, his sister Christina in "Monna Innominata," George Meredith in Modern Love, and William Morris in The Earthly Paradise. Although Tennyson most obviously tries to shore up fragments against his ruin in In Memoriam, all three works employ the fragment as a truer embodiment of phenomenological and spiritual truth than narrative. This questioning of narrative anticipates late-twentieth-century Postmodernism.

All four works privilege imaginative and experiential truth, and both Aurora Leigh and The Ring and the Book self-consciously make it the centre of explicitly stated theories of poetry. Tennyson's In Memoriam, like The Idylls of the King, implicitly shows that it is the province of poetry. Having constructed a poetic form of fragments, the works by Tennyson and Browning juxtapose panels, set pieces, or tableaux arranged in a climactic narrative.

Although emphasizing fragments less than does Tennyson's epic elegy, Browning's twelve-part mystery-novel poem functions in the same way by constructing a poem and a reality of fragments, each of which contains part of the truth and each of which the reader must traverse to experience the world as the poet sees it.

Each of these segmented poetic structures dramatizes a conversion experience or confirmatory vision — that of the speaker in In Memoriam, Caponsacchi in The Ring and the Book, and Bedivere, Guinevere, and a host of others in The Idylls of the King. Aurora Leigh, which employs a more conventionally unified narrative structure, also features the conversion of Romney.

In all four poems the problem of faith appears as the relation between having faith and keeping faith, between belief and right conduct (or right identity). This relation, which makes conversion experience central to the meaning of the work, appears embodied in relations of men and women, especially that of marriage.

Having abandoned narrative as the dominant principle of literary structure and organization, these works employ chains of images, motifs, and paradigms to inform their climactic segmented poetic structure, and even Aurora Leigh, which makes greater use of narrative, relies heavily on skillfully deployed organizing motifs.

In three of these poems biblical allusion provides a major source of such motifs. In Memoriam uses it to resolve the problem of God in history, The Ring and the Book to reveal the moral stature of individual characters, and Aurora Leigh to present Barrett Browning's poetic theory and seize the high ground for women in their battle with oppressing men.

Finally, all four poems present of the inspired prophetic poet. The four-part religious structure of In Memoriam, which takes the reader from despair to doubt and then to hope before he arrives at faith, also leads us progressively to discover a final definition of the role of the poet and justification of his enterprise.

Although the emphases on art in The Idylls of the King take the less explicit form of Merlin and even Arthur's own attempts to create order, in Aurora Leigh and The Ring and the Book they clearly occupy centre stage. Definitions of the dramatic monologue, a form invented and practiced principally by Robert Browning, Alfred Tennyson, Dante Rossetti, and other Victorians, have been much debated in the last several decades.

Everyone agrees that to be a dramatic monologue a poem must have a speaker and an implied auditor, and that the reader often perceives a gap between what that speaker says and what he or she actually reveals.

In one of the most influential, though hotly contested definitions, Robert Langbaum saw the form as a continuation of an essentially Romantic "poetry of experience" in which the reader experiences a tension between sympathy and judgment. One problem with this approach, as Glenn Everett has argued, lies in the fact that contemporary readers of Browning's poems found them vastly different from Langbaum's Wordsworthian model. Many writers on the subject have disagreed, pointing out that readers do not seem ever to sympathize with the speakers in some of Browning's major poems, such as "Porphria's Lover" or "My Last Duchess." Glenn Everett proposes that Browninesque dramatic monologue has three requirements:

- The reader takes the part of the silent listener.
- The speaker uses a case-making, argumentative tone.
- We complete the dramatic scene from within, by means of inference and imagination.

HIS OTHER WORKS

MEN AND WOMEN

Men and Women is a collection of English poems published by Robert Browning in 1855. Although now generally regarded as featuring his best shorter pieces, the collection sold poorly and was not well received critically at the time.

Circumstances Leading up to Publication

Men and Women was Browning's first published work

for five years, and his first collection of shorter poems since his marriage to Elizabeth Barrett in 1846. His reputation had still not recovered from the disastrous failure of Sordello fifteen years previously, and Browning was at the time comprehensively overshadowed by his wife in terms of both critical reception and commercial success.

Away from the spotlight, Browning was able to work on a long-considered project. He had long been associated with the dramatic monologue, having written two early volumes of poems entitled Dramatic Lyrics and Dramatic Romances and Lyrics, but with Men and Women he took the concept a step further.

The volume consists of fifty-one unrelated poems, all of which are monologues spoken by different narrators, some identified and some not; the first fifty take in a very diverse range of historical, religious or European situations, with the fifty-first - One Word More - featuring Browning himself as narrator and dedicated to his wife.

The title of the collection came from a line in her Sonnets from the Portuguese. Browning himself was very fond of the collection, referring to the poems as "My fifty men and women" (from the opening line in One Word More), and today it has been described as one of Victorian England's most significant books.

Poems in the Collection

- Love Among the Ruins
- A Lover's Quarrel
- Evelyn Hope
- Up at a Villa – Down in the City
- A Woman's Last Word
- Fra Lippo Lippi
- A Toccata of Galuppi's
- By the Fire-Side
- Any Wife to Any Husband
- An Epistle Containing the Strange Medical Experience of Karshish, the Arab Physician
- Mesmerism

- A Serenade at the Villa
- My Star
- Instans Tyrannus
- A Pretty Woman
- "Childe Roland to the Dark Tower Came"
- Respectability
- A Light Woman
- The Statue and the Bust
- Love in a Life
- Life in a Love
- How It Strikes a Contemporary
- The Last Ride Together
- The Patriot
- Master Hugues of Saxe-Gotha
- Bishop Blougram's Apology
- Memorabilia
- Andrea del Sarto
- Before
- After
- In Three Days
- In a Year
- Old Pictures in Florence
- In a Balcony
- Saul
- "De Gustibus—"
- Women and Roses
- Protus
- Holy-Cross Day
- The Guardian-Angel
- Cleon
- The Twins
- Popularity
- The Heretic's Tragedy
- Two in the Campagna
- A Grammarian's Funeral
- One Way of Love
- Another Way of Love
- "Transcendentalism - A Poem in Twelve Volumes"*

- Misconceptions
- One Word More

DRAMATIS PERSONAE

Dramatis Personae is a poetry collection by Robert Browning. It was published in 1864.

Poems in the collection

- James Lee's Wife
- Gold Hair: A Story of Pornic
- The Worst of It
- Dis Aliter Visum
- Too Late
- Abt Vogler
- Rabbi Ben Ezra
- A Death in the Desert
- Caliban upon Setebos
- Confessions
- May and Death
- Deaf and Dumb
- Prospice
- Eurydice to Orpheus
- Youth And Art
- A Face
- A Likeness
- Mr. Sludge, "The Medium"
- Apparent Failure
- Epilogue
- Ben Karshook's Wisdom
- Sonnet

Browning wrote the collection in London, after returning there with his son because of his wife's death. It was his first publication after a nine-year hiatus. During this time, Browning's reputation was fluctuating, and Dramatis Personae along with The Ring and the Book, which is widely considered his greatest work, were enough to begin a critical re-evaluation of the writer.

The poems in Dramatis Personae are dramatic, with a

wide range of narrators. The narrator is usually in a situation that reveals to the reader some aspect of his personality. Instead of speeches that are intended for others' ears, most are soliloquies.

They are generally darker than the poems found in Men and Women, his previous collection, and along with The Ring and the Book these poems embody a turning point in Browning's style. Browning's poetry after this point most notably touches on religion and marital distress, two potent issues of his time period. This new style was appreciated, as Dramatis Personae sold enough copies for a second edition to be published, which was a first in Browning's career. However, though he gained respect, Browning didn't have much commercial success as a poet. The sales of this work and most notably his Collected Poems were helped by public sympathy after the death of his wife.

Caliban upon Setebos

Caliban upon Setebos is an 1864 poem written by the British poet Robert Browning. It deals with Caliban, a character from Shakespeare's The Tempest, and his reflections on Setebos, the brutal god he believes in. Some scholars see Browning as being of the belief that God is in the eye of the beholder, and this is emphasized by a barbaric character believing in a barbaric god.

Others feel that he was satirizing theologians of his time, who attempted to understand God as a reflection of themselves; this theory is supported by the epigraph, Psalm 50:21, "Thou thoughtest that I was altogether such a one as thyself." This could be taken as God mocking Caliban (and Browning's contemporaries) for their methods of attempting to understand Him.)

The poem is referred to in Dan Simmons' science fiction books Ilium and Olympos, in which Caliban and Setebos are villains.

THE RING AND THE BOOK

The Ring and the Book is a long dramatic narrative poem

of 21,000 lines written by Robert Browning. It was published in four installments from 1868 to 1869.

The book tells the story of a murder trial in Rome in 1698, whereby an impoverished nobleman, Count Guido Franceschini, is found guilty of the murders of his young wife Pompilia Comparini and her parents, having suspected his wife was having an affair with a young cleric, Giuseppe Caponsacchi.

Having been found guilty despite his protests and sentenced to death, Franceschini then appeals - unsuccessfully - to Pope Innocent XII to overturn the conviction. The poem comprises twelve books, each a dramatic monologue spoken by a different narrator involved in the case, usually giving a different account of the same events.

The Books

1. The Ring and the Book
2. Half-Rome
3. The Other Half-Rome
4. Tertium Quid
5. Count Guido Franceschini
6. Giuseppe Caponsacchi
7. Pompilia
8. Dominus Hyacinthus de Archangelis
9. Juris Doctor Johannes Baptista Bottinius
10. Pope Innocent XII
11. Guido
12. The Book and the Ring

Major Characters

- Count Guido Franceschini
- Pompilia Comparini, his wife
- Giuseppe Caponsacchi, a priest
- Pope Innocent XII

The poem is based on a real-life case. Under Roman law at the time, trials were not held in open court but rather by correspondence, whereupon each witness was required to submit a written statement for future adjudication. Browsing in a flea market in Florence in 1860, Browning came across a large volume of these written statements relating to the 1698 Franceschini case, and bought it on the spot.

This volume - later known as the Yellow Book, after the colour of its aged covers - struck Browning as an excellent basis for a poem, but he was unable to get any further than the basic idea and often offered it as a subject to other writers, notably Alfred Tennyson, upon which to base a poem or novel.

Luckily for posterity, there were no takers, and following his wife's death and his return to England, Browning revived his old plan for a long poem based on the Roman murder case almost eight years after the idea had first struck him. The first book features a narrator, possibly Browning himself, who relates the story of how he came across the Yellow Book in the market and then giving a broad outline of the plot. The next two books give the views and gossip of the Roman public, apparently divided over which side to support in the famous case, who give differing accounts of the circumstances surrounding the case and the events which took place. Book 4 is spoken by a lawyer, Tertium Quid, who has no connection to the case but gives what he claims is a balanced, unbiased view of proceedings.

Book 5 sees the start of the testimony from the trial, allowing the accused murderer Franceschini to give his side of the story, Book 6 is the young priest who was accused of being Pompilia's lover, and who asserts no affair took place, that he simply tried to help Pompilia escape her abusive husband; Book 7 is the account of the dying Pompilia, mortally wounded but not killed in the attack. The next two books are dry, academic depositions by the two opposing trial lawyers, and are filled with pedantic legal bickering and infinite discussion of tiny, irrelevant points; these are darkly humorous attacks by Browning on the quibbling, unproductive legal system, and have practically no bearing whatsoever on events.

Book 10 is perhaps the best-known of the monologues in the poem, as Pope Innocent considers Franceschini's appeal against a wider backdrop of moral issues, and a deep reflection on the nature of good and evil, before rejecting the condemned man's plea. Book 11, which features Franceschini in his cell on "death row" the night before his execution, is similarly well-regarded, with the narrator veering from near-psychotic spleen to begging for his life. Book 12 returns to Browning's own voice, wrapping up the aftermath of the trial and ending the poem.

The Ring and the Book was, by some margin, the best-selling of all Browning's works during his lifetime. The depth of its philosophical, psychological and spiritual insight is a step up from anything Browning produced before or since, and the poem was almost universally hailed as a work of genius, restoring the pioneering reputation among the first rank of English poets which Browning had lost with Sordello nearly thirty years previously.

The book lost popularity with readers during the 20th century, but has recently been reprinted and sold reasonably well. Facsimile copies of the Yellow Book (the source documents for the poem) are also available, and they reveal the extent of conjecture and invention Browning used when writing the poem.

After Browning's death, a cache of documents relating to the case almost twice the size of the Yellow Book was found in an Italian library in the 1920s; the true story of the murder is told in Derek Parker, 'Roman Murder Mystery', London, Sutton, 2001.

The actual ring and book which inspired Browning—and which are described at the start and end of the work—are preserved at Balliol College, Oxford University, having been donated by Browning's son Pen.

In July 2008, a two part play adaptation of this story, set in poetry and prose by Martyn Wade and starring Anton Lesser as Browning, Roger Allam as Guido Franceschini and Loo Brealey as Pompilia, was broadcast as the BBC Radio 4 "Classic Serial". Abigail le Fleming produced and directed.

PRINCE HOHENSTIEL-SCHWANGAU, SAVIOUR OF SOCIETY

"Prince Hohenstiel-Schwangau, Saviour of Society" is a

long poem by Robert Browning, first published in 1871. The poem, which takes the French Emperor Napoleon III as its subject, was largely written in Florence in the early 1860s before apparently being abandoned.

It appears that the poem was largely forgotten while Browning worked on Dramatis Personae and The Ring and the Book, which raised his profile and commercial appeal. In 1871, following the Franco-Prussian War and the forced end of Napoleon's reign, Browning dusted off his lengthy poem and made some revisions and additions before publishing it as Prince Hohenstiel-Schwangau in December 1871.

Sales were initially very strong, with more than one and a half thousand copies being sold in the first week, but they soon tailed off sharply; the poem's length and complexity apparently put off prospective readers, and the first printing run failed to sell out.

No second edition was ever required. Some critics have called this poem the least-read of all Browning's works, though unlike Sordello 31 years earlier, the poem's reception had no discernible damaging effect on his continued popularity and strong critical reputation.

PACCHIAROTTO, AND HOW HE WORKED IN DISTEMPER

Pacchiarotto, and How He Worked in Distemper is a short collection of English poems by Robert Browning, published in 1876. The collection marked Browning's first collection of short pieces for more than twelve years, and was well-received.

The title poem, which ostensibly discusses the life and works of 15th Century Italian painter Giacomo Pacchiarotti, is actually a thinly-veiled attack on Browning's own critics, and many other pieces in the collection take the same tone.

Contents

- Prologue
- Of Pacchiarotto, and How He Worked in Distemper
- At the "Mermaid"
- House

- Shop
- Pisgah-Sights
- Fears and Scruples
- Natural Magic
- Magical Nature
- Bifurcation
- Numpholeptos
- Appearances
- St. Martin's Summer
- Hervé Riel
- A Forgiveness
- Cenciaja
- Filippo Baldinucci on the Privilege of Burial
- Epilogue

JOCOSERIA

Jocoseria is a collection of short poems by Robert Browning, first published in 1883. Effectively a continuation of the Dramatic Idyls series, the book was not well-received by critics at the time and has continued to be considered one of the poet's least effective collections, aside from the famous prologue to the collection.

The prologue, which has no official title but is usually referred to by its first line, Wanting is what?, became one of Browning's favourite short lyrics and is a standard fixture in anthologies.

Jocoseria—whose title comes from a 1598 collection of jokes and anecdotes, referring to its jocose and serious contents—was released in late 1883, and enjoyed decent sales despite the lack of critical plaudits, to such an extent that Browning's already-completed follow-up Ferishtah's Fancies was delayed for nearly a year so as not to crowd it out of the shops.

Contents

- Untitled Prologue (Wanting is what?)
- Donald
- Solomon and Balkis

- Cristina and Monaldeschi
- Mary Wollstonecraft and Fuseli
- Adam, Lilith, and Eve
- Ixion
- Jochanan Hakkadosh
- Never the Time and the Place
- Pambo

FERISHTAH'S FANCIES

'Ferishtah's Fancies' is a book of poetry by Robert Browning first published in 1884. Technically the book is one long poem divided into twelve parts, but the parts are so disparate that many critics have considered it a collection of shorter pieces rather than a lengthy whole. The book is narrated by Browning in the thinly-disguised persona of the Persian soothsayer Ferishtah, who tells several parables (the titular "fancies") to students that illustrate his/Browning's opinions on a number of religious and moral topics.

Browning had finished the book by late January 1884, but his publisher chose to delay its release until the end of the year so as not to compromise the sales of his recently-released collection Jocoseria.

Reviews were mixed, some critics opining that there was "too much preaching and not enough poetry" in the book, but sales were good, due in part to the prevailing fashion for Orientalism in England at the time. The book is nowadays considered a very minor work in the Browning canon and selections from it are rarely included in Browning anthologies.

Contents

- Prologue
  1. The Eagle
  2. Melon-Seller
  3. Shah Abbas
  4. The Family
  5. The Sun
  6. Mihrab Shah
  7. A Camel-Driver

8. Two Camels
9. Cherries
10. Plot-Culture
11. A Pillar at Sebzevah
12. A Bean-stripe; also Apple-Eating

- Epilogue.

SORDELLO

Sordello da Goito or Sordel de Goit (sometimes Sordell) was a 13th-century Lombard troubadour, born in the municipality of Goito in the province of Mantua.

He is perhaps best remembered for the praise heaped on him by other poets: he is praised by Dante Alighieri in the De vulgari eloquentia, and in the Purgatorio of The Divine Comedy is made the type of patriotic pride. He is the hero of a well-known poem by Robert Browning. He is also praised for his passion in Oscar Wilde's poem "Amor Intellectualis".

The real Sordello, so far as we have authentic facts about his life, hardly seems to justify these idealizations, though he was the most famous of the Italian troubadours. About 1220 he was in a tavern brawl in Florence; and in 1226, while at the court of Richard of Bonifazio in Verona, he abducted his master's wife, Cunizza, at the instigation of her brother, Ezzelino da Romano.

The scandal resulted in his flight (1229) to Provence, where he seems to have remained for some time. He entered the service of Charles of Anjou, and probably accompanied him (1265) on his Naples expedition; in 1266 he was a prisoner in Naples. The last documentary mention of him is in 1269, and he is supposed to have died in Provence.

His appearance in Purgatory among the spirits of those who, though redeemed, were prevented from making a final confession and reconciliation by sudden death, suggests that he was murdered, although this may be Dante's own conjecture.

His didactic poem, L'ensenhamen d'onor, and his love songs and satirical pieces have little in common with Dante's presentation, but the invective against negligent princes which

Dante puts into his mouth in the 7th canto of the Purgatorio is more adequately paralleled in his sirventes-planh (1237) on the death of his patron Blacatz, where he invites the princes of Christendom to feed on the heart of the hero.

Sordello is briefly referred to in Samuel Beckett's 1951 novels Molloy and Malone Dies. Ezra Pound also references him in the Cantos. Numerous references occur in Roberto Bolano's novella By Night in Chile.

DRAMATIC LYRICS

Dramatic Lyrics is a collection of English poems by Robert Browning, first published in 1842 as the second volume in a series of self-published books entitled Bells and Pomegranates. It is most famous as the first appearance of Browning's poem The Pied Piper of Hamelin, but also contains several of the poet's other best-known pieces, including My Last Duchess, Soliloquy of the Spanish Cloister, Porphyria's Lover, and Johannes Agricola in Meditation.

Many of the original titles given by Browning to the poems in this collection, as with its "follow-up" collection Dramatic Romances and Lyrics, are different from the ones he later gave them in various editions of his collected works.

Since this book was originally self-published in a very small edition, these poems really only came to prominence in the later collections, and so the later titles are given here.

- Cavalier Tunes:
  - Marching Along
  - Give a Rouse
  - Boot and Saddle
- My Last Duchess
- Count Gismond
- Incident of the French Camp
- Soliloquy of the Spanish Cloister
- In a Gondola
- Artemis Prologuizes
- Waring
- Rudel to the Lady of Tripoli
- Cristina

- Johannes Agricola in Meditation
- Porphyria's Lover
- Through the Metidja to Abd-El-Kadr
- The Pied Piper of Hamelin

Porphyria's Lover

"Porphyria's Lover" is a poem by Robert Browning and that was first published as "Porphyria" in the January 1836 issue of Monthly Repository. Browning later republished it in Dramatic Lyrics (1842) paired with "Johannes Agricola in Meditation" under the title "Madhouse Cells." The poem did not receive its definitive title until 1863.

"Porphyria's Lover" is Browning's first short dramatic monologue, and also the first of his poems to examine abnormal psychology. Although its initial publication passed nearly unnoticed and it received little critical attention in the nineteenth century, the poem is now heavily anthologised and much studied.

A possible inspiration for the poem is John Wilson's "Extracts from Gosschen's Diary", a lurid account of a murder published in Blackwood's Magazine in 1818. A man knives a woman to death, talks of the corpse's blue eyes, golden hair, and white breasts, and describes the feeling of perfect happiness the murder gives him.

Although he stabs her repeatedly, the woman never cries out. Browning's friend and fellow poet Bryan Procter acknowledged basing his 1820 "Marcian Colonna" on this source, but added a new detail; after the murder, the killer sits up all night with his victim.

The poem consists of one long stanza, written in a simple, conversational style, but with a strictly maintained rhyme and meter, of ABABB. The persona is an apparent madman who sits embracing a woman he claims to have murdered the night before. Porphyria, he says, came to his cottage, kindled a fire, then sat beside him and told him she loved him.

It is suggested that Porphyria is richer than he is, presumably the "vainer ties" she speaks of are financial ones. The speaker assumes that if she could, she would want to be with him forever. As the persona adores Porphyria (as shown by the calming power she holds as she enters) he strangles her to preserve the moment in which she loves him.

Although "Porphyria's Lover" is a short poem written in straightforward language, interpretations have been many and various. Most readers, however, tend to focus on the insane persona and to define the poem as a portrait of abnormal psychology.

Browning's monologues are frequently voiced by eccentrics, lunatics, or people under emotional stress. Their ramblings illustrate character by describing the interactions of an odd personality with a particularly telling set of circumstances.

In both "Porphyria's Lover" and "My Last Duchess", Browning uses this mode of exposition to describe a man who responds to the love of a beautiful woman by killing her. Each monologue offers the speakers' reasons for transforming the desired woman from subject to object: in "My Last Duchess", the Duke may have jealously murdered his wife, but keeps a portrait of her behind a curtain so none can look upon her smile without his permission; in "Porphyria's Lover", the persona wishes to stop time at a single perfect moment and so kills his lover and sits all night embracing her carefully arranged body.

It should be noted that in "My Last Duchess" the woman's murder is at best implied, while in "Porphyria's Lover" it is described quite explicitly by the speaker. The "Porphyria" persona's romantic egotism leads him into all manner of monstrously selfish assumptions compatible with his own longings.

He seems convinced that Porphyria wanted to be murdered, and claims "No pain felt she" while being strangled, adding, as if to convince himself "I am quite sure she felt no pain." He may even believe she enjoyed the pain, because he, her lover, inflicted it. When she's dead, he says she's found her "utmost will," and when he sees her lifeless head drooping on his shoulder, he describes it as a "smiling rosy little head", possibly using the word "rosy" to symbolise the red roses of love, or to demonstrate his delusion that the girl, and their relationship, are still alive.

More likely, however, is the thought that blood returning to her face, after the strangulation, makes her cheeks "rosy." Her "rosy little head" may also be a sly reference to the hymen; Porphyria leaves a "gay feast" and comes in from the outside world wearing "soiled gloves"; now her blue eyes, open in death, are "without a stain."

Another interpretation for Porphyria's improbable rosy cheeks, laughing eyes, and smiling face is that she is still alive: her lover did not commit murder, but performed an act of Erotic asphyxiation. The lover may also be a fetishist, indicated by the fact that he refers to her hair numerous times throughout the poem, and strangles her with it.

Since the speaker may (as many speculate) be insane, it is impossible to know the true nature of his relationship to Porphyria. Theories, some of them rather bizarre, abound: some contemporary scholars suggest, for example, that the persona may be a woman; if so, the strangulation could stem from frustration with the world.

An incestuous relationship has also been suggested; Porphyria might be the speaker's mother or sister. Another possibility is that she is a former lover, now betrothed, or even married, to some other man.

Alternatively, she may simply be some kind lady who has come to look in on him, or even a figment of his imagination. Other sources note that the lover might be impotent, disabled, sick, or otherwise inadequate, and, as such, unable to satisfy Porphyria.

There is much textual evidence to support this interpretation: he describes himself as "one so pale/ for love of her, and all in vain." At the beginning of the poem, the persona never moves; he sits passively in a cold, dark room, sadly listening to the storm until Porphyria comes through "wind and rain", "shuts the cold out and the storm," and makes up his dying fire.

Finally, she sits beside him, calls his name, places his arm around her waist, and puts his head on her shoulder;

interestingly, she has to stoop to do this. At the poem's midpoint, the persona suddenly takes action, strangling Porphyria, propping her body against his, and boasting that afterward, her head lay on his shoulder.

In line with the persona's suggested weakness and sickness, other scholars take the word "porphyria" literally, and suggest that the seductress embodies a disease, and that the persona's killing of her is a sign of his recovery. Porphyria, which usually involved delusional madness and death, was classified several years before the poem's publication; Browning, who had an avid interest in such pathologies, may well have been aware of the new disease.

Much has been made of the final line: "And yet, God has not said a word!" Possibly, the speaker seeks divine condonement for the murder. He may believe God has said nothing because He is satisfied with his actions.

God may be satisfied because: He recognises that the persona's crime is the only way to keep Porphyria pure; or, because He doesn't think her life and death are important compared to the persona's. The persona may also be waiting in vain for some sign of God's approval. Alternatively, the line may represent his feelings of emptiness in the wake of his violence; Porphyria is gone, quiet descends, and he's alone. The persona may also be schizophrenic; he may be listening for a voice in his head, which he mistakes for the voice of God. It has also been postulated that this is Browning's statement of "God's silence," in which neither good nor bad acts are immediately recompensed by the deity.

The final line may also register the persona's sense of guilt over his crime. Despite his elaborate justifications for his act, he has, in fact, committed murder, and he expects God to punish him - or, at least, to take notice. The persona is surprised, and a little uneasy, over God's continued silence.

The mirrored effect produced by Porphyria's modelling of the persona in the first half, and the persona's reciprocal modelling of her after strangulation is indicative of a popular Victorian art form called Tableaux Vivant in which humans were used as art in order to recreate actual paintings.

This is indicative of the allegorical content of "Porphyria's Lover" in which both characters imitate the process of artistic creation: when art is created or published, it is dead and forever unchanging. In the last few lines of the poem, Porphyria is manipulated in much the same way as the speaker was in the first few lines of the poem.

Tennyson shares similar ideas in "The Lady of Shalott", as do other Victorian authors who contribute to the popular conversation about the artistic processes.

Soliloquy of the Spanish Cloister

Soliloquy of the Spanish Cloister is a comic dramatic monologue written by Robert Browning, first published in his collection Dramatic Lyrics (1842). It is written in the voice of an unnamed Spanish monk. The poem consists of nine eight-line stanzas and is written in iambic tetrameter. The plot of the poem centers around the speaker's hatred for Brother Lawrence, a fellow monk in the cloister.

The speaker notes the trivial ways in which Brother Laurence fails in his Christianity, and then plots to murder or damn the soul of Brother Laurence. However, the poem ends before the speaker can finish.

My Last Duchess

"My Last Duchess" is a poem by Robert Browning, frequently anthologized as an example of the dramatic monologue. It first appeared in 1842 in Browning's Dramatic Lyrics.

The poem is written in 28 rhymed couplets of iambic pentameter. The poem is preceded by the word Ferrara:, indicating that the speaker is most likely Alfonso II, fifth Duke of Ferrara (1533–1598) who, at the age of 25, married the 14-year-old Lucrezia di Cosimo de' Medici, the daughter of Cosimo I de' Medici, Grand Duke of Tuscany, and Eleonora di Toledo.

Lucrezia was not well educated, and the Medicis' status could be termed "nouveau riche" in comparison with that of the venerable and distinguished Este family. The Duke's remark regarding his gift of a "nine-hundred-years-old name" clearly indicates that he considered his bride beneath him socially. She came, however, with a sizeable dowry.

The couple married in 1558, and she died three years later, on April 21, 1561, at age 17. There was a strong suspicion of poisoning. The Duke then sought the hand of Barbara, eighth daughter of the Holy Roman Emperor Ferdinand I and Anna of Bohemia and Hungary and the niece of the Count of Tyrol.

The count was in charge of arranging the marriage; the chief of his entourage, Nikolaus Mardruz, a native of Innsbruck, was his courier. Mardruz is presumably the silent listener in the poem. The other characters named in the poem, painter Frà Pandolf and sculptor Claus of Innsbruck, are fictional.

The poem is set during the late Italian Renaissance. The narrator (presumably the Duke of Ferrara) is giving the emissary of his prospective second wife a tour of the artworks in his home. He draws a curtain to reveal a painting of a woman, explaining that it is a portrait of his late wife; he invites his guest to sit and look at the painting.

As they look at the portrait of the late Duchess, the Duke describes her happy, cheerful and flirtatious nature, which had displeased him. He says, "She had a heart -- how shall I say? -- too soon made glad..." He goes on to say that his complaint of her was that "'twas not her husband's presence only" that made her happy. Eventually, "I gave commands; then all smiles stopped together." He now keeps her painting hidden behind a curtain that only he is allowed to draw back, meaning that now she only smiles for him.

The Duke then resumes an earlier conversation regarding wedding arrangements, and in passing points out another work of art, a bronze statue of Neptune taming a sea-horse. In an interview, Browning said, "I meant that the commands were that she should be put to death . . . Or he might have had her shut up in a convent."

The Pied Piper of Hamelin

The Pied Piper of Hamelin is a legend about the abduction

of many children from the town of Hamelin (Hameln), Germany. Famous versions of the legend are given by the Brothers Grimm and, in English, by Robert Browning. Pied refers to patches of two or more colors, typical dress for minstrels and entertainers in the middle ages.

In 1284, while the town of Hamelin was suffering from a rat infestation, a man dressed in pie appeared, claiming to be a rat-catcher. He promised the townsmen a solution for their problem with the rats. The townsmen in turn promised to pay him for the removal of the rats. The man accepted, and thus played a musical pipe to lure the rats with a song into the Weser River, where all of them drowned.

Despite his success, the people reneged on their promise and refused to pay the rat-catcher. The man left the town angrily, but returned some time later, seeking revenge. On Saint John and Paul's day while the inhabitants were in church, he played his pipe yet again, this time attracting the children of Hamelin.

One hundred and thirty boys and girls followed him out of the town, where they were lured into a cave and never seen again. Depending on the version, at most two children remained behind (one of whom was lame and could not follow quickly enough, the other one was deaf and followed the other children out of curiosity) who informed the villagers of what had happened when they came out of the church. Other versions (but not the traditional ones) claim that the Piper lured the children into the river and let them drown like the rats or led the children to a cave on Köppen Hill or Koppelberg Hill (outside of Hamelin) or a place called Koppenberg Mountain and returned them after payment or that he returned the children after the villagers paid several times the original amount of gold.

The earliest mention of the story seems to have been on a stained glass window placed in the Church of Hamelin c. 1300. The window was described in several accounts between the 14th century and the 17th century. It was destroyed in 1660. Based on the surviving descriptions, a modern reconstruction of the window has been created by Hans Dobbertin (historian).

It features the colorful figure of the Pied Piper and several figures of children dressed in white.

This window is generally considered to have been created in memory of a tragic historical event for the city. Also, Hamelin town records start with this event. The earliest written record is from the town chronicles in an entry from 1284 which states:

"It is 10 years since our children left"

Although research has been conducted for centuries, no explanation for the historical event is agreed upon. In any case, the rats were first added to the story in a version from c. 1559; they are absent from previous accounts.

Theories that have gained some support can be grouped into the following categories:

In William Manchester's A World Lit Only by Fire, suggests that the Pied Piper was a psychopath pedophile. Manchester asserts that on June 20th, 1484, this criminal kidnapped 130 children from the Saxon village of Hammel and used them in "unspeakable ways."

He adds that "some of the children were never seen again. Others were found dismembered and scattered in the forest underbrush or hanging from tree branches." The incident he refers to has not been documented anywhere but in his book and he offers no citations for the asserted facts. His account discounts versions of the story that appear to date from at least 120 years earlier.

The children fell victim to an accident, either drowning in the river Weser or being buried in a landslide.

The children contracted some disease during an epidemic and were led out of town to die in order to protect the rest of the city's population from contracting it:

An early form of Black Death has been suggested. (After the initial epidemic of the Black Death across Eurasia, subsequent outbreaks took a greater toll on children than on adults, as young children had not been exposed to the disease and so had no immunity to it.)

Others attribute the dancing of the children to be an early reference to Huntington's disease; however, this is an inherited disorder, and the statistical probability of that many unrelated children having the same genetic condition is very low.

Another possibility would be the outbreaks of dancing mania, or communal dancing mania, which are recorded in a number of European towns during the period of general distress which followed the Black Death. The 'Verstegan/ Browning' date, 1376, would be consistent with this. These theories perceive the Piper as a symbolic figure of Death. Death is often portrayed dressed in motley, or "pied" clothing. Analogous themes which are associated with this theory include the Dance of Death, Totentanz or Danse Macabre, a common medieval type. Various ecstatic outbreaks were associated with the Plague, such as the Flagellants, who wandered from place to place while scourging themselves in penance for sins that presumably brought the plague upon Europe. The rat is the preferred host for the plague vector, the rat flea. When the rats die, the fleas seek humans as a substitute host. Children might be especially vulnerable to the disease.

The Pied Piper leads the children.

The children left the city to be part of a pilgrimage, a military campaign, or even a new Children's crusade (which occurred in 1212, not long before) but never returned to their parents. These theories see the unnamed Piper as their leader or a recruiting agent.

> The children willingly abandoned their parents and Hamelin in order to become the founders of their own villages during the colonization of Eastern Europe. Several European villages and cities founded around this time have been suggested as the result of their efforts as settlers. This claim is supported by corresponding placenames in both the region around Hamelin and the eastern colonies where names such as Querhameln ("mill village Hamelin") exist. Again the Piper is seen as their leader.

The tradition that the children emigrated in 1284 is so old and well-reported that explanations associated with the Black Death seem unlikely.

Modern scholars regard the emigration theory to be the most probable, i.e. that the Pied Piper of Hamelin was a recruiter for the colonization of Eastern Europe which took place in the 13th century and that he led away a big part of the young generation of Hamelin to a region in Eastern Europe. A version of the theory was published in the Saturday Evening Post.

The Emigration theory is supported by writings found on the walls of old homes in Hameln which say that on July 26, 1284, a Piper led 130 children out of town and that the piper was possibly an agent of Bruno von Schaumburg, the Bishop of Olmutz who was organizing a drive to populate parts of Moravia (which is now within the Czech Republic). The Bishop was acting on behalf of the Bohemian King Ottokar II.

Added speculation on the migration is based on the idea that by the 13th century the area had too many people resulting in the oldest son owning all the land and power, leaving the rest as serfs. The Black Death later destroyed that balance. In any case, the motivation to leave was high and very much like the motivation for emigration to America in the 18th century i.e. freedom, opportunity, and land.

It has also been suggested that one reason the emigration of the children was never documented was that the children were sold to a recruiter from the Baltic region of Eastern Europe, a practice that was not uncommon at the time.

In her essay Pied Piper Revisted, Sheila Harty states that surnames from the region settled are similar to those from Hamelin and that selling off illegitimate children, orphans or other children the town could not support is the more likely explanation. She states further that this may account for the lack of records of the event in the town chronicles.

In his book, The Pied Piper: A Handbook, Wolfgang Mieder states that historical documents exist showing that people from the area including Hameln did help settle parts of Transylvania. Transylvania had suffered under the Mongol invasions of central Europe that date from around the time of the earliest appearance of the legend of the piper.

In the version of the legend posted on the official website for the town of Hameln, another aspect of the emigration theory is presented:

"Among the various interpretations, reference to the colonization of East Europe starting from Low Germany is the most plausible one: The "Children of Hameln" would have been in those days citizens willing to emigrate being recruited by landowners to settle in Moravia, East Prussia, Pomerania or in the Teutonic Land. It is assumed that in past times all people of a town were referred to as "children of the town" or "town children" as is frequently done today. The "Legend of the children's Exodus" was later connected to the "Legend of expelling the rats". This most certainly refers to the rat plagues being a great threat in the medieval milling town and the more or less successful professional rat catchers."

This version states that "children" may simply have referred to residents of Hameln who chose to emigrate and not necessarily to youths.

Historian Ursula Sautter, citing the work of Linguist Jurgen Udolph, offers this hypothesis in support of the emigration theory:

"After the defeat of the Danes at the Battle of Bornhoved in 1227," explains Udolph, "the region south of the Baltic Sea, which was then inhabited by Slavs, became available for colonization by the Germans." The bishops and dukes of Pomerania, Brandenburg, Uckermark and Prignitz sent out glib "locators," medieval recruitment officers, offering rich rewards to those who were willing to move to the new lands. Thousands of young adults from Lower Saxony and Westphalia headed east. And as evidence, about a dozen Westphalian place names show up in this area. Indeed there are five villages called Hindenburg running in a straight line from Westphalia to Pomerania, as well as three eastern Spiegelbergs and a trail of etymology from Beverungen south of Hamelin to Beveringen northwest of Berlin to Beweringen in modern Poland."

Udolph favors the hypothesis that the Hamelin youths wound up in what is now Poland. Genealogist Dick Eastman cited Udolph's research on Hamelin surnames that have shown up in Polish phonebooks:

"Linguistics professor Jurgen Udolph says that 130 children did vanish on a June day in the year 1284 from the German village of Hamelin (spelled Hameln in German). Professor Udolph entered all the known family names in the village at that time and then started searching for matches elsewhere. He found that the same surnames occur with amazing frequency in Priegnitz and Uckermark, both to the north of Berlin. He also found the same surnames in the former Pommeranian region, which is now a part of Poland. Professor Udolph surmises that the children were actually unemployed youths who had been sucked into the German drive to colonize its new settlements in Eastern Europe.

The Pied Piper may never have existed as such, but, says the professor, "There were characters known as Lokator who roamed northern Germany trying to recruit settlers for the East." Some of them were brightly dressed, and all were silver-tongued. Professor Udolph can show that the Hamelin exodus should be linked with the Battle of Bornhoeved in 1227 which broke the Danish hold on Eastern Europe.

That opened the way for German colonization, and by the latter part of the thirteenth century there were systematic attempts to bring able-bodied youths to Brandenburg and

Pommerania. The settlement, according to the professor's name search, ended up near Starogard in what is now northwestern Poland.

A village near Hamelin, for example, is called Beverungen and has an almost exact counterpart called Beveringen, near Pritzwalk, north of Berlin and another called Bewerungen, near Starogard. Local Polish telephone books list names that are not the typical Slavic names one would expect in that region. Instead, many of the names seem to be derived from German names that were common in the village of Hamelin in the thirteenth century. In fact, the names in today's Polish telephone directories include Hamel, Hamler and Hamelnikow, all apparently derived from the name of the original village."

Fourteenth Century Decan Lude Chorus Book

Decan Lude of Hamelin was reported, c. 1384, to have in his possession a chorus book containing a Latin verse giving an eyewitness account of the event. The verse was reportedly written by his grandmother. This chorus book is believed to have been lost since the late 17th century. The odd-looking name 'Decan Lude' may possibly indicate a priest holding the position of Dean (Latin: decanus, modern German: Dekan or Dechant) whose name was Ludwig; but as yet he has proved impossible to trace.

Fifteenth Century Lueneburg Manuscript

The Lueneburg manuscript (c. 1440–50) gives an early German account of the event:

Anno 1284 am dage Johannis et Pauli
war der 26. junii
Dorch einen piper mit allerlei farve bekledet
gewesen CXXX kinder verledet binnen Hamelen gebo[re]n
to calvarie bi den koppen verloren
In the year of 1284, on the day of Saints John and Paul
on 26 June
130 children born in Hamelin were seduced
By a piper, dressed in all kinds of colours,
and lost at the place of execution near the koppen.

This appears to be the oldest surviving account. Koppen (Old German meaning "hills") seems to be a reference to one of several hills surrounding the city. Which of them was intended by the verse's author remains uncertain.

Reportedly, there is a long-established law forbidding singing and music in one particular street of Hamelin, out of respect for the victims: the Bungelosenstrasse adjacent to the Pied Piper's House. During public parades which include music, including wedding processions, the band will stop playing upon reaching this street and resume upon reaching the other side.

Sixteenth and Seventeenth Century Sources

In 1556, De miraculis sui temporis (Latin: Concerning the Wonders of his Times) by Jobus Fincelius mentions the tale. The author identifies the Piper with the Devil.

Somewhere between 1559 and 1565, Count Froben Christoph von Zimmern included a version in his Zimmerische Chronik. This appears to be the earliest account which mentions the plague of rats. Unfortunately von Zimmern dates the event only as 'several hundred years ago' (vor etlichen hundert jarn [sic]), so that his version throws no light on the conflict of dates.

The Lame Child

The earliest English account is that of Richard Rowland Verstegan (1548-c. 1636), an antiquary and religious controversialist of partly Dutch descent, in his Restitution of Decayed Intelligence (Antwerp, 1605); unfortunately he does not give his source. (It is unlikely to have been von Zimmern, since his manuscript chronicle was not discovered until 1776.) Verstegan includes the reference to the rats and the idea that the lost children turned up in Transylvania.

The phrase 'Pide [sic] Piper' occurs in his version and seems to have been coined by him. Curiously enough his date is entirely different from that given above: July 22, 1376; this may suggest that two events, a migration in 1284 and a plague of rats in 1376, have become fused together.

Verstegan's account was copied in Nathaniel Wanley's Wonders of the Little World (1687), which was the immediate source of Robert Browning's well-known poem. Verstegan's account is also repeated in William Ramesey's Wormes (1668) — "...that most remarkable story in Verstegan, of the Pied Piper, that carryed away a hundred and sixty Children from the Town of Hamel in Saxony, on the 22. of July, Anno Dom. 1376. A wonderful permission of GOD to the Rage of the Devil".

Nineteenth Century Versions

In 1803, Johann Wolfgang von Goethe wrote a poem based on the story that was later set to music by Hugo Wolf. He incorporated references to the story in his version of Faust. The first part of the Drama was first published in 1808 and the second in 1832.

Jakob Grimm and Wilhelm Grimm, siblings known as the Brothers Grimm, drawing from eleven sources included the tale in their collection "Deutsche Sagen", first published in 1816. According to their account two children were left behind as one was blind and the other lame, so neither could follow the others. The rest became the founders of Siebenbürgen (Transylvania).

Using the Verstegan/Wanley version of the tale and adopting the 1376 date, Robert Browning wrote a poem of that name which was published in 1842. Browning's verse retelling is notable for its humour, wordplay, and jingling rhymes.

Verse 2

Rats! They fought the dogs and killed the cats,
And bit the babies in the cradles

Allusions in linguistics

In linguistics pied-piping is the common, informal name for the ability of question words and relative pronouns to drag other words along with them when brought to the front, as part of the phenomenon called Wh-movement. For example, in "For whom are the pictures?", the word "for" is pied-piped by "whom" away from its declarative position ("The pictures are for me"), and in "The mayor, pictures of whom adorn his office walls" both words "pictures of" are pied-piped in front of the relative pronoun, which normally starts the relative clause.

Some researchers believe that the tale has inspired the common English phrase "pay the piper", although others disagree. To "pay the piper" means to face the inevitable consequences of one's actions, possibly alluding to the story where the villagers broke their promise to pay the Piper for his assistance in ridding the town of the rats. The phrase sometimes refers to a financial transaction but often does not.

Also, some experts on pedophilia, such as Ken Lanning, in writing about the seduction of children by some pedophiles, have used the term the "Pied Piper effect" to describe a "unique ability to identify with children."

Contemporary Renditions

In The Wonderful Adventures of Nils (1907) by Selma Lagerlöf, the main protagonist, Nils, performs the same task that the Pied Piper: he mesmerizes rats with his flute and leads them into water.

The military interpretation of the Pied Piper story is used as a foreshadowing device in Rainbow Valley (1919) by Lucy Maud Montgomery. The story is told on two occasions by young Walter Blythe, son of Anne of Green Gables, who will later be called to fight in World War I, and fall in the Battle of the Somme (1916).

The Pied Piper story is heavily referenced by the Russian poet Marina Tsvetaeva in her poem The Ratcatcher, first published in 1925.

Eric Frank Russell's short story "The Rhythm of the Rats", published in the July 1950 issue of Weird Tales, is a retelling of the Pied Piper legend as a 20th century horror story.

In Beverly Cleary's children's novel Ellen Tebbits (1951), the school puts on a version of the story, in which the Pied Piper brings the children back.

Ellen says that her mother had not said the piper brought the children back, but the teacher called it a "creative" play. Ellen got a part in the play as a "substitute rat," and that was the title of that chapter in the book.

An allusion to the folk tale appears in the poem The Drunk in the Furnace (1960) by W. S. Merwin. Children "flock like piped rats" to the noises of a drunk in a furnace while their parents are at church.

In his poem, "The One Who Stayed" (in the collection Where the Sidewalk Ends, 1974) Shel Silverstein tells the story of a child who stayed behind while the rest of Hamelin's children followed the piper's song.

Harlan Ellison's "Emissary from Hamelin" (included in his collection Strange Wine, 1978) tells of a descendant of the original pied piper coming back seven hundred years later to lead all the adults away as punishment for centuries of "making the world a bad place".

While the piper does not explain what he means, the narrator understands this to mean violence, pollution, lying, crime, and a lack of empathy.

In the Belgian comic book Le Bal du rat mort (1980), the title of which means "The Ball of the Dead Rat",[24] police inspector Jean Lamorgue is like a pied piper who has to deliver the city of Ostend from thousands of invading rats who attack people and kill them, but in the end he fails because he is possessed by his own demons.

The Ratastrophe Catastrophe (1990) by David Lee Stone is a parody based on the Pied Piper about a boy called Diek who takes away the children of a town because a voice in his head told him to.

What Happened in Hamelin (1993) by Gloria Skurzynski is a young adult novel in ergotism from contaminated rye crops helps explain the mystery of what happened there.

Don Paterson referenced the Pied Piper tale in his poem "00:00: Law Tunnel" (published in the collection "God's Gift to Women", 1997).

The story provides the basis for the central plot and several characters in the 1998 debut novel King Rat by China Miéville.

After Hamelin (2000) by Bill Richardson is a children's book that picks up the story where Browning's poem left off. It is written in the voice of the deaf child in the poem, whom Richardson names Penelope.

Terry Pratchett's The Amazing Maurice and His Educated Rodents (2001) is a humorous take on the Pied Piper. A talking cat engineers the plagues (and subsequent removals by his sidekick piper). The story lampoons the fairy tale conventions of the original tale while providing thoughtful commentary on the motives that drive people to act as they do in the real world.

Danish writer Lars Jensen and artist Flemming Andersen created "The Ghost Rats of Hamelin" (2001), a Donald Duck comics adventure published in English in Donald Duck Adventures Take-Along Comic 6 (2004).

In it, Hamelin is plagued once a year by the marauding, giant-size ghosts of the Pied Piper's rat victims. Donald and Fethry Duck, members of a Ghostbusters-like organization, are sent to destroy these ghosts.

Michael Moorcock produces his own theory of the Hamelin tale in his book, The Dreamthief's Daughter (2002), where the cavern that the children escape into is actually a secret entrance to the Mittelmarch.

In the Donna Jo Napoli novel Breath (2003) the protagonist, Salz, is the disabled boy who did not catch up with the pied piper.

In the fifth book of The Dark Tower Series, Wolves of the Calla (2003), by Stephen King, the town robot Andy leads the children through the town playing a song, and a reference is made to the Pied Piper of Hamelin.

German author Wolfgang Hohlbein uses the Pied Piper as a secondary antagonist (as the slave of a demon) in his fantasy novel Dreizehn ("Thirteen") (2003).

The Piper is also mentioned as an antagonist in Garth Nix's series, the Keys to the Kingdom (2003).

In 2005, children's author Jane Yolen wrote a young adult novel about the tale: Pay the Piper, a rock and roll fairy tale.

In 2005, Adam McCune and Keith McCune, a father–son

writing team, published The Rats of Hamelin, in which an eighteen-year-old Pied Piper faces a hidden enemy with powers like his own.

In the Mary Higgins Clark novel Two Little Girls in Blue (2006), the main antagonist is until the end referred to as the Pied Piper, for his plot involves the kidnapping of a pair of twin children.

The tale is alluded to in George R.R. Martin's short story "Guardians" (1981) from his Tuf Voyaging series.

Australian author, Bryce Courtenay, has written a novel, Sylvia, (Penguin, 2006), about a peasant girl, who comes from a humble beginning, and eventually meets a flute player, Reinhardt, who finally calls himself The Pied Piper of Hamelin. They become principal characters in the tragedy of a Children's Crusade, marching from Cologne in Germany, right down to Italy, where the leading evangelist drowns as he is about to walk across the water. The story gets under way in the year 1212, and includes many remarkable events, such as the calling of the birds, the appearance of a fish on Sylvia's back, the plague of the crows, and others, all of which were interpreted as miracles by some of the public.

James Finn Garner wrote a "politically correct" version of the Pied Piper fairy tale, that satirizes anti-capitalism.

In the novel by James Owen, 'The Imaginarium Geographica: The Search for the Red Dragon', the antagonist was a Voice with no body, who got Clockwork Men to enchant the children one night to follow them into a cave, whereafter it closed behind them. This was most likely inspired by The Pied Piper. One little girl, kept her ears sealed with wax so as to not be seduced, like the Lame Child.

In the novel by Chimamanda Ngozi Adichie, "Half of a Yellow Sun" the child narrator Ugwu cites part of the Robert Browning poem towards the beginning of his novel. This foreshadows this character being led to the "new nation" of Biafra by the "Pied Piper" intelligentsia whose house he works in, and who have sent him to school in the first place.

Pied Piper is enbedded in 'Music Is A Time-Art', a story by Maythil Radhakrishnan. The author has it that the story of Pied Piper is actullay the story of Black Death (Bubonic Plague) retold in an allegorical form (Clue: First rats and then humans). The reluctnace of the city authorities to pay the promised amount to Pied paper indicates their total disregard to sanitary conditions - one reason why the Black Death was so effective.

Theatre

The 2006 DVD version "O Flautista", choreographer by Iolanda Rodrigues, dance show performed by CeDeCe - Companhia de Danca Contemporanea. This DVD was directed by Joao Tocha.

In the play The Pillowman written by Martin McDonagh, the main character had written a story explaining the origin of the lame child who could not follow the Piper. He claimed that it was the Piper himself who chopped off the child's toes, because the child had showed him kindness, and the Piper did not want to punish the child.

A musical entitled The Pied Piper of Hamelin, written and composed by Harvey Shield and Richard Jarbot, was produced and performed at the Olio Theater in Los Angeles in 1984; the original title was 1284, the year in which the actual Pied Piper visited Hamelin. A recording of the soundtrack was released in 1984 on Panda Digital with Harvey Shield, John Mostetter, Jodi Mitchell, J.D. Ellis, Joey Sheck, Susan Holmes, Del Appleby and Lesley Sachs.

In 2002, the ballet The Contract (The Pied Piper) composed by Michael Torke, libretto by Robert Sirman and choreographed by James Kudelka was created to celebrate the National Ballet of Canada's 50th Anniversary season. Taking as its inspiration the story of the Pied Piper, The Contract centers its story around the character of "Eva", a charismatic faith healer who is contracted to rid a small community of a mysterious illness that afflicts the town's young people.

She succeeds, but when the town's elders find reason to disapprove of her private conduct, they refuse to honor the contract, precipitating an even greater tragedy. In May 2003, the National Ballet of Canada Orchestra recorded a CD of

Michael Torke's original music for The Contract. Pleasantville, New York's Little Village Playhouse children's theatre group performed a retelling of the piper story from the point of view of the children, "New Hamelin" (2007).

In the musical, the children having been seduced to a cave by the music of the piper, return to their town and vengefully kill their parents for not coming to their rescue. The show was written by director Adam David Cohen and partner Kevin Laub.

Opera

Der Rattenfänger von Hameln, a grand opera in five acts by Viktor Nessler to a German libretto by Friedrich Hofmann based on a poem by Julius Wolff (Leipzig, 19 March 1879).

Another opera of the same name by German-American composer Adolf Neuendorff to a German libretto was produced in 1880 but has disappeared from the repertoire. However, a recording of one of the arias from this opera, "Wandern, ach, Wandern," by Fritz Wunderlich is to be found on the EMI album, Fritz Wunderlich – Der Grosse Deutsche Tenor, a three CD set.

An opera entitled The Piper of Hamelin, written and composed by Nicolas Flagello in 1970, was performed and recorded live by the Manhattan School of Music Preparatory Division in March 1999 and released on Newport Classics [NCD 60153]. The production was conducted by Jonathan Strasser, and the performers included Bob McGrath of Sesame Street fame as "The Narrator", Brace Negron as "The Piper", Troy Doney as "The Mayor" and Nicole McQuade as "The First Woman (soloist)". This opera differs in its ending from the Browning poem; while the Piper leads the children from town, he later returns alone and is freely given the promised 1,000 guilders by the distraught and repentant townspeople, and the children are reunited with their parents.

Friedrich Cerha's 1987 opera Der Rattenfänger is based on Carl Zuckmayer's 1975 play.

Mark Alburger's opera, "The Pied Piper of Hamelin" (2004), with a libretto after the Robert Browning poem, was premiered at Thick House Theater in San Francisco (2006), with the Piper in the guise of George W. Bush and the Rats as terrorists.

Music

John Corigliano composed The Pied Piper Fantasy (1979-82), a concerto for flute and orchestra. The work, by flute virtuoso James Galway, premièred on February 4, 1982 at the Hollywood Bowl in Los Angeles performed by Galway (as the flutist) and the Los Angeles Philharmonic.

The world première recording was made on December 8 and December 9, 1985 and released on RCA Victor, performed by Galway and the Eastman Philharmonic, conducted by David Effron. Another version is available on Koch International Classics, performed by Alexa Still and the New Zealand Symphony Orchestra and conducted by James Sedares. The Pied Piper Fantasy consists of seven parts:

1. Sunrise and The Piper's Song
2. The Rats
3. Battle with The Rats
4. War Cadenza
5. The Piper's Victory
6. The Burghers' Chorale
7. The Children's March.

Folk singer Donovan, who starred in the 1972 film The Pied Piper as the title character, recorded the song "People Call Me the Pied Piper" which was included in his album Pied Piper, released on the Music for Little People label (another version of this song was included in the film).

Stairway To Heaven by Led Zeppelin contains the Lyric - "the piper is calling you to join him", as well as "the piper will lead us to reason".

"Pied Piper" is a song composed by Ian Anderson, released on Jethro Tull concept album Too Old to Rock 'n' Roll: Too Young to Die! (1976).

Italian singer and songwriter Edoardo Bennato recorded the album E' arrivato un bastimento based on the Pied Piper fairy tale.

The Megadeth song "Symphony of Destruction" contains lyrics referencing the piper, in the lines "Just like the pied piper led rats through the street."

The Radiohead song "Kid A" contains clear references to the Pied Piper tale, including the lyrics "Rats and children follow me out of town" and "Come on, kids."

The Jason Webley song "Broken Cup" contains lyrics referencing the piper in the lines, "After so many pipers have played in these streets, who is missed more? The children or the rats?"

In the song "Lose Yourself" by the rapper Eminem, he says "Best believe somebody's payin' the Pied Piper".

1970's pop group ABBA recorded a song called 'The Piper' influenced by the Pied Piper of Hamelin.

Crispian St. Peters had a 1966 hit calling for us to follow him as 'The Pied Piper'

The song, Supper's Ready by Genesis contains the line: "the Pied Piper takes his children underground..."

In the Queen song "My Fairy King", writer and lead vocalist Freddie Mercury borrowed some lines from the poem.

The song "Ogre Battle", also by Queen, makes a reference to the story "Now once upon a time, An old man told me a fable, When the piper is gone, And the soup is cold on the table."

In Extremo have recently put Goethe's verse to music in their song, "Der Rattenfänger" on their album, Sünder ohne Zügel. The Demons & Wizards song "The Whistler" from their self-titled debut album.

R. Kelly often refers to himself as the Pied Piper. (In 2002, R. Kelly was indicted on charges of child pornography)

"The Piper Never Dies", the second track from the German power metal band Edguy's Hellfire Club album.

Dune song "Let's go hand in hand". The Hooters song "Where do the Children Go?" asks "..and who's that deadly piper, who leads them away?" Bob Dylan's song "Tombstone Blues", released on the 1965 album Highway 61 Revisted says the king of the Philistines "Puts the pied pipers in prison and fattens the slaves".

Film

The story has been depicted many times on film: 1903, 1911, 1913, 1918, 1924, 1926, 1933, 1957, 1972, 1981, 1982 and 1985. The 1933 adaptation was produced as an animated Walt Disney Silly Symphony short. Changes to the story include the rats being lured by a mirage of cheese created by the Piper's music and made to disappear into thin air (rather than being drowned in the river), and the children being "rescued" by the Piper from the bad upbringing being given by their selfish parents.

The 1957 made-for-television special The Pied Piper of Hamelin was a musical version in colour, using the music of Edvard Grieg, and starring Van Johnson in the title role. Claude Rains and Jim Backus also star in this film. The dialogue for this film was in rhyme, and included generous chunks of Browning's poem.

A happy ending was added, in which the children are returned after the entire village offers up a prayer of repentance.

Subplots were also added in this version, with the mayor (Rains) exhorting the children to work helping to build a clock-tower rather than attend school so that the town may win a contest, the reward being a banner bestowed by the King; a rival town, Hamelout, being devastated by both floods and the rats and being forced to beg for help from Hamelin's mayor and council (who naturally don't intend to lift a finger to help); and the mayor's daughter (Lori Nelson) being in love with the handsome schoolteacher Trueson (i.e. true son), also played by Johnson, who bitterly opposes the harsh and greedy methods imposed by the mayor.

The film was first shown by NBC as a Thanksgiving special, and later syndicated to local stations. In the early 1960s, it was briefly shown in theatres.

The 1972 film The Pied Piper was not a musical per se, although it contained music by Donovan, who also played the title role. This was an especially dark and realistic version of the tale, set this time in the 14th Century during the time of the Black Plague. The film was directed by Jacques Demy and also starred Jack Wild, Michael Hordern, Donald Pleasance and John Hurt. A stop-motion "claymation" half-hour version was made in 1981 in the United Kingdom by Cosgrove Hall, directed by Mark Hall and narrated by Robert Hardy, following the Browning poem exactly and told within the framework of a story related to a child by a cloaked stranger on a winter's evening outside the church where the Pied Piper's tale is painted on the great church window; after the story is told, the stranger reveals himself to be the Piper, who then vanishes. This version was shown on PBS.

In 1985, Shelley Duvall's Faerie Tale Theatre adapted the story in the episode The Pied Piper of Hamelin, written and directed by Nicholas Meyer with original music by James Horner, and starring Eric Idle in both the title role and as "Robert Browning".

The story is told within the framework of a subplot in which Robert Browning tries to get a boy named Willie to go to sleep by telling him the story, and emphasizes the morality of always keeping promises. This is probably the closest live-action adaptation of the story to date, with all of Browning's poe

Chapter 10

Browning's Dramatic Monologues

The first distinguishing characteristic of Browning's dramatic monologues is the point of entry, which, I argue, is not through an empathetic relationship with the speaker. The experience Browning offers us is not the same as that offered by the Wordsworthian lyric, although the poets begin the same way. In both cases, the poet's subject is the psychology of the speaker, and in both cases the author explores the speaker's point of view by means of imaginative sympathy — Einfuhlung.

With the Wordsworthian lyric, the reader's job is to achieve that sympathy; with the Browningesque monologue the reader may instead take the part of the listener, and this point of view is always available within the form. Indeed, the auditor may appear to be absent (as in "Johannes Agricola"), dead ("Porphyria's Lover"), out of earshot ("Soliloquy of the Spanish Cloister"), or simply inattentive ("Andrea del Sarto").

Second, whether this auditor is present does not matter so long as we find the speaker using the same kind of case-making, argumentative tone that marks "My Last Duchess" and which is the second definitive characteristic of the type. In all these instances the real listener (that is, the target of the argument) is the speaker's "second self"; and it becomes clear that in many monologues the putative auditor within the poem is less important than this Other.

The arguments in "Karshish" are not really intended for Abib's eye, but for Karshish's own, as the rationalizing in "Cleon" is not intended to dissuade Protus's interest in Paulus and in Christ, but Cleon's own. The tone of the argument tells us that there is a second point of view present, and it is that point of view which we take.

It is this strongly rhetorical language which distinguishes the dramatic monologue from the soliloquy, for it shows the speaker arguing with a second self. We are coaxed out of our natural sympathy with the first-person speaker by the vehemence of the arguments made; and if Abib or Lucrezia are not impressed by the arguments, we take their places within the monologues and listen as they should.

As its third important distinction, the form requires that we complete the dramatic scene from within, by means of inference and imagination, and thus these texts are rules by which the reader plays an imagined drama. The clues which Browning's speakers provide to their obsessions are observable only if we imagine ourselves within the dramatic situation, with the speaker there before us. (Because Wordsworth intends to put us within the mind of the *speaker*, his poems remain essentially lyric.)

In order to read the poems in this way, we must often sacrifice our certainty about which way to take them: do the Bishop's sons really give him cause for worry that they will substitute travertine for his antique-black and make off with his lapis lazuli, or is he paranoiac? What word did Porphyria's lover expect to hear from God? Was there any truth to the "lie" that Count Gauthier told and Gismond made him swallow? We and the listeners in these dramatic monologues can only speculate, for within the text neither they nor we can find conclusive proofs.

This indeterminacy, which his first readers found so distressing, accords with Browning's own "uncertainty" about what happens in his poems: most famously his comment to Hiram Corson that the Duke might have had his Duchess put to death — "or he might have had her shut up in a convent" (Corson viii). Since the envoy cannot know conclusively, neither can we.

VICTORIAN REACTIONS

To twentieth-century readers of Robert Browning's

poetry, the reactions of his contemporaries may seem startling. One is prepared to see Browning disliked for his obscure references and difficult syntax, but the critics of the 1830s, '40s, and '50s were more extreme: it was impossible to make sense of his poetry, they said, he must have gone mad, he was unreadable.

This charge of "unreadability" is curious, for today the standard view of his work is that it is a variety of the Romantic "poetry of experience," the kind of thing with which his critics should have been most familiar.

Something is amiss. Whereas modern criticism sees more similarities between Browning and his predecessors than differences, his contemporaries react as if they are facing something new and alien. Clearly, they did not know what strategies to use in reading Browning's poems.

The same fundamental lack of comprehension of Browning's appears even in the reactions of major critics, such as John Stuart Mill and John Ruskin, both of whom incidentally made the Wordsworthian lyric central to their notions of poetry. Witness Browning's remarks in the copy of Pauline that has both John Stuart Mill's marginal notations and the young Browning's responses to them. In his comments beside lines 971-75,

So, when spring comes
With sunshine back again like an old smile,
And the fresh waters and awakened birds
And budding woods await us, I shall be
Prepared, and we will question life once more. . .

Mill wants to know what it is that the Poet is preparing himself for. Browning's reply is, "Why, 'that's tellings,' as schoolboys say" (Peterson and Standley 169). The rules for his poetry are the same as those for schoolboys' games: the participant has to infer the truth without actually being told it, from "a set of governing rules" (Iser, Act 108).

Certainly, some readers — perhaps we should say players — will find some games more difficult, even bewildering, as John Ruskin did Browning's poetry. This statement of his poetic practice is taken from a December 1855 "thank you" letter to Ruskin, who had written some friendly criticisms of Men and Women:

For your bewilderment more especially noted — how shall I help *that*? We don't read poetry the same way, by the same law; it is too clear. I cannot begin writing poetry till my imaginary reader has conceded licences to me which you demur at altogether. I *know* that I don't make out my conception by my language, all poetry being a putting in infinite within the finite.

You would have me paint it all plain out, which can't be; but by various artifices I try to make shift with touches and bits of outlines which *succeed* if they bear the conception from me to you. (Litzinger and Smalley 14-15) In other words, the reader must fill in the gaps, and can do so better from the standpoint of the auditor than from that of the speaker.

THE FIGURE OF THE LISTENER

The distinguishing characteristic of Browning's dramatic monologues is that they make new demands of the reader, and those extra-textual demands are signalled within the text by the figure of the auditor. That listening figure and the tone which the speaker adopts in order to make his or her case are the most important new ingredients in the Browningesque dramatic monologue.

Because the listener is not always physically present, most critical assessments have misunderstood its significance. In fact, the presence of the auditor determines how the reader must react to the speaker, and thus the proper questions about the poem are not those which ask about the relationship between the speaker's ideas and the poet's; instead we must ask about the speaker's effect upon his listener.

From this rhetorical effect we can infer the dramatic situation, and it is the interplay among the characters in these scenes which Browning wishes us to imagine. Observing the speakers as their listeners do, we find we have to piece together scraps of information to complete a picture of the speaker, and even, sometimes, simply to figure out what is going on. Thus, in each re-reading we must relive the process of discovery which the listener experiences. Rather than a balance of sympathy and judgment, a better description of this process of discovery is engagement, then detachment: we readers must become engaged in the game of imagination which the poem asks us to play before we can attain a detached, critical view of the whole work.

THE SILENT LISTENER

Why indeed do the listeners never speak; or, if they do, why do we hear their words only as rephrased by the monologist? Although we might expect them to be very similar, the dynamics of dialogue differ quite markedly from those of monologue.

All dramatic monologues tend toward dialogue because we continue to expect the auditor to interrupt the speaker, but when the auditor actually becomes a second speaker, we lose our entry into the poem; he or she no longer serves as a proxy for us. It seems odd that the presence of a second speaker should force a change in genre until we realise that unless the inscribed listener remains silent, we cannot see the action through the Other's eyes. As Woolford explains:

The fact that . . . the second-consciousness never speaks. . . points, in the most radical fashion possible, to meaning as being or including absence or silence. To complete the construal of the dramatic monologue's meaning, we require access to the response of the person to whom it is addressed, and for whom its rhetorical manoeuvres are intended.

In withholding that response Browning forces the reader himself to provide it, and thus compels him to hypostasise a meaning beyond the periphery of the persona's intention. The listener must be left blank so that we can create him or her, within the parameters Browning has left us—our very own colour-by-numbers character.

That Other, wholly passive presence gives us a place to stand within the narrative and respond. Much of the experience of reading is the creating of that other side of the picture from the poem's hints and implications. This is why those monologues by Tennyson in which we are supplied information in a prefatory note belong to a different poetic genre.

If the work has been done for us, we do not have to become so involved. Other seemingly similar poems like Yeats's "Michael Robartes and the Dancer" or "Dialogue of Self and Soul," where both personalities are parts of the poet's self, leave no room for us to stand; when the second character also speaks, we are no longer able to impose ourselves upon that character and take its role in the poem.

When the speaker restates the listener's stated or anticipated question, giving the suggestion of a dialogue, as in "Fra Lippo Lippi," "Bishop Blougram's Apology," and "Mr. Sludge, the Medium," the other side of the conversation must, if the poet wishes to employ the dynamics of the dramatic monologue, be relayed to us by the speaker's restatement of what the auditor has said or might say. We are left uncertain whether the questions to which the monologist appears to respond have actually been voiced.

On the contrary, the Duke actually states that he is answering questions which his guests have seemed to want to ask, "if they durst"; and the questions asked in "Mr. Sludge" and "Bishop Blougram" may be not just restated but rephrased. Bishop Blougram, David Ewbank observes, "often puts words in Gigadibs' mouth". These words are unvoiced, hypothetical objections that Gigadibs would raise — Ewbank calls it the "illusion of dialogue".

To take it a step further: the Bishop uses Gigadibs to create an idealized critic, who raises the most cogent objections that he himself can anticipate, and charges himself with responding to them — as if Gigadibs had raised them. The test is that the questions teach us nothing about the character of Gigadibs, but much about the Bishop.

With St. Praxed's Bishop, there are only the barest suggestions that his "nephews" intend to rob him; he assumes that they want to, and we have no other source of information about them, but his view of them (and of Gandolf) is certainly tainted by his own obsessions — as is the lover's judgment about what Porphyria really wants (to put it mildly).

FIRST-PERSON SPEAKER CREATES FOR INTERPRETATION

J. T. Best's ingenious reading of "Porphyria's Lover" raises central questions about interpreting the dramatic monologue, that quintessentially Victorian poetic genre or form developed by Robert Browning, Alfred Tennyson, and Dante Gabriel Rossetti in the 1830s and '40s.

Victorian poetry, which often displays radical experimentation with poetic form, presented numerous problems for contemporary readers, but the fundamental difficulties associated with interpreting dramatic monologues derive from three closely associated facts:

- These poems have a first-person speaker.
- This first-person speaker may or may not voice the opinions of the poet.
- First-person narration (or presentation) provides no sure way of authenticating the speaker's statements.

These defining characteristics of this poetic form created major problems for early Victorian readers, who had little idea how to read such poems because they were accustomed to assuming that all poems spoken in the first person represented either the poet or an idealized version or persona of the poet.

Readers tend strongly to identify with — that is, give their credence to — the speakers of first-person narration, and as Wayne C. Booth's The Rhetoric of Fiction demonstrated a half century ago, the main problem with first-person narration appears in its either/or nature: either one takes the speaker to be a completely reliable narrator, accepting everything that he or she says as true, or, less frequently, one understands the speaker to be completely unreliable and takes everything he or she says with a grain of salt or outright disbelief, such as occurs as soon as the reader realizes that the speaker in Swift's "A Modest Proposal" does not represent the author; many readers, especially students new to satire, in fact never do come to this realization.

First-person narration, in others words, allows little room for subtlety about the narrator or speaker. But as Booth further pointed out, first-person speakers create another fundamental problem for interpreting the texts in which they appear — the reader has no sure way of getting outside the speaker's statements to determine whether they are true!

THE TURN OF THE SCREW

Booth makes these points in the midst of a discussion of Henry James's The Turn of the Screw, which has had an interesting critical history: at the time the novella appeared in print, readers assumed that James had written a suitably creepy ghost story and nothing more.

As the years passed James's reputation as a prose master rose in the literary academy, in large part because of his supposed combination of high seriousness, complex analyses of personal motives, and sophisticated, often difficult, modes of narration in which irony played a large role. As Vivian in Oscar Wilde's "The Decay of Lying" put it satirically,

Mr. Henry James writes fiction as if it were a painful duty, and wastes upon mean motives and imperceptible 'points of view' his neat literary style, his felicitous phrases, his swift and caustic satire.

Mid-twentieth-century readers of James, however, couldn't get enough of these qualities, which came to define his greatness. Soon enough academic critics decided that such a master of prose would not, could not, stoop to write a mere ghost story, a pop form, and since these were also the decades in which Freud's writings became far widely accepted than they have been recently, some ingenious critics read The Turn of the Screw as a sophisticated pyscho-sexual case study in which the governess who narrates the tale, driven by her sexual needs, herself kills her young charge.

This interpretation, which soon dominated the way the novella was taught, had the several great advantages: It perfectly matched contemporary fashion, it served to make James, the great canonical author, appear even more sophisticated and wise in the ways of the human psyche, and it also permitted the critics who made this interpretation to seem very smart, certainly more intelligent than James's contemporaries. Only one problem: looking at James's notebooks shows that he thought he was writing . . . a ghost story.

The critical history of The Turn of the Screw has several important implications for the interpretation of dramatic monologues, which like the James novella, have a first-person speaker:

(1) Since such texts provide no evidence other than that provided by the speaker, any reading that seems consistent with this evidence will appear plausible.
(2) Readers tend to choose interpretations that match popular intellectual fashions, their own deep beliefs, or self-interest.
(3) Going outside the poem for external evidence, such as the writer's own public or private remarks, may provide the only convincing way to resolve alternate self-consistent readings, though not everyone may be willing to be convinced: a reader could counter the evidence of James's own notebooks with the claim that he may have began with sole intention of writing a ghost story but somewhere along the way he changed his mind and did not feel it necessary to record that decision in his notebooks (what kind of evidence would make this claim more or less likely? at what would you have to look?)

"ULYSSES"

Tennyson's poem has an even more complex history with not two but four possible — that is more or less self-consistent — interpretations. By far the most popular reading of the poem matches the popular Victorian one, builds to the famous final line: "To strive, to seek, to find, and not to yield." According to this reading, "Ulysses" embodies the Victorian stiff-upper lip, the need to endure when things get difficult and unpleasant.

Going outside the poem, we recall that Tennyson stated he wrote it shortly after learning of Arthur Henry Hallam's death, so "Ulysses" turns out to be — along with "Tithonus" and "Morte d'Arthur" — in some sense a reaction to the traumatic death of his closest friend. "Tithonus," like the Struldbugs in the third book of Gulliver's Travels, argues for the necessity of death just as Bedivere in the "Morte d'Arthur" dramatizes the necessity, if difficulty, of having faith, keeping faith, and carrying on after the death of a loved one.

According to the usual reading of "Ulysses," then, the poem's final line fits perfectly with the poet's situation as a mourner. As I have pointed out elsewhere in VW, Victorians tended to read this poem pretty straightforwardly, as an avowal of faith in the necessity of striving ever onward.

They were supported by Tennyson's own statement that this poem "gave my feeling about Hallam's death perhaps more simply than anything in In Memoriam," his great elegaic lament. But modern critics have found "Ulysses" anything but simple. Perhaps more than any other single poem, how you read it depends upon your theoretical assumptions about the nature of poetry.

In 1954 E. J. Chiasson called the accepted reading of the poem into question when he pointed out the speaker's

marital and social irresponsibility, pursuit of sensation, and adoration of the naked intellect, [which] is thoroughly opposed to In Memoriam's glorification of the marriage bond as symptomatic of and contributory to social solidarity. . . . It is especially surprising that the pivotal doctrine of In Memoriam, namely the belief in immortality, the belief which serves as sanction for all other beliefs, and without which life becomes mere rutting and social disintegration, should become in 'Ulysses' at best a subject for the display of a kind of jovial agnosticism.

According to Chiasson, then, the poem, which so many take to be an uplifting call to courageous perseverance, is in fact a form of intellectual satire, which "can be read as the dramatic presentation of a man who has faith neither in the gods nor consequently in the necessity of preserving order in his kingdom or in his own life", and thus, like Tithonus and the mariners in "The Lotus-Eaters" dramatizes an intellectual position that the poet wishes to explore but not accept.

Chiasson's reading depends upon two points, the first of

which is the speaker's apparently scornful treatment of his wife, son, and people — so unlike the protagonist of The Odyssey. Second, Chaisson assumes that Tennyson speaker is the Ulysses of Dante's Inferno, which condemns him to hell for overreaching pride, rather than the main character of the Homeric epic. The justification for making this assumption was the statement by the poet's son that his father referred to Dante's, not Homer's, Ulysses.

To the standard reading of Ulysses character and Chiasson's more sharply negative one with their consequent effects upon the meaning of the poem, I offer a third possibility: Like Browning's "The Bishop Orders His Tomb at St. Praxed's," "Ulysses" is a deathbed poem, which treats death as the last great adventure into the unknown — a reading that fits perfectly with Tennyson's statements about the occasion on which he wrote the poem as well as the other poems the explore the nature of death.

According to this interpretation, Tennyson's speaker is the character who appears in Homer rather than Dante, and I would justify this assertion with the argument that unlike so many statements in the poet's memoirs edited by his son, Hallam Tennyson, not his father, asserts that "Ulysses" refers to Dante's version. (Quite frankly, this is the weakest point in the argument for my interpretation.) In this reading of the poem, the mariners Ulysses addresses are the ghosts of his crew from the The Odyssey, all of whom perish.

Considering all three readings, one can argue that Chiasson's and mine have the advantage over the more popular one that they are self-consistent; that is, they fit the text of the poem. Nonetheless, it is difficult proving which one might be correct because both arguments appeal to contradictory external evidence. James Kincaid, who has written perhaps the finest book-length study of Tennyson, follows Robert Langbaum and takes yet another tack, arguing that in the dramatic monologue

the removal of context makes it extremely difficult not only to know how to judge but to be sure if one should judge at all. Certainly, the creation of a solid position from which one can observe how the speaker "contradicts himself" or is subject to the poet's satire is a critical fiction, a convenience that distorts the effects of the poem.

Robert Langbaum's The Poetry of Experience, a brilliant discussion of the problem of perspective in the dramatic monologue, uses a very open appeal to our experience in the poem to demonstrate that an overtly satiric reading of a dramatic monologue is a possible, but rather crude and uninteresting response.

To see that Ulysses's comments on Telemachus are contemptuous is one thing; to argue that this contempt acts to condemn Ulysses is something else. 'there is no way we can find within the poem a morality that allows for such certain judgments. By removing rhetorical securities, the dramatic monologue does, as Langbaum insists, force us to experience the speaker himself, not a meaning which is external to him.

Still, the tendency of this form to find the extreme case, in fact to be generally effective in direct proportion to the outrageousness of its argument and the distance of the speaker and action from conventional moral and social norms, means that our instinct to make judgments is very strongly activated. . . . Contrary to what I take to be the implications of Langbaum's argument, judgment is not an attendant or superficial response but an immediate and powerful one. But it is also given no place to rest, no terms with which to deal, and this very fact accounts for the ironic rhetoric.

We are asked to respond simultaneously on two contradictory levels: that of distant critical judgment and that of absorbed, direct experience. We must and we cannot do both; and we realise, therefore, the tension between the now disjoined meaning and experience.

Such an essentially agnostic approach to interpreting those dramatic monologues that treat the speaker ironically certainly has appeal, if only because of its ingenious novelty. But for me such interpretations of "Ulysses" and similar dramatic monologues has one fatal flaw: it takes for granted the not very credible assumption that Tennyson writes this kind of themeless poetry — dramatic monologues in which he does not make any points about the subjects that most concern him — only in those poems that we have difficulty interpreting.

The conclusion seems a bit too convenient. Certainly, this fundamental difficulty of interpretation does not exist in poems in which the speaker more or less speaks for or in place of the author. In Browning's case we have the example of speakers whom the author treats unironically, such as Abt Vogler, Rabbi ben Ezra, and the Pope in The Ring and the Book. One could of course argue that this new kind of themeless poetry occurs only when the author of the dramatic monologue treats the speaker critically or ironically, but that doesn't work either, for plenty of examples of dramatic monologues come to mind in which both Tennyson and Browning treat their speakers ironically and yet their points of view appear quite clearly in the resulting intellectual satires: Tennyson's "Tithonus" and "The Lotos Eaters," Browning's "Andrea del Sarto," "Soliloquy of the Spanish Cloister," "The Bishop Orders His Tomb at St. Praxed's," and "Cleon."

INTERPRETING A DRAMATIC MONOLOGUE

The dramatic monologue is a literary genre, and like all genres it relies upon certain techniques that signal the reader how to read it. Browning, Tennyson, and other authors or use this form use some or all of the following means of helping readers interpret the words of the fictional speaker who is unreliable:

- Having a character's actions or own words contradict his assertions ("Porphyria's Lover")
- Appeal to a common morality, belief system, or set of assumptions that authors believe, correctly or not, that they and their readers share ("Porphyria's Lover," "My Last Duchess," Hopkins's "A Soliloquy of one of the Spies left in the Wilderness") .
- Use of epigraphs and allusions that position the poem (Hopkins's "The Windhover")
- Titles ("The Windhover," "An Epistle Concerning

the Strange Medical Experience of Karshish, the Arab Physician"")

- Placement of poem in a particular section or category in a book ("Porphyria's Lover" as a "Madhouse Cell")
- A character's use or misuse of material, such as the symbolic interpretation of well-known biblical passages, that serve to define the character's moral status. For example, Guido in The Ring and the Book thinks he's presenting himself as a Christ-figure when in fact he continually uses images that refer to Satan, and the speaker misuses commonplace symbols of heaven in "The Bishop orders His Tomb at St Praxed's." Hopkins uses this methode in his early "A Soliloquy of one of the Spies left in the Wilderness")

"PORPHYRIA'S LOVER"

Considering both internal and external evidence, one might think that the speaker of "Porphyria's Lover" exemplifies the most unambiguous and easily understood of all unreliable speakers in dramatic monologues: first, the poem was originally published as one of two "Madhouse Cells," clearly and unabiguously pointing to the fact that the words of the insane speaker are not to be trusted; second, every assertion or judgment the speaker makes is quickly disproved by his own words:

- Using what Ruskin termed the pathetic fallacy to show how the speaker falsifies nature, Browning has him project his own feelings upon the wind and rain, which is, of course, not "sullen" or full of "spite."
- The speaker falsely asserts that his "love of her . . . [is] all in vain," but in fact she does think of him and she does come!
- He claims that's she's proud, but she gives no sign of being so, and he admits that he is proud of what he's done.

- He claims she neglects him, but the first thing she does, even before removing her wet outer clothing, is to light a fire and comfort him.

Then there's the central fact of the poem, the chief source of its power — this madman, who today would be labelled a paranoid schizophrenic, strangles his beloved, asserts on the basis of no evidence that she felt no pain, and sits all night with the dead body wondering why God hasn't spoken to him in praise for his act.

When discussing this poem in class, the first question I ask students is, "At what point in the poem did you begin to distrust the speaker?" For almost all of us that point comes with the great shock of reading that he has strangled the beloved with her own hair. At that point (or upon completing the poem) one can go back through the poem and note all the previously missed hints of what was to come.

The sensationalism of the poem is enough to tempt one to take it at first as a poem without much more of a point than that young women should probably not date homicidal maniacs, but on reflection it soon becomes clear that Porphyria's lover is another one of those Browning male characters who objectify, use, and abuse woman by projecting their wishes upon them — the Duke of Ferrara and Count Guido Franceschini being the most obvious examples.

Chapter 11

The Difficulties of Victorian Poetry

Dick Sullivan raises a really important point when he asks, "What might have happened to English-language poetry if [Hopkins had] been published in his lifetime and had to compete with Tennyson, Swinburne, and Browning?" ["Hopkins and the Spiritual"] Looking at the reception of the early, radically experimental poetry of Tennyson and Browning, the answer seems fairly obvious: almost certainly nothing would have happened unless Hopkins had resolutely kept publishing and been lucky enough to find a few critics who would defend his work in print.

Like these other poets, Hopkins would have been greeted with complete non-comprehension when he was noticed or reviewed at all, and if and when he was reviewed, he would probably have received the same kind of mockery they did. Now that the three poets to whom Sullivan compares Hopkins have become canonical — which means in practice "read in secondary schools and universities" — we forget how the Victorians at first found them amazingly difficult to read.

Let's begin with Browning because in some ways his difficulties for the reader have so much in common with Hopkins's. Readers long found Browning's poetry incomprehensible for the following reasons:

- He created a radically new form for which his audience did not know the rules.
- He used difficult, often arcane words.
- He made difficult, often obscure allusions.
- He did not, in other words, write with a conventional sense of audience.

Taking the second and third points, I should point out that both Swinburne and Tennyson present the same difficulties, Tennyson, for example, anticipating e.e. cummings by a century and coining new words, using nouns as verbs, and so on. Browning, unlike the other two poets, was home-schooled and self taught, and he enjoyed reading obscure biographies and reference works with the result that he had an unsure sense of what he could expect his readers to know. (He didn't always realise when he was being difficult!)

The scholarly and equally well-read Swinburne similarly often showed little attention to the needs of his audience, characteristically attempting to popularize his political and poetic hero Victor Hugo with a poem filled with dozens of allusions to the French author's works that only a someone who had practically memorized them could possible recognize.

What we see here with all four poets, in other words, is the Modernist elitist attitude toward the audience that assumes it's the reader's job to work hard to understand the text or work of art. Or as one of the great twentieth-century novelists (Joyce? Faulkner?) put it, "You can't read my novels. You can only re-read them." Don't expect to get it on the first read!

As difficult as might be these poets' choice of words and allusions, their novel poetic forms created the most serious problems for readers. Let's look at Browning, who used a radically new poetic form — essentially a new genre with its own rules — and readers simply did not know what to do.

Along with Tennyson and Rossetti, Browning invented the dramatic monologue, particularly that form of it in which the speaker does not represent the poet and, therefore, his statements were certainly not those that the poet himself believed.

Accustomed to taking it for granted that the first-person speaker was either the poet or his idealized persona, audiences did not know what to do when they encountered the homicidal maniac of "Porphyria's Lover" and the even more terrifying Duke in "My Last Duchess." It's as hard to over-estimate the importance of this point as it is even to realise it after so many years of teaching Browning in secondary schools as an exercise in close reading: Early and mid-Victorian readers simply had no clue what to do first when encountering a speaker in a poem who did not serve as an obvious stand-in for the author and whose statements therefore had to be received with scepticism or at least reservation of judgment.

If this statement doesn't seem obvious, go back to those two famous Browning dramatic monologues and take note of the point at which you first realized you could not trust the speakers.

Browning, as contemporary anecdotes demonstrate, was simply unreadable for most in his intended audience: all biographies of Browning tell the story of a well-known person who was given a copy of Browning's admittedly difficult Paracelsus while recovering from an illness; horrified by the fact that he could not understand the poem at all, the invalid thought that the illness had destroyed his mind and was considering suicide until others assured him they couldn't understand it either.

What happened so that secondary school students can now read — and understand — Browning (or at least the shorter dramatic monologues)? Are we so much more intelligent than the Victorians? Hardly. Wordsworth explains it all when he stated in the 1815 edition of Lyrical Ballads that great poets have to "create the taste by which they are to be enjoyed." In other words, readers have to learn the new rules — the signals to the readers — that let them know what to do next.

The idea of combining two different forms or modes in the dramatic monologue (drama and lyric) was just as unsettlingly unexpected as Wordsworth and Coleridge's similarly joining two supposedly opposed ones in lyrical ballads, since the lyric was a non-narrative form while the ballad was essentially narrative. But readers learn.

Remember, although early twentieth-century readers found stream-of-consciousness narration of James Joyce and Virginia Wolfe initially incomprehensible, after three or four decades undergraduates learned the rules, and now pop genres, such as detective stories and science fiction novels, use the technique. Tennyson and Swinburne also write with new forms. In addition to his early use of the then-novel dramatic monologue, Tennyson wrote radically experimental challenges to narrative in his two great long poems, In Memoriam and Idylls of the King. Anticipating (and certainly heavily influencing T. S. Eliot), he builds a poetry of fragments in In Memoriam that challenges all previous elegies, calling into question their too-easy linear movement from grief to consolation. (His use of poetic segments containing moments of illumination and climax incidentally provides the model for Hopkins's "Wreck of the Deutchland.")

In Memoriam makes such a radical challenge to both conventional poetic form and narrative that more than any other work intended for print — more even than Cortazar's Hopkscotch, Sterne's Tristram Shandy, or Coover's "The Babysitter" — this poem anticipates computer-based hypermedia.

When I teach and write about the ways one can both satisfy readers with the individual blocks of texts (or lexias) in hypertext and yet make them want to continue (i.e. follow links), I point students to In Memoriam, which also shows how chains of imagery, such as the poems's use of "hand," "dream," and "type," can provide a new kind of unity in a networked text. Tennyson continues his experimental poetic project in The Idylls of the King (1859-1888), in which his characteristic use of flashbacks, parabolic commentary, and complex plotting anticipates the modernist narrative of Faulkner.

And then there is Swinburne, probably the Victorian poet as far from Hopkins in just about every way one can imagine: whereas Hopkins published almost nothing, Swinburne, the leading expert of his time on Jacobean drama, published many critical books, including one of the first on Blake, as well as many volumes of poetry and poetic drama; whereas Hopkins was a politically conservative, devout christian who led a celibate, abstemious life, Swinburne, the radical democrat and atheist, first became known as the bard of perversion before he became the bard of the great leftist cause of the Victorian period — the liberation and unification of Italy. Perhaps the one poetic quality that most separates the two authors appears starkly in the length of their poems.

Many of Hopkins's finest works take the form of the sonnet and its variants — extremely dense poems with layers of imagery; with the exception of Swinburne's Dirae (curses), bitterly satirical sonnets on political themes, all of his major poems are very long, and, unlike those of both Hopkins and Tennyson, they do not build towards moments of vision but employ a circular structure that returns again and again to a provisional imaginative centre, adding layer after layer of image and meaning.

Nonetheless, one must not overemphasize the differences between the poets, for a comparison reveals surprising similarities. In their early careers both wrote fine dramatic monologues — Swinburne's "Hymn to Proserpine" and Hopkins's "A Soliloquy of one of the Spies left in the Wilderness."

Both frequently employ sophisticated biblical allusions — both in fact draw upon the types of Christ and Satan in Genesis 3:15 — though Swinburne usually does so satirically and Hopkins as a centre to his devotional poetry. Perhaps surprisingly, both men use masochism and masochistic imagery as a means of expressing their sense of being in the world. Both men went through periods of intense depression and personal crisis that significantly marked their poetry.

Finally, both men create a poetry of meditation that provides multiple ways into a main point of belief, and to do so both employ dense layering of allusion as a means of overcoming the shortcomings of language. Of course, devout belief and fervent atheism divide them pretty sharply, allowing us to see certain parings of their poems as binary opposites, at least on this one point.

Thus, just as Rossetti's House of Life is (as Dick Fredeman pointed out long ago) an anti-In Memoriam, so Swinburne's brilliant landscape meditation, "Evening on the Broads" (text), is very much an anti-"Windhover." But "Evening on the Broads" nonetheless reveals points of convergence with

Hopkins. This dense poem, which presents the brief moment the sun hovers on the horizon before plunging into night as an image of human life, struggles to find language adequate to a transient existence, as does Hopkins's "Spring and Fall;" Hopkins, like the Tractarian poets, such as Keble and early Newman, believes earthly phenomena to be divinely intended symbols of Christ, heaven, and spiritual truths. Swinburne, in contrast, finds that such phenomena symbolize nothing, except perhaps death, time, and change.

In some ways Hopkins's best poetry has turned out to be easier to read and therefore more widely read than Swinburne's finest works, and this fact derives significantly from their length: the brevity of Hopkins's poems made them perfectly suited to the word-by-word and line-by-line close reading of the New Criticism (whose adherents created Hopkins's fame and position in the canon).

The poetry of Hopkins, far more than that of Swinburne, has that most crucial of qualities: it is teachable and therefore frequently taught. In contrast, because Swinburne really doesn't fit any pedagogical method, he creates hard work for teachers.

Both Hopkins and Swinburne write a poetry of meditation, but the very brevity of Hopkins's best poems makes ruminating on individual words and lines seem more attractive than trying to unravel Swinburne's individual lines, in which he builds metaphors upon metaphors, emphasizing both the shortcomings of human language and the fact that poetry really exists only in the language; for him it's all we have.

y definition, any work of fiction must not be "real," in that no work of fiction has ever really happened just as it was written. But there are clearly differences between an obvious work of realism, like Anthony Trollope's The Warden, and an obvious fantasy, like Lewis Carroll's Alice in Wonderland. And yet, Alice contains characters like those one could meet in "real life," and its characters (predominately) speak English, and Alice breathes air and has two legs like any other nine-year old girl.

By examining a few works of fiction, of various styles, I intend to create a working definition of fantasy in the Victorian era — not an all-inclusive one, but one that would apply to most fantasies of the era.

The works to be addressed are George MacDonald's Phantastes, Christina Rossetti's "Goblin Market," Carroll's Alice in Wonderland and Through the Looking-Glass, Alfred Tennyson's Idylls of the King, and Robert Browning's "Childe Roland to the Dark Tower Came." These works are by no means identical. Aside from the obvious fact that they include both poetry and prose, they cover a variety of styles and literary techniques.

They all have something in common, however, and that is a fantastic element — an element which I will address in this essay. These works share both fantastic setting and characterization. The settings of these works vary from Carroll's Wonderland to Tennyson's Camelot, but they all differ from the world that surrounds us. In addition, the works frequently describe a process of transition from a realistic world to the fantastic — and when they do not, travel of another sort often plays a significant role.

Perhaps the most obvious sign of the fantastic to a reader is the setting of a work. And perhaps the most obvious examples of this are Carroll's Alice books. Both Alice in Wonderland and Through the Looking-Glass are set in very different worlds, and Alice must make a transition between her own world and the new.

In Alice in Wonderland, she famously goes "down the rabbit-hole," and once underground she attempts to make another transition, this time through a small hole in the wall. In the second book, she goes "through the glass...into the Looking-glass room," which is simply the anteroom to an entire looking-glass world.

The worlds of both books are essentially normal, yet slightly off — a dichotomy present in other fantasies as well. Eric Rabkin writes that this is what differentiates a true fantasy from a fairy tale, that it "continues to reserve its ground rules again and again" (quoted in George P. Landow, "Fantasy and Conceptions of the Real"). Alice's worlds are defined by ground rules: the world of Through the Looking-Glassis governed by a complex adherence to the rules of chess (as described in Carroll's "Preface to the 1897 Edition," 105), and Alice in Wonderland's world is frequently concerned with issues of size (certain objects make one larger, while others make one smaller).

While these worlds have rules, they are unlike those of reality. MacDonald's Phantastes resembles the Alice books in this regard, in that his protagonist, Anodos, finds a "path to Fairy Land" (Phantastes, 23) that takes him to another world. Rossetti's "Goblin Market" is similar, yet forms an interesting departure from this trope.

The titular market is just "down the glen" (l.47), but after Laura tastes the goblins' forbidden fruit, she is forbidden to return, or even see the market: Listening ever, but not catching The customary cry, "Come buy, come buy," ...Not for all her watching Once discerning even one goblin (ll.230-236)

Thus Rossetti shifts Carroll and MacDonald's travel structure, for Laura travels to a world she could see but not experience and then craves that experience but cannot return or even see the fantastic world. This is, again, an example of the "ground rules" of the goblin market: look, but don't touch.

Tennyson's Idylls of the King and Browning's "Childe Roland to the Dark Tower Came" also take place in different worlds: Tennyson's in a mythic Camelot and Browning's in a world created from a "great variety of sources" (Donald Smalley, Notes, 500).

What these works have in common (and what separates them from Carroll, MacDonald and Rossetti) is that these worlds are enclosed. Arthur does not travel from Victorian England to Camelot, and neither does Browning's narrator make the sort of transition described above. The worlds of these works are, like the previous ones, defined in certain ways.

Tennyson's Camelot has its rules of conduct and chivalry as well as premonitions and dreams, and Browning suggests a similar sort of world, albeit in vaguer terms, mentioning "knights," "failure prophesied," and a "quest" (ll.37-39). But while these works do not have the sort of transition the previous four do, they do describe travel.

Browning's narrator has been performing a "world-wide wandering...thro' years" (ll.19-20), and in fact, the poem is a sort of travelogue following the narrator on his quest. Since Tennyson's Idylls is a sequence of poems, each telling a separate story, there is no overarching journey. Travel does play a role in the poems, however, especially in the conclusion, "The Passing of Arthur." Arthur's death is actually a journey, as Tennyson writes,

The barge with oar and sail
Moved from the brink, like some full-breasted swan ...
Long stood Sir Bedivere
Revolving many memories, till the hull
Look'd one black dot against the verge of dawn,
And on the mere the wailing died away. ["The Passing of Arthur," ll. 433-440]

The figure of the journey is mentioned elsewhere, as several other characters make voyages. Neither of these examples (Browning or Tennyson) represent the same idea of transition that the previously discussed works do, but their presence denotes some sort of shift in place in these works.

The settings of all these works clearly position them as fictions, but it is not simply that which makes them fantastic. All the works create a sense of reality even in their most fantastic moments, because they have internal rules that they follow.

These rules are not the rules of the real world, but they still dictate the actions of characters in the work. These works are also characterized by travel — in most of them, it is a transition from the real world to the fantastic. This transition is important (and the travel as well, because to a lesser degree it denotes the same thing) because, as George Landow writes, "something...must signal us that we are meant to take certain elements as fantastic" ("Fantasy and Conceptions of the Real"). By showing their characters traveling, these writers "prove" to their readers that they are creating fantasies.

The characters that inhabit these fantasy lands are the

second sign to the reader. As with setting, there are varying degrees of reality in the characters of these works. But even where the characters may be drawn very true to life, there are other elements that create a world of fantasy.

As with setting, Carroll, MacDonald and Rossetti create characters that are plainly of another world. Carroll's books are full of anthropomorphic animals, human playing cards, and the like. Phantastes takes place in Fairy Land, and is thus populated with fairies, as well as goblins and other creatures.

Finally, Rossetti's "Goblin's Market" features many goblins as well. Rossetti's goblins are more along the lines of Carroll's white rabbit as she describes them:

One had a cat's face,
One whisked a tail,
One tramped at a rat's pace,
One crawled like a snail,
One like a wombat prowled obtuse and furry,
One like a ratel tumbled hurry skurry. [ll.71-76]

Like setting, these characters follow Rabkin's requirement for "ground rules" in fantasy. In Carroll's Alice books, the frequent use of anthropomorphic animals (i.e., animals that speak, think and act like humans) is always housed in realistic terms.

When Alice first meets some talking animals, she frightens away a group of birds by mentioning her cat. While Carroll describes the birds in very human terms — they all find "various pretexts" to leave Alice (Alice in Wonderland, 26) — they do so only because they are birds, who fear cats as predators.

Even with the more abstract characters, like the animated playing cards, they follow a version of the real world's rules. The queen card is, indeed, the queen of Wonderland, and the king and jack play their appropriate roles as well.

Rossetti's goblins are similarly anthropomorphic, but those characteristics only manifest themselves in their outward nature, rather than in their motivations (as in Carroll). The snail-like goblin is slow as if he were a snail, and the cat-faced goblin "purr'd", but the cat-faced goblin does not chase the rat-like one. These creatures still follow a fantastic logic in their actions, however. They tempt Laura and Lizzie, in an effort to entrance them. Their actions follow rules: they do not accept payment for their fruits, and they only appear to those who have not tasted their product.

MacDonald's creatures are also slightly different, of course. The Fairy Land of Phantastes has its own taxonomy of creatures, from fairies and goblins to living trees and ogres. Each has its own motivations and natures, as MacDonald makes a point to mention. Early in Anados' Fairy Land adventure, he makes an observation about fairies and plants.

I may as well mention here, that the conclusion I arrived at from the observations I was afterwards able to make, was, that the flowers die because the fairies go away; not that the fairies disappear because the flowers die. The flowers seem a sort of houses for them, or outer bodies, which they can put on or off when they please.

Just as you could form some idea of the nature of a man from the kind of house he built, if he followed his own taste, so you could, without seeing the fairies, tell what any one of them is like, by looking at the flower till you feel that you understand it. [Phantastes, 36]

MacDonald's narrator makes what almost seems like a scientific observation in this passage, making it clear that there are rules in Fairy Land — as there are in the goblin market and Wonderland.

Again, as with setting, Tennyson and Browning create characters that are closer (physiologically, at least) to what we consider real. When the characters in these works approach realism, the things that surround them become stranger, reminding the reader of their fantastic qualities. In Browning, for example, inanimate objects are given human qualities — a strategy that may be a form of pathetic fallacy, but nevertheless serves to stress the strangeness of the narrator's surroundings. He describes grass as growing "scant as hair/In leprosy" ("Childe Roland to the Dark Tower Came," ll.73-74); he addresses Nature, who responds "peevishly"; and the titular tower is "blind as the fool's heart".

These personifications (and apostrophe) are another form of Rabkin's "ground rules," this time working in reverse. Browning's poem starts with the accepted ground rules (grass grows on the ground, etc.) and moves away from them, but maintains that realistic basis.

Tennyson performs a similar task in making everyday objects seem fantastic, but he uses a different method. In "The Last Tournament," realistic objects like a necklace and suit of armor become fantastic when described.

The necklace that serves as the inspiration for the tournament is discovered in a manner that seems to deserve its own epic poem — Lancelot climbs up a cliff to find a necklace around the neck of an untouched infant sitting in an eagle's nest.

This series of events is described matter-of-factly, in the space of a few lines, suggesting to the reader that this sort of adventure is entirely commonplace in the fantastic world of Camelot. Later, Tennyson describes Tristram's garb:

...armor'd all in forest green, whereon
There tript a hundred tiny silver deer,
And wearing but a holly-spray for crest,
With ever-scattering berries, and on shield
A spear, a harp, a bugle... ["The Last Tournament," ll.170-174]

The idea that a knight would wear such an elaborate suit of armor into a battle is entirely fantastic, and even for elaborate ceremonial garb, this would be an impressive sight. Yet Tristram is not the king, nor the most prominent knight (that being Lancelot).

In The Idylls of the King, Tennyson injects the elements of the fantastic into an apparently realistic setting by imbuing every object with a dramatic story or ornate style. Thus both Browning and Tennyson use characterization (that of inanimate objects, though) to create fantasy in their works.

The literary devices addressed here are used in different ways throughout these six works. Tennyson and Browning create essentially realistic worlds that diverge from reality in their settings and characterizations. Carroll, Rossetti, and

MacDonald create almost entirely unrealistic worlds that are rooted in (quasi-)realistic settings and characterizations.

The interplay between reality and fantasy in these books is emblematic of Rabkin's "problem of Knowing" (quoted in Landow, "Fantasy and Conceptions of the Real") which he describes as characteristic of fantasy. Victorian fantasy created a world that was at once familiar and strange, and perhaps these works gained their popularity due to the drastic changes in society, politics and technology of the time, which created a truly real "real world" that was at once familiar and strange.

Chapter 12

Use of Biblical Typology in "The Bishop Orders His Tomb"

The almost inevitable disparities between type and fulfillment in the life of a fictional character, like a character's misapplication or misinterpretation of such symbolism, produces a range of ironic commentary on fictional personages. Since the time the Wife of Bath argued for female superiority with wonderfully twisted allusions to scripture, English authors have long employed such subjective distortions of interpretive procedures as a means of creating and occasionally satirizing figures in their own works.

As Barton demonstrates, such uses of commonplace types can produce gentle, if far-reaching, satire. They can also induce the reader to make far harsher judgments of a fictional character, and Rochester's misapplication and misreading of Achan's tent exemplifies such an earnest condemnation.

The double perspective or context provided by typology makes it particularly useful to the writer of dramatic monologues, since the disparity between literal and symbolical (or type and antitype) provides him with an effective means of allowing his character to convey more than he intends. Robert Browning, who is the great typologist among Victorian poets, frequently employs types for this purpose.

For instance, "The Bishop Orders His Tomb at Saint Praxed's Church. Rome, 15 — " (1845) uses a number of types to emphasize the precise nature of the prelate's characterizing attitudes towards life and death, matter and spirit. The Bishop, whom Ruskin took to be a brilliantly achieved emblem of the

Renaissance, persistently confuses matter and spirit in a most blasphemous manner, for having no true belief in Christian immortality, he yet tries to secure himself a kind of bizarre life after death. Browning's many citations of types in the poem reveal his speaker continually misinterpreting heavenly spiritual matters which he appropriates and misapplies to his passionate yearning to make himself immortal.

As George Monteiro has pointed out, "in ordering his tomb — and the entire poem is organized around this piece of business — the Bishop in effect parodies the Lord's command to Moses to build him a sanctuary: "According to all that I show thee, after the pattern of the tabernacle"". The Bishop, who sees himself as "an object worthy of worship", wishes his tomb to be constructed of stones from the Tabernacle, moreover, which were types of Heaven.

Furthermore, the very details, such as the nine pillars supporting his tomb, turn out to be allusions to passages in Exodus which were commonly read as prefigurative images of Heaven as well. "Without hope for personal salvation and with no faith in the Christian Resurrection, the Bishop reduces references to John the Baptist and the Madonna to nothing more than aesthetic comparisons for his beloved lapis lazuli. At the same time, taking over metaphors which emblematize salvation, he attempts to remake them into the letter of an earthbound immortality of sorts".

We may add that the Bishop's many blasphemies find their centre in his complete inability to comprehend the nature of matter, spirit and the relationship between them. In particular, he cannot interpret the literal expression of spiritual matters properly.

Augustine's Confessions tell that during his earlier Manichaean stage when he accepted the sect's belief in philosophical materialism, he could not conceive symbolic interpretation, and that as he came to believe in a world of the spirit, he also came to accept and understand symbolic reading of texts. In fact, the connection of the two remains so close for Augustine that he terms "spiritual" what we today would subsume under the broad category "symbolical".

Browning's Bishop finds himself in the predicament of a Manichaean who can only accept the material and yet passionately desires immortality which requires a belief in spirituality. As a result, he collapses matter and spirit into each other, now calling upon the capacities of the one and now the other.

This fusion and confusion of states of being which his passionate desire for immortality produces, is well suited to the psychological state of a dying man, and perhaps this suitability provides another reason why Browning chose to set this character portrait within the context of a death-bed scene.

BIBLICAL TYPOLOGY IN THE RING AND THE BOOK

The dying prelate in "The Bishop Orders His Tomb" provides the most extreme example from Browning's work of a character who can neither interpret nor apply types properly, but the preacher in "Christmas Eve" (1850), like many in The Ring and the Book (1868-9), embodies an equally effective use of this method of character definition.

His long poems also depict characters by means both of these figures's self-conscious distortion of types for dishonest ends and of their apparently unconscious citation of such biblical images. For example, in The Ring and the Book the villainous Count Guido Francheschini represents himself as an innocent, selfless man by dramatizing himself as Christlike.

But when he refers to "God's decree,/ In which I, bowing bruised head, acquiesce" (4.1410-11), he reminds us that he is, in fact, far more like Satan than like Christ. Guido's Satanic nature is recognized by other characters in the poem, including Caponsacchi, who, realizing his adversary's dangerous scheming, had thought to himself: "No mother nor brother Viper of the [Francheschini] brood/ Shall scuttle off without the instructive bruise" (6.677-8).

The authoritative statement of Guido's nature in terms of this image is made, of course, by the old Pope, who sees Pompilia acting analogously to Christ when she treads this

Satan-figure into hell and, the reader adds, is herself "bruised". Browning uses the same typological allusions in The Inn Album (1875).

When the evil nobleman mentions in passing that "Head and feet/ Are vulnerable both, and I, foot-sure,/ Forgot that ducking down saves brow from bruise", the reader might not perceive this as an allusion to Genesis 3:15. But when his former mistress describes him more elaborately, we cannot miss the allusion:

Let him slink hence till some subtler Eve
Than I, anticipate the snake — bruise head
Ere he bruise heel — or, warier than the first,
Some Adam purge earth's garden of its pest
Before the slaver spoil the Tree of Life.

Browning has his characters employ typological allusions to locate his villain for the reader, thus providing a means of authorial commentary even in the midst of forms modeled on dramatic monologue in which he cannot speak in his own person.

THE SMITTEN ROCK

When the Israelites were desperate from thirst during their desert wanderings, the Lord instructed Moses: "Behold, I will stand before thee there on the rock in Horeb; and thou shalt smite the rock, and there shall come water out of it, that the people may drink" (Exodus 17:6). As Numbers 20:1-13 tells, the prophet brought forth water again when he struck a second rock, even though this time he had been instructed only to pray for water.

Henry Melvill, the "Evangelical Chrysostom" who was the favourite preacher of Ruskin and Browning, makes the standard Victorian interpretation of the first incident when he holds that "this rock in Horeb was typical of Christ" and its yielding water when struck by Moses signifies "that the Mediator must receive the blows of the law, before he could be the source of salvation to a parched and perishing world."

Melvill also cites the New Testament authentication of this type when he explains that "it is to this that St. Paul refers, when he says of the Jews, 'They did all drink of the same spiritual drink; for they drank of that spiritual rock that followed them, and that rock was Christ' [1 Corinthians 10:4]."

English literature alludes to the smitten rock in several chief ways, the most obvious of which is the embodiment of God's sustaining the Israelites and all human beings.

Less common in literature is Paul's use of it as type of baptism, although this interpretation occurs in the visual arts. The smitten rock appears most often as (1) a type of Christ, who when struck (crucified) produces waters of grace or as (2) the stony heart of the believer that when struck by God or Christ produces waters of grace. Both these typological readings appear in secularized forms.

Seventeenth-century poets characteristically make ingenious variations on these typological applications. George Herbert, for example, presents the smitten rock in "The Sacrifice" as the type of the saviour's sufferings when Christ himself describes how his tormentors "strike my head, the rock from whence all store/ Of heav'nly blessing issue evermore" (ll. 169-71).

The same poet's "Love Unknown," on the other hand, invokes the second major intonation of this typological commonplace when it describes in visionary terms how a servant of his lord seized his heart "And threw it in a font, wherein did fall/ A stream of blood, which issu'd from the side/ of a great rock" (ll. 12-15).

This concatenation of biblical images, types, and emblems turns the waters of the Old Testament scene into the blood of Christ's sacrifice, thus making explicit the prophetic blending of times and beings always potential in a type. In "Easter Day," Richard Crashaw most unusually makes the smitten rock a type of Christ's tomb, from which issues forth the risen Christ and immortality for all believers.

Eighteenth- and nineteenth-century hymns and devotional verse make extensive use of the smitten rock to generate a typological universe surrounding the reader.

Like Gerard Manley Hopkins's dramatic monologue, "Soliloquy of One of the Spies left in the Wilderness" (c. 1864),

Isaac Watts's "Go, worship at Immanuel's feet" (1709), William Williams's "Guide me, O Thou great Jehovah!" (1774), and John Newton's "When Israel, by Divine command" (1799) make the general situation rather than the smitten rock itself a type and thus emphasize the contemporary believer's postfiguration of the sinful wandering Israelites.

In contrast, John Newton's "That Rock was Christ" (1772), Augustus Montague Toplady's "Rock of Ages" (1776), and Horatius Bonar's "The Cross" present the smitten rock simply as a type of the Crucifixion.

Another, perhaps less strictly orthodox type occurs when poets use Moses striking the rock to prefigure Christ bringing forth tears of repentance from the stony heart of the individual worshipper. This version of the type, which has had a long history in English verse, appears in the "author's emblem of himself," which opens the first part of Henry Vaughan's Silex Scintillans (1650), and in book six of The Excursion (1814), where Wordsworth has Ellen explain that God "'at whose command the parched rock/ Was smitten, and poured forth a quenching stream' has softened her hardness of heart" (VI, 920-21).

This use of the smitten rock, which occurs again in John Ruskin's "The Broken Chain," John Keble's "Sixth Sunday after Trinity" and "Easter Eve," and Tennyson's "Supposed Confessions" (1830), provides the climax and poetic centre of Tennyson's In Memoriam (1850), (section 131) and of Christina Rossetti's "Good Friday" (1862).

Purely secular applications of the type — those that require the reader to perceive the existence of the Christian reading of the Old Testament event as a prefiguration of Christ and his dispensation but that have no religious theme — appear occasionally throughout the nineteenth century.

Robert Calder Campbell's untitled love sonnet, which appeared in the Pre-Raphaelite periodical The Germ (1850), tells the speaker's beloved that when she departs he has "no speech — no magic that beguiles/ The stream of utterance from the harden'd rock," and Emily Dickinson in "A Wounded Deer — leaps highest" makes the "Smitten Rock that gushes" one of several instances of sharp reaction to a blow. Both these examples, like the following from Meredith's The Egoist (1879), draw upon commonplace traditions of biblical exegesis primarily for emphasis: "We cannot quite preserve our dignity when we stoop to the work of calling forth tears. Moses had probably to take a nimble jump away from the rock after that venerable Law-giver had knocked the water out of it" (Ch. 31). The allusion achieves it full effect only if one recognizes the traditional association of Christ's calling forth tears of repentance from the sinner.

A more elaborate allusion to Moses striking the rock appears in Robert Browning's "One Word More" (1855), which emphasizes that just as the ungrateful Jews failed to appreciate Moses's bringing forth water from the rock, so, too, the Victorian audience fails to appreciate what the poet produces on its behalf. A characteristically complex multiple use of the smitten rock appears in A.D. Hope's "An Epistle from Holofernes" (1946), when the ghost of Israel's enemy meditates upon myth, truth, and poetry.

When the Israelites were desperate from thirst during their desert wanderings, the Lord instructed Moses: "Behold, I will stand before thee there on the rock in Horeb; and thou shalt smite the rock, and there shall come water out of it, that the people may drink" (Exodus 17:6).

As Numbers 20:1-13 tells, the prophet brought forth water again when he struck a second rock, even though this time he had been instructed only to pray for water. Henry Melvill, the "Evangelical Chrysostom" who was the favourite preacher of Ruskin and Browning, makes the standard Victorian interpretation of the first incident when he holds that "this rock in Horeb was typical of Christ" and its yielding water when struck by Moses signifies "that the Mediator must receive the blows of the law, before he could be the source of salvation to a parched and perishing world."

Melvill also cites the New Testament authentication of this type when he explains that "it is to this that St. Paul refers, when he says of the Jews, 'They did all drink of the same spiritual drink; for they drank of that spiritual rock that followed them, and that rock was Christ' [1 Corinthians 10:4]." English literature alludes to the smitten rock in several chief ways, the most obvious of which is the embodiment of God's sustaining the Israelites and all human beings. Less common in literature is Paul's use of it as type of baptism, although this interpretation occurs in the visual arts.

The smitten rock appears most often as (1) a type of Christ, who when struck (crucified) produces waters of grace or as (2) the stony heart of the believer that when struck by God or Christ produces waters of grace. Both these typological readings appear in secularized forms.

Seventeenth-century poets characteristically make ingenious variations on these typological applications. George Herbert, for example, presents the smitten rock in "The Sacrifice" as the type of the saviour's sufferings when Christ himself describes how his tormentors "strike my head, the rock from whence all store/ Of heav'nly blessing issue evermore" (ll. 169-71).

The same poet's "Love Unknown," on the other hand, invokes the second major intonation of this typological commonplace when it describes in visionary terms how a servant of his lord seized his heart "And threw it in a font, wherein did fall/ A stream of blood, which issu'd from the side/ of a great rock" (ll. 12-15).

This concatenation of biblical images, types, and emblems turns the waters of the Old Testament scene into the blood of Christ's sacrifice, thus making explicit the prophetic blending of times and beings always potential in a type. In "Easter Day," Richard Crashaw most unusually makes the smitten rock a type of Christ's tomb, from which issues forth the risen Christ and immortality for all believers.

Eighteenth- and nineteenth-century hymns and devotional verse make extensive use of the smitten rock to generate a typological universe surrounding the reader. Like Gerard Manley Hopkins's dramatic monologue, "Soliloquy of One of the Spies left in the Wilderness" (c. 1864), Isaac Watts's "Go, worship at Immanuel's feet" (1709), William Williams's "Guide me, O Thou great Jehovah!" (1774), and

John Newton's "When Israel, by Divine command" (1799) make the general situation rather than the smitten rock itself a type and thus emphasize the contemporary believer's postfiguration of the sinful wandering Israelites.

In contrast, John Newton's "That Rock was Christ" (1772), Augustus Montague Toplady's "Rock of Ages" (1776), and Horatius Bonar's "The Cross" present the smitten rock simply as a type of the Crucifixion.

Another, perhaps less strictly orthodox type occurs when poets use Moses striking the rock to prefigure Christ bringing forth tears of repentance from the stony heart of the individual worshipper.

This version of the type, which has had a long history in English verse, appears in the "author's emblem of himself," which opens the first part of Henry Vaughan's Silex Scintillans (1650), and in book six of The Excursion (1814), where Wordsworth has Ellen explain that God "'at whose command the parched rock/ Was smitten, and poured forth a quenching stream' has softened her hardness of heart" (VI, 920-21).

This use of the smitten rock, which occurs again in John Ruskin's "The Broken Chain," John Keble's "Sixth Sunday after Trinity" and "Easter Eve," and Tennyson's "Supposed Confessions" (1830), provides the climax and poetic centre of Tennyson's In Memoriam (1850), (section 131) and of Christina Rossetti's "Good Friday" (1862).

Purely secular applications of the type — those that require the reader to perceive the existence of the Christian reading of the Old Testament event as a prefiguration of Christ and his dispensation but that have no religious theme — appear occasionally throughout the nineteenth century.

Robert Calder Campbell's untitled love sonnet, which appeared in the Pre-Raphaelite periodical The Germ (1850), tells the speaker's beloved that when she departs he has "no speech — no magic that beguiles/ The stream of utterance from the harden'd rock," and Emily Dickinson in "A Wounded Deer — leaps highest" makes the "Smitten Rock that gushes" one of several instances of sharp reaction to a blow.

Both these examples, like the following from Meredith's

The Egoist (1879), draw upon commonplace traditions of biblical exegesis primarily for emphasis: "We cannot quite preserve our dignity when we stoop to the work of calling forth tears.

Moses had probably to take a nimble jump away from the rock after that venerable Law-giver had knocked the water out of it" (Ch. 31).

The allusion achieves it full effect only if one recognizes the traditional association of Christ's calling forth tears of repentance from the sinner.

A more elaborate allusion to Moses striking the rock appears in Robert Browning's "One Word More" (1855), which emphasizes that just as the ungrateful Jews failed to appreciate Moses's bringing forth water from the rock, so, too, the Victorian audience fails to appreciate what the poet produces on its behalf.

A characteristically complex multiple use of the smitten rock appears in A.D. Hope's "An Epistle from Holofernes" (1946), when the ghost of Israel's enemy meditates upon myth, truth, and poetry. Much of Robert Browning's legacy to poets writing after him in the nineteenth and twentieth centuries comes from his vitalization of the dramatic monologue.

Victorian and modern poets have found it liberating to assume other personae (often quite alien to their own values and beliefs) and by looking through those characters' eyes, allow them to speak for themselves.

It follows logically that an author who has taken so much trouble to assume a role and keep it consistent is much less likely to step into the text in his own person and point the reader down the "right" interpretive path.

But this puts a greater burden on the reader, and may be the source of the idea that literature, especially poetry, is not a popular form, and is really only to be enjoyed by specialists.

It is also possible to argue that the withdrawal of the author from the text constitutes a secularization of literature. If the author refuses to give you moral guidance after placing difficult questions before you, he must believe one of three things:

(1) That no guidance is needed, because the case is obvious;
(2) That no guidance is possible, because you must see the truth for yourself; or
(3) That it doesn't really matter if you come up with the same answer he does.

This last alternative, assuming that the author cares about his fellow human beings and acknowledges his responsibility as an author, must mean that he does not believe in the possibility of salvation or damnation.

Chapter 13

Verse Tragedy A Blot on the 'Scutcheon'

Burletta and melodrama form the theatrical context of the officially-sanctioned dramatic adaptations of Charles Dickens's Christmas Books which took the London stage by storm in the mid-1840s. According to the "Chronological Table" of Frederick and Lise-Lone Marker in sixth volume of The Revels History of Drama in English (pp. xv-xliv), few notable plays debuted on stages in the United Kingdom during most of the first half of the nineteenth century, except in the period 1832-42, which preceded the new Theatre Regulation Act (1843).

By the terms of this act, which Sir Edward G. D. Bulwer-Lytton sponsored, the Office of the Lord Chamberlain acquired licensing authority over all playhouses in Great Britain; Lord Chamberlain's powers up to that time had extended only to the "legitimate" theatres of London's Covent Garden and Drury Lane.

THE STAGE CONTEXT OF THE 1830S AND BROWNING'S DRAMATIC WRITINGS

Among that period's major dramatic events were Dion Boucicault's Legend of Devil's Dyke (1838) and comedy of manners London Assurance (1841), Bulwer Lytton's historical pieces The Lady of Lyons (1838), Richelieu (1839) — showing the influence of The Three Musketeers — and Money (1840), and three unsuccessful tragedies by Robert Browning, who "in those days . . . was struggling for recognition" (Ley 35).

One may speculate that the failure on the commercial stage (despite the involvement of William Macready) contributed to Browning's throwing his creative energies into the development of the dramatic monologue through the medium of the magazine Bells and Pomegranates.

Some of the finest examples of the form such as "My Last Duchess" and "Soliloquy in A Spanish Cloister" Browning published in 1842.

The 1836 poems "Johannes Agricola in Meditation" and "Porphyria's Lover" are arguably of the new genre also, but predate Browning's historical drama Strafford by a year, while his last play intended for the stage, Colombe's Birthday he wrote in 1844, somewhat after his chief period of dramatic production and commercial failure.

DICKENS, BULWER-LYTTON, AND BROWNING

Oddly enough, Dickens's interest in Browning's verse dramas rather than in the highly popular historical romances of the novelist-cum-dramatist Bulwer Lytton seem of more significance to Dickens's novel-writing. In particular, Browning's failed A Blot in the 'Scutcheon is relevant to Dickens's works during that period (1841's Barnaby Rudge alone qualifying as an historical novel). Bulwer-Lytton achieved his three great theatrical successes with the aid of Drury Lane's chief actor and manager W. C. Macready, a friend of Dickens and producer of Browning's unsuccessful plays. While Browning was failing in his attempts at reviving verse tragedy (at least partly because his notion of a play was not dialogue "but a succession of monologues" (Lounsbury 69), Dickens and Lytton were succeeding on stage and in print with works more congruent with the tastes and spirit of the early Victorian period:

With the 1840's a change came over comedy. Not only was it becoming gradually more domestic and realistic, though still with a strong admixture of rhetoric. . . . The major themes explored in comedy over the next thirty years were those of wealth and social ambition; the virtues of rustic and domestic simplicity; the artificiality and moral inferiority of Society;

the idealizing of womanhood, the marriage bond, and domestic harmony. . . . (Booth, vol. 3, page 21)

BROWNING'S A BLOT IN THE 'SCUTCHEON (1842)

Were it not for Dickens's privately expressing to their mutual friend John Forster his great admiration for Browning's A Blot in the 'Scutcheon, a work which he apparently was responsible for Macready's producing at Drury Lane, the theatrical historian might be inclined to dismiss the play as an utter failure: like his Strafford (1837), a verse drama influenced as much by Shelley's The Cenci (1819) as by Forster's biography of the 17th-century nobleman, the second Browning tragedy closed after a few nights.

Edmund Gosse defends Strafford as stageworthy, and blames the poor reception on Macready's production: the piece "was produced when the finances of Covent Garden Theatre were at their lowest ebb, and nothing was done to give dignity or splendor to the performance". In fact, the great actor-manager William Macready had not been confident of the play's reception because the principal's passion seemed baseless and, consequently, implausible.

Although it, too, is set in eighteenth-century, rural England, Browning's tragedy of familial love and honour is a far cry from Dickens's Christmas Book for 1846, The Battle of Life, which the novelist, modeling the novella on The Vicar of Wakefield, deliberately set in Goldsmith's period "for the sake of anything good in the costume" (Pilgrim Letters, IV, 648) for illustration.

Whereas Browning's 1842 tragedy concerns a hot-blooded and impulsive aristocratic family and a pair of star-crossed lovers, Dickens's five Christmas Books (1843-1848) are firmly grounded in the middle-class realities of hearth, home, and family. Although the first two of the series share a contemporary urban setting, the third moves to the country.

The fourth, The Battle of Life, is set in the previous century, like Browning's play, but in a typical country village rather than in a patrician's hunting lodge or mansion. In fact, few of the characteristics of the period's bourgeois melodrama (including a village setting, poverty afflicting a noble and honest peasantry, a hard-hearted or negligent landowner or employer, and a ruthless steward) seem applicable to Browning's Blot, while such elements are detectable even in the urban-based fiction of Dickens.

Despite its three-act structure, the plot of A Blot in the 'Scutcheon (written in 1842; finally produced in 1843) is relatively simple, involving as it does a single action based on the forbidden love of Mildred, sister and ward of Lord Tresham, and Henry, Earl Mertoun, a young neighbour.

Until the couple's romantic indiscretion is revealed by Mertoun's climbing in Mildred's window at the close of the first act, the action is both slow and confusing. Tedious speeches such as those by Mildred's sister, Guendolen, harp on Tresham's "find[ing] no flaw, /No slightest spot" in one who wishes to graft himself into this peerless stock".

Browning delights in putting such archaisms as "poursuivant" and "varlets" into the mouths of the retainers, who serve as a chorus in much the same manner that contemporary melodramas used villagers, to introduce the opening situation and principal characters.

Unlike Benjamin and Clemency in Dickens's The Battle of Life, these minions never become characters in their own right, whereas Dickens develops the quirky servant couple into thriving middle-class entrepreneurs. The play's chief source of interest is neither of the lovers, but Tresham, who is so obsessed with his family's honour that he is "the one scarer of [Mildred's] dreamsÓ (201).

A secondary villain is the old huntsman, Gerard, who informs his inflexible master of Mildred's affair. There is, however, less of Webster's malcontented henchman of The Duchess of Malfi about Gerard than there is of such contemporary misanthropes as Buckstone's Luke the labourer and Dickens's Tackleton the toymaker in the Christmas Book for 1845, The Cricket on the Hearth, both of whom anticipate W. S. Gilbert's malignant Dick Deadeye in H. M. S. Pinafore thirty years later.

In fact, although Browning's poetic and dramatic models

may have been Shakespeare's Romeo and Juliet and Webster's The Duchess of Malfi, there is still more of nineteenth-century melodrama than of Elizabethan and Jacobean tragedy in Browning's A Blot in the 'Scutcheon.

Browning has, for example, a humourous female, Guendolen, and pasteboard antagonists, Tresham, agonizing over his sister's lack of chastity, and Mertoun, feeling guilty about his duplicity with Mildred's brother.

Something of the dramatic tastes of young Charles Dickens, whose first literary work was the Tragedy of Misnar, Sultan of India (1820) must have stayed with England's foremost novelist in the 1840s. Although attuned to the popular taste, Dickens greatly admired the anguished lines from Mildred's soliloquy that closes the first act (and in the original appeared once more in the second act) when he read the Browning manuscript Forster had lent him — "I was so young, loved him so, I had / No mother, God forgot me, and I fell". "I know no love like it, no passion like it, no moulding of a splendid thing after its conception, like it" (Pilgrim Letters, III, 381). However, the most compelling aspect of the play as theatre is the intense irony of the second act.

Browning produces great dramatic and situational irony when Tresham, angered by his sister Mildred's refusing to divulge the identity of her clandestine lover, believes that in accepting Mertoun's marriage proposal she is deceiving "an unconscious trusting youth.

The audience is aware (as Dickens's reader is not in the case of Dot's supposed infidelity in The Cricket on the Hearth) that Mertoun is the unknown lover. (Guendolen's brother possesses an inflexible pride and jealousy of his family name analogous to those of Alfonso D'Este, the imfamous Duke of "My Last Duchess.") After Guendolen has guessed at and informed her brother of the lover's identity, Tresham, the older and superior fencer, waylays and slays Mertoun in a one-sided duel not unlike the fencing match between Tybalt and Mercution in Romeo and Juliet.

Tresham is then bitten by remorse as the youth, dying, reveals — improbably — that he had never properly come to know the Treshams socially because his admiration of Tresham's person had rendered him diffident.

Even more improbably, to preserve the family's honour (apparently) Tresham takes poison and dies. Mildred unexpectedly dies, too — the audience surmizes of a broken heart — when she learns of Mertoun's death. As he joins his sister, Tresham enjoins the survivors to uphold the familial Ôscutcheon and remember that "Vengeance is God's, not man's".

"The grossest improbabilities were therefore to be accepted" (Lounsbury 142) by Browning's audience in both the behaviour of the principal characters and the plot of the piece, which seems totally divorced from reality in both motivation and action. However, ever the sentimental romantic, Dickens in reading the manuscript in November, 1842, was affected deeply by Browning's poetic rendering of the Romeo-and-Juliet theme:

I swear it is a tragedy that MUST be played; and must be played, moreover, by Macready. There are some things I would have changed if I could (they are very slight, mostly broken lines); and I assuredly would have the old servant [Gerard] begin his tale upon the scene [II, i]; and be taken by the throat, or drawn upon, by his master, in its commencement. But the tragedy I never shall forget, or less vividly remember than I do now. And if you tell Browning that I have seen it [ms.], tell him that I believe from my soul there is no man living (and not many dead) who could produce such a work . . . . [Pilgrim Letters, III, 381-3]

Subsequently, thanks to the combined efforts of Forster and Dickens in persuading Macready as manager of Drury Lane to stage it (although Browning in a 15 December, 1884, letter to Hill, the editor of the Daily News, ridiculed the notion that it was these two rather than the work's merit that had influenced Macready), performances of A Blot in the ÔScutcheon were given on 11, 15, and 17 February, 1843. While most London weeklies criticized the play's structural defects, lack of probability, and unpleasantness of subject (even though Macready had made Browning's fourteen-year-old

Mildred eighteen to stifle such objections), the Examiner's dramatic critic (probably Forster) defended the play. In his Introduction to Browning (1906), Symons describes the American productions of A Blot in the 'Scutcheon. A Tragedy in Three Acts:

Symons characterizes A Blot in the 'Scutcheon as the simplest, and perhaps the deepest and finest of Browning's plays. The Browning Society's performances, and Mr. Barrett's in America, have proved its acting capacities, its power to hold and thrill an audience.'

The language has a rich simplicity of the highest dramatic value, quick with passion, pregnant with thought and masterly in imagination; the plot and characters are perhaps more interesting and affecting than in any other of the plays; while the effect of the whole is impressive from its unity. The scene is English; the time, somewhere in the eighteenth century; the motive, family honour and dishonour.

The story appeals to ready popular emotions, emotions which, though lying nearest the surface, are also the most deeply-rooted. The whole action is passionately pathetic, and it is infused with a twofold tragedy, the tragedy of the sin, and that of the misunderstanding, the last and final tragedy, which hangs on a word, spoken only when too late to save three lives.

This irony of circumstance, while it is the source of what is saddest in human discords, is also the motive of what has come to be the only satisfying harmony in dramatic art. It takes the place, in our modern world, of the Necessity of the Greeks; and is not less impressive because it arises from the impulse and unreasoning wilfulness of man rather than from the implacable insistency of God. It is with perfect justice, both moral and artistic, that the fatal crisis, though mediately the result of accident, of error, is shown to be the consequence and the punishment of wrong.

(Note) A contemporary account, Written by Joseph Arnould to Alfred Domett, says "The first night was magnificent . . . there could be no mistake at all about the honest enthusiasm of the audience. The gallery (and this, of course, was very gratifying, because not to be expected at a play of Browning) took all the points quite as quickly as the pit, and entered into the general feeling and interest of the action far more than the boxes. . . Altogether the first night was a triumph.'

Although Dickens never saw the play produced on stage, reading it in manuscript undoubtedly left its mark upon him, for he pronounced it "at once the most tender and the most terrible story I have ever read" (Pilgrim Letters, III, 383) to his artist-friend Maclise the day after he had appraised the play in writing to Forster on 25 November, 1842.

It seems peculiar that Dickens, whose own works were often so perfectly attuned to the Victorian taste, had completely overestimated the power of so slight an action to hold the stage. What affected his judgment was the purity of the lovers' passions and their anguish (which, to Browning, mitigates their having sinned).

These same features Dickens utilized two years later in A Cricket on the Hearth in which the lady's immorality mercifully turns out to have been illusory; however, John Peerybingle's distress at the supposed infidelity of his young wife is far more powerfully described. In the second Christmas Book, more viciously realistic than either A Christmas Carol, with its talk of prisons and workhouses, or Browning's A Blot in the 'Scutcheon, Trotty Veck's terrible premonition of Meg's moral decline and eventual suicide may also echo the turbid passions of Browning's characters.

However, Dickens in The Chimes (1844) utilizes such feelings to enlist the support of his middleÑclass readership for the cause of the urban and rural poor, and not merely (as with Browning) as an exercise in voyeurism. Higher though his purpose be, Dickens provides means of averting disaster in the Christmas Books as improbable as Browning's bringing it to fruition in A Blot in the 'Scutcheon.

In the first two of the series Dickens resolves the problem — the wretched futures of Scrooge, Tiny Tim, Trotty's daughter and friends by the dream mechanism, a device which was then not so hackneyed. Similarly, he explains at the conclusion of Cricket that Dot's affection for the disguised stranger was innocent, after all, and at the conclusion of Battle that Marion's dishonourable elopement was a mere ruse. In the last of the series, The Haunted Man, Dickens manipulates the supernatural machinery so that the 'gift' of perception utterly devoid of sentiment may be recalled.

Although, for example, in The Cricket on the Hearth (1845) the disguised stranger's turning out to be Caleb's long-lost son and May Fielding's childhood sweetheart returned just in time to rescue her from marriage to the odious Tackleton seems to be as incredible as the multiple deaths that close of Browning's A Blot in the 'Scutcheon, Victorian audiences and theatre critics alike, nurtured on such melodramatic fare as Buckstone's Luke the Labourer or, The Lost Son (1826), would have accepted Dickens' denouements as being well within the conventions of the contemporary stage, which in turn sprang from those of the eighteenth-century stage and novel.

For example, in Luke the Labourer the plot-line resembles that of The Cricket on the Hearth superficially: Farmer Wakefield's son, stolen in youth by Gypsy Mike and the malevolent Luke, returns just in time to save the honour of his sister, Clara, from the lecherous Squire Chase and his sordid henchmen.

The Victorian audience, then, was prepared to countenance an action as improbable as Browning's if the dramatist provided an entertainment that conformed to the contemporary formula for melodrama: an attractive hero and heroine of the middle class who, although threatened by the machinations of upper-class villains and lower-class thugs, marry or are reunited after separation. In short, what a successful play provided in the 1840s was domestic sentiment and a happy ending in which virtue is triumphant.

Despite the quality of his verse and his improved sense of dialogue in this second play for Macready, Browning again failed because, especially in the young earl's song "There's a woman like a dewdrop" that he jauntily sings as he proceeds to his mistress's chamber, it contradicted the temper of the

Victorian age. The scene so affronted the audience's sensibility "that on the first night of its performance the play came near being wrecked on this particular scene" (Lounsbury 140).

"With the emphasis on commercial and domestic reality and the concern in much drama to depict the minutiae of everyday existence, legitimate tragedy was doomed" (Booth, II, 13) because of the tendency of such dramatists as Browning and Knowles to violate "the truth of life" (Lounsbury 145) with characters and situations that bore little relationship to bourgeois, urban, and contemporary realities.

As Booth explains, what Browning's audience would have more readily accepted would have been the sort of compromise between tragedy and melodrama that Lytton effected in The Lady of Lyons (1838) and Richelieu (1839). Even the friendly reviewer in The Examiner was doubtful of the play's continuing because "People are already finding out . . . that there is a great deal that is equivocal in its sentiments, a vast quantity of mere artifice in its situations, and in its general composition not much to Ôtouch humanity".

This, of course, was Dickens's gift, making appealing the lives and even the hardships of ordinary people from the working and middle classes.

Browning himself had recognized that his dramatic construction was deficient in the sort of action that Dickens had advocated interpolating; in his 1837 preface to the printed version of Strafford he conceded that in his "eagerness to freshen a jaded mind by diverting it to the healthy natures of a grand epoch, may have operated unfavourably on the represented play, which is one of Action in Character rather than Character in Action."

The 1842-43 tragedy exhibits the same tendency. In an age that demanded theatrical spectacle and effect, a play dependant upon the poetry of the dialogue could hardly be expected to succeed, even though the plot offered a denouement as violent and sensational as that of Sheridan Knowles's Virginius (1820).

Macready's proposed cuts run to approximately 310 lines, or about oneÑfourth of the play. . . almost all the changes are understandable or justifiable the Drury Lane audience could hardly be expected to sit quietly through a five act discussion of family pride. Browning still had not mastered the idiom of the stage; he did not understand that it was impossible to convey closet drama subtlety in the spoken theatre . . . Macready was revising for the recently enlarged Drury Lane, where most of the gallery could see only part of the action and hear very little of the dialogue even when it was shouted (as most of it was).

This version of the play's reception is corroborated by a personal friend of Browning, Joel Arnould, who with his wife attended the play for all three nights, that is, on the opening Saturday (11 February), Wednesday (15 February), and Friday, 17 February.

These dates, incidentally, do not square with Browning's 1884 recollection that his play's production was contemporary with those of two other fresh and unconventional pieces, The Patrician's Daughter and Plighted Troth.

Macready all this time was struggling with pecuniary difficulties. It is not likely that a manager so beset, whatever might be his personal feelings, would risk the chances with two new and untried plays while a third one, with which he could be sure of attracting large audiences, was suffered to remain unacted.

Arnould, as reported by Lounsbury, recalled that, although the opening night of A Blot in the 'Scutheon was a triumph, on the second night a mere seventy occupied the pit while the boxes were empty.

The third night I again took my wife to the boxes. It was evident at a glance that it was to be the last. . . .the miserable great chilly house with its apathy and emptiness produced in us both the painful sensation which made her exclaim that she 'could cry with vexation at seeing so noble a play so basely marred.'

Browning had interfered by insisting that Samuel Phelps, an unknown quantity to London audiences, instead of Macready, the foremost actor of his day, should take the leading role of Tresham. "To have a new play brought out at

Macready's theatre, without Macready in it, was courting failure, no matter whether much or little money was spent on the accompaniments of its representation".

In contrast, Dickens's advice on the production of The Battle of Life (Lyceum, 1846), a novella which the Times had scorned as "trash" but which within a month of publication had outsold its predecessors, compensated for weakness with in the cast and produced some interesting special effects.

In particular, Dickens proposed a recent addition to the Lyceum company, Leigh Murray (who had made his London debut on 19 April, 1845, in Knowles's Hunchback at the Princess's) for Alfred Heathfield, in which capacity he gave an "Intelligent, gentlemanly performance . . .".

That Dickens chose him particularly for the role of Alfred indicates the novelist's sound theatrical sense, for Murray's "comic acting was marked by refined vivacity, as his serious acting was by refined feeling" (Marston 391). He possessed both grace and charm on stage as well as correct elocution and a "prepossessing appearance" (Marston 391) admirably suited to juvenile leads.

For the production of The Battle of Life the author, Charles Dickens, had likewise intervened by vetoing the Keeley management's choice of the too-broadly-comic and notoriously inept W. H. Oxberry for either Snitchey or Craggs. Within a week of his return to London he had made the company "very quick and excited in the passionate scenes, and so [infused some appearance of life into those parts of the play".

The reviews affirmed Dickens's judgments about the production, singling out for censure the actresses who played the sisters and for unbounded praise Mrs. Keeley, who had brought Clemency Newcome to life: "it was certainly beyond her well-recollected explanation of her conduct as Dot Peerybingle last year; and that is no poor compliment" the Illustrated London News remarked.

However, if the effectiveness of the production was indebted to Mrs. Keeley, it was indebted no less to Dickens himself, who had selected the Lyceum for the adaptations of his third and fourth Christmas Books on account of the comedic talents of its star-managers, Robert and Mary Ann Keeley. With the parts of Benjamin and Clemency ready-made for the couple, Albert Smith was the only one of the novella's seven London adaptors to score a theatrical hit with a vehicle artificial in plot and deficient in character.

Whereas Browning's A Blot in the 'Scutcheon possessed similar failings and lasted three nights, Dickens's The Battle of Life with a generally strong cast and the coaching and snow scenes that were Dickens's own innovations, managed forty-two performances as a Christmas play, despite the fact that it has neither the supernatural machinery nor the yuletide atmosphere of A Christmas Carol. The difference between the Christmas Books generally and Browning's plays lies in the motivation and credibility of character:

The story taken as the groundwork of the drama may be as unreal and impossible as one found in the Arabian Nights. But that once accepted, what is required is that the personages should act as they would were it probable and true. But in no work produced by any great poet have these principles been more systematically violated.

Through his participation in the dramatisations of the Christmas Books Dickens accomplished far more than the introduction to the stage of less stereotypical characters and more natural dialogue. Continuing where Douglas Jerrold in Black-Ey'd Susan (1829) and The Rent-Day (1832) had halted in developing socially realistic yet popular plays, through his assisting with the dramatic adaptations of the Christmas Books in the 1840s Dickens helped create a drama that arose from neither the arid streambed of traditional, aristocratic tragedy, "cut off from the mainsprings of modern English life and thought", nor the upstart, working-class, domestic melodrama, vibrant but awkward.

He helped restore drama to the status of respectable, middle-class entertainment, and assisted in laying the basis for the more realistic dramas of Tom Robertson, Henry Arthur Jones, and Arthur Wing Pinero. It is probably no accident that Robert son, like Boucicault, learned his dramatic trade by first serving an apprenticeship as a stage adaptor of Dickens. Like Robert Browning, Charles Dickens had attempted to bridge the gulf between literature and the stage, but while Browning's static and confusing Strafford and his improbable and wooden A Blot in the 'Scutcheon failed to gain popular acceptance, Dickens's Christmas Books, like his Pickwick Papers and Oliver Twist earlier, were enormously successful on stage.

The writing and staging of the Christmas Books, then, mark a significant point not only in Dickens' progress as a writer, but also as a period halfway between the old, aristocratic comedy of Sheridan and the new, middle class comedy of Wilde and Shaw.

Dickens was, in fact, one of the few great Victorian literary personalities to achieve commercial as well as critical success on the stage. He did so, first of all, by grudgingly recognizing that he was not a true dramatist, and that his genius was better fitted to the novel than to the popular dramatic forms of his day.

That Browning never arrived at a similar realisation about his dramatic talents is attested to by his refusal to accept Macready's judgment about the necessity for editing A Blot in the 'Scutcheon for the stage and by his inability even years later to recognize the limitations imposed on drama by the physical realities of the Victorian theatre, as well as by the tastes of its patrons.

In the second place, Dickens was content to advise the theatrical companies to whom he gave (for a nominal hundred pounds) his sanction and his proofs of the Christmas Books. Demanding a new sensitivity of playing, Dickens also made suggestions that produced coherent realizations of his work in terms of setting and effect.

While accepting that theatrical 'hacks' would pare down his dialogue, convert his descriptions to action and scenery, and hew his plot to meet popular expectations, he endeavoured to have the actors and actresses with whom he worked retain the sense of his words and the essential conceptions of his characters as these existed in the original.

With Edward Stirling, who gave the first sanctioned adaptation of a Christmas Book, he probably had too little control of the actual scripting, embarking upon the enterprise after the script was complete; with his friends Lemon and A' Beckett at the Adelphi in December, 1844, he probably exercised too great a degree of control, compelling them to retain dialogue that, while excellent in the printed version of The Chimes would become tedious on stage. Stirling had wanted, above all, to create novel effects. Dickens seems to have wanted to translate his characters and situations faithfully to the stage — uncanonical interpretations deeply upset him, as his letter to Forster on 21 February, 1844, suggests.

In his (or the Keeleys') choice of Albert Smith for his adaptator Dickens was most fortunate. It was with the versatile Smith that Dickens dramatized attained the zenith of popular success with The Cricket on the Hearth (1845) and The Battle of Life (1846) at the Lyceum, under the management of the Keeleys.

Certainly, the star-system influenced the composition (and success theatrically) of the works that Dickens wrote for Smith's adaptation, the writer making sure that there were strong comic parts for Robert and Mary Ann Keeley in both The Cricket on the Hearth and especially The Battle of Life. It may be argued that Browning's lack of knowledge about this system doomed A Blot in the 'Scutcheon from the start, since he rejected the vastly popular Macready in favour of the unknown Phelps. Dickens' "one or two expensive notions. . .about Scenery" (Letters, IV, 662) contributed to the success of The Battle of Life while a fine cast and interesting effects were even able to rescue the static, undramatic The Haunted Man from failure on stage.

Another compensation for lack of external action in the Adelphi's 1863 revival of The Haunted Man, as in the Surrey's 1819 production of Home's Douglas was spectacle. The gimmick of Professor Pepper's optical illusion made the play, despite its static talkiness, acceptable entertainment once again. Generally speaking, however, spectacle was an adjunct to rather than a replacement for dramatic action in the sanctioned

Christmas Book plays. Since the dramatisations were, in part, realisations of the illustrations in these novellas, the dramatists' tableaux were based on the plates by Leech, Doyle, Stanfield, and Maclise. However, Dickens, despite his manifest interest in visual effects in The Battle of Life felt that an adaptation ought to be more than simply a realization.

To Dickens the actors' understanding of the dialogue was essential to the success of the production. Smith seems to have possessed the happy knack, which Lemon and A'Beckett did not, of balancing the dramatic requirements of spectacle, dialogue, and action. Dickens's great contribution to early Victorian drama was his placing character and motivation (which Browning neglected) above contrived incident, and internal conflict above the tension between idealized innocence and unredeemed villainy.

As a novelist sensitive to contemporary taste Dickens taught the dramatists of his age how to utilize contemporary life, with its characters, problems, and settings, as the basis for a new, realistic type of drama which simultaneously could reveal Character in Action, as well as Action in Character.

Chapter 14

"My Hunger Both To Be And Know The Thing I Am"

The different points of view exemplified in the series of dramatic monologues which makes up The Ring and the Book gave Browning an opportunity to synthesize all the dominant tendencies in his thinking. His later work introduces no new themes, although the reader who is principally interested in the poet's ideas will here find them reaffirmed with increasing conviction and specificity.

Thus, "La Saiziaz," "A Pillar at Sebzevar" from "Ferishtah's Fancies," and the Parleying "With Bernard de Mandeville" extend the intuitional foundations of the poet's religious faith; and the Parleying "With Charles Avison" is his strongest statement of the supremacy of instinct over intellect in the creative act.

The loss of individual integrity through submission to the tyranny of institutions continues to elicit his anti-social bias. "Prince Hohenstiel-Schwangau," "Saviour of Society" and the Parleying "With George Bubb Dodington" are mordant studies of political temporizers, while Léonce Miranda, the protagonist of "Red Cotton Night-Cap Country"; or "Turf and Towers," is destroyed by religious superstition. Browning's unorthodox theories about love and the relations between the sexes are set forth in such poems as "Fifine at the Fair," The Inn Album, "A Forgiveness," and the Parleying "With Daniel Bartoli."

And a very large number of poems touch on one or another aspect of his aesthetic theories. The interpenetration of reality by imaginative insight informs the important critical pronouncements in the two works constructed around translations of Euripidean tragedies, and in the Parleyings "With Francis Furini" and "With Gerard de Lairesse." The concept of the poet-seer, directly inspired by and owing primary allegiance to God, accounts for the treatment of René Gentilhomme in "The Two Poets of Croisic" and also for the Parleying "With Christopher Smart."

If, however, Browning was content in his later poetry to reformulate themes which we have already sufficiently explored in his better-known work, he continued to the end of his career to invent new forms for the projection of those themes. This constant technical experimentation is the most interesting and suggestive critical problem relating to his final literary period.

Tennyson's last poems reflect a divided intent; part are transparently popular in tone, while others have the quality of private utterance. Browning, on the other hand, continued to try to resolve the artistic dilemma posed by a double awareness, through his search for poetic forms responsive to both conditions of sensibility.

In the dramatic monologue, as practised in his period of greatest achievement, the poet might be supposed to have found his rightful manner; and the wonder is that after The Ring and the Book his writing in this vein shows such a falling off. The explanation lies in a failure in dramatic sense, disastrous for a poet who saw all life as conflict.

Just as Browning's dramas are deficient in external action, so the later monologues lack internal action of the kind produced by emotional intensity. Ironically enough in one who so distrusted the theorizing faculty, intellect comes to preponderate over feeling.

What these poems offer is not the throb of passion, but the psychoanalytic investigation of motives behind impulses which never themselves get actualized. Having previously dispensed with incident, Browning now tends at one further remove to refuse emotional involvement in the situations he evokes.

And, correspondingly, the reader finds it more and more difficult to care very greatly why a character acts in a given way when the act itself, anticipated or retrospective, has not been made to seem interesting or significant.

"Fifine at the Fair" is a case in point. After reading it (and the other long and intricate monologues of the period), one cannot help thinking that had Browning seen fit to take up the writing of novels he might have foreshadowed the accomplishments of Meredith, Conrad, and James.

But for all the fascination of its protagonist, a latter-day Don Juan, and the subtle relevance of his arguments to modern habits of mind, the dialectics of "Fifine at the Fair" are too diffuse and centrifugal to answer the demands of poetic form.

The emotional conflict created in the hero by the rival attractions of the spiritual Elvire and the fleshly Fifine is a valid one; but long before the final choice is made, the initial tension has become slack, weighted down under an excessive burden of intellectual speculation.

Browning has perfected his skill in special pleading to the point of over-sophistication, and the reader finds himself wondering whether the Don's ambiguous nature may not after all reflect his creator's own inability to make up his mind. Browning clearly sympathizes with the libertine's restiveness under a system of individually repressive social conventions, for he puts into his character's mouth many of his own opinions about love and society and art.

Like Bishop Blougram, the Don has a faculty for calling true things by false names; only in "Fifine at the Fair" Browning overreaches himself and so loses control over his argument. For such appeal as the poem makes rests in the very skill with which the protagonist rationalizes his selfish desires and thereby reduces morality to conform to private convenience.

Deprived of any ethical sanction, the emotions become the plaything of intellectual casuistry; and this too often seems to be the case in those later monologues where the dramatic conflict enacts itself on a level of abstract ideas.

The obscurity in which Browning's sophistries too often

involved him in such poems as "Fifine at the Fair" was in the nature of a return to the manner of Pauline and Sordello; and his reputation suffered accordingly. It was clearly in an effort to free himself from this subjective vein that the poet turned to straight narrative in the two series of "Dramatic Idyls."

As the use of the term Idyls indicates, Browning was here following Tennyson's lead, although with the intention of showing up the laureate's timid avoidance of actuality. The handling of realistic details in these poems does not, however, compensate for the author's technical inferiority to Tennyson as a story-teller.

If the springs of motivation in "Fifine at the Fair" and Red Cotton Night-Cap Country are unduly complex, many of the Dramatic Idyls suffer from the opposite failing of inadequate motivation. The climactic events of "Ivàn Ivànovitch," "Clive," and "Muléykeh," for cxample, seem arbitrary to the point of improbability.

Whereas the resolution of a poem like "The Glove" arouses the reader to self-recognition, the Browning of the later monologues often seems content with the short-lived shock produced by a surprise ending.

Other groups of poems show that Browning was continuing his search for ways of enlivening recondite material. "Ferishtah's Fancies" is a variation on the formula of "Pippa Passes." Indeed, as early as Paracelsus he had inserted lyric interludes into other types of poetry as a kind of emotional leitmotiv.

The use of lyrics to comment on philosophic discourse in "Ferishtah's Fancies," however, is a good deal less effective than the handling of this device in the more dramatic circumstances of Paracelsus and "Pippa Passes." In Parleyings with Certain People of Importance in Their Day, Browning had recourse to another early method for the projection of his ideas: namely, the study of historical individuals in the context of cultural movements.

As W. C. DeVane has conclusively demonstrated, the Parleyings are of unparalleled value in analyzing tne origin and development of Browning's characteristic theories; but their appeal is limited to those whose interest is in the man rather than the artist.

The peevish and spiteful treatment of his critics in Pacchiarotto, with Other Poems evidences the poet's anxiety about his erratic bold on the reading public. In defence of his later work he constantly makes two assertions which have the appearance of special pleading in his own behalf. If his poetry seems difficult, that is because his audience, expecting cowslip-wine, gets nettle-broth instead.

To express this concept he employs the further metaphors of the nut in "Jochanan Hakkadosh" and of the ortolan in the "Prologue to Ferishtah's Fancies." The external appearance of neither is inviting; he who would savor their true flavor must bite through a resistant covering. Browning offers a more elevated version of his artistic intent at this time in the Epilogue to the second series of Dramatic Idyls, in which the lyric poet of the first stanza harks back to Aprile and Eglamor:

"Touch him ne'er so lightly, into song he broke
Soil so quick-receptive-not one feather-seed,
Not one flower-dust fell but straight its fall awoke
Vitalizing virtue: song would song succeed
Sudden as spontaneous-prove a poet-soul!"
Indeed?
Rock's the song-soil rather, surface hard and bare:
Sun and dew their mildness, storm and frost their rage
Vainly both expend,-few flowers awaken there:
Quiet in its cleft broods-what the after-age
Knows and names a pine, a nation's heritage.

Concurrently, the poet makes much of the fact that his writing is founded in actuality. Its life-principle is the "sap of prose experience"; his "fancy wells up through corrective fact."

So, in his later poems, such as the Prologue to Asolando, the author constantly affirms the all-importance of seeing things as they are:

Friend, did you need an optic glass,
Which were your choice? A lens to drape
In ruby, emerald, chrysopras,
Each object-or reveal its shape

Clear outlined, past escape,
The naked very thing?-so clear
That, when you had the chance to gaze,
You found its inmost self appear
Through outer seeming-truth ablaze,
Not falsehood's fancy-haze?

And here once again the concept of a double awareness enters in. With Browning's emphasis on fact the Victorian age could take no issue; however, it might well do so with his undisguised "sense" of fact.

In "Pacchiarotto, with Other Poems" the poet had insisted on the rigorous objectivity of his attitude; but coupled with an admission of the difficulties offered by his work, this defence stands self-convicted of disingenuousness.

Fact may be, indeed usually is, Browning's starting-point; but when submitted to analysis by his inquiring and subtle mind and interpreted in the light of this process, the original fact acquires highly subjective meanings and becomes principally significant as an index to the poet's individual consciousness.

It is all very well for Don Juan to say in "Fifine at the Fair":
And-consequent upon the learning how from strife
Grew peace-from evil, good-came knowledge that, to get
Acquaintance with the way o'the world, we must not fret
Nor fume, on altitudes of self-sufficiency,
But bid a frank farewell to what-we think-should be,
And, with as good a grace, welcome what is-we find.

But how is this statement to be squared with the Don's earlier confession of intense self-consciousness: "My hunger both to be and know the thing I am," a statement which might stand as the epigraph to the history of Browning's mind? For the poet, while professing dependence on the outer world, could never accept its evidences until they had first passed through the filter of his imagination.

Thus, he addresses Gerard de Lairesse as follows:

. . . for sense, my De Lairesse,
Cannot content itself with outward things,
Mere beauty: soul must needs know whence there springs

How, when and why-what sense but loves, nor lists
To know at all.

And again, further elaborating the necessity for the artist to probe beneath the surface of outward seeming, the poet has the protagonist of "Red Cotton Night-Cap Country" say:

Along with every act-and speech is act-
There go, a multitude impalpable
To ordinary human faculty,
The thoughts which give the act significance.
Who is a poet needs must apprehend
Alike both speech and thoughts which prompt to speak.
Part these, and thought withdraws to poetry:
Speech is reported in the newspaper.

Browning, as we have seen, asserted that intuition is the ultimate means of knowledge, and that the faculty which enables the artist to approach truth is imaginative insight. In his own case these faculties operated most successfully through a form of dramatic perception in which the fact and its ulterior meaning become fused into unity by a single act of apprehension.

But with the decline of dramatic sensibility in his later work, fact and meaning draw apart, so that he depends increasingly on the rationalizing intellect to set up correspondence between them.

Whether the successes of his middle period are attributable to the glow of emotional maturity, or to the perfecting of a suitable form, or to both, it is only in the poems of these years (and perhaps occasionally in the Indian summer of Asolando) that we find the inner and outer consciousness held in equipoise.

In the later poetry as in the early efforts, the split in awareness is manifest. Into the character of Euripides, as conceived in "Balaustion's Adventure" and "The Last Adventure of Balaustion," Browning incorporated his reading of the dilemma which tormented the Victorian artist.

The evidence is contained not only in the partisan words of Balaustion, but also, with surprising impartiality, in Aristophanes' criticism of his rival.

Euripides, coming in the wake of Sophocles, is made to say: "I, his successor, . . ./ Incline to poetize philosophy,/ Extend it rather than restrain."

And Aristophanes then proceeds to describe Euripides' introspective habit of mind in terms that clearly echo Browning's own rueful recognition of the unpredictable and alienating ways of his imagination:

His task is to refine, refine,
Divide, distinguish, subtilize away
Whatever seemed a solid planting-place
For footfall,-not in that phantasmal sphere
Proper to poet, but on vulgar earth
Where people used to tread with confidence.
There's left no longer one plain positive
Enunciation incontestable
Of what is good, right, decent here on earth.

Chapter 15

"And Then I First Explored Passion and Mind"

IN ORDER to trace the operation of a double awareness in Browning's poetry, allowance must at the outset be made for three complicating factors which do not occur in a parallel study of Tennyson. Browning was a much more original artist than the laureate. Whereas Tennyson was content to locate his themes in a familar context, whether literary or relating to comtemporary life, and generally speaking, to present this material in converntional forms, Browning naturally inclined to recondite subject-matter and to experimental methods.

Secondly, Tennyson's habit of mind was introspective, with the result, as we have seen, that the matrices of interest in his poetry are comparatively few and easy to identify. Browning, on the other hand, combined with greater intellectual self-confidence a multiple curiosity about man's external relationships.

Tennyson could never have written as Browning did in the Epilogue to "Pacchiarotto, with Other Poems": "Man's thoughts and loves and hates!/ Earth is my vineyard." Finally, where Tennyson was diffident about private convictions and careful to express them in as uncontroversial a way as possible, Browning, out of enthusiasm for his own highly individualistic beliefs, was unwilling to make concessions to the aptitudes and predilections of his readers.

Browning's most characteristic ideas are traceable to certain psychological assumptions adumbrated in the three substantial poems with which he inaugurated his career.

These are: "Pauline" (1833), "Paracelsus" (1835), and "Sordello" (1840; although not published until three years after "Strafford," "Sordello" was begun on the completion of Pauline in 1833.)

These works are in a sense variations on a single theme: the evolution of the creative impulse in artists beset by uncertainty as to the genuineness of their inspiration and the best uses that can be made of their talents. In "Pauline" these problems are formulated in terms of a conflict between reason and instinct. The poem introduces a youthful poet restive under the yoke of received opinion:

How should this earth's life prove my only sphere?
Can I so narrow sense but that in life
Soul still exceeds it?
In their elements
My love outsoars my reason...

To the voice of common sense, recommending subordination of this idealizing tendency to the way of the world, the speaker protests:

There's some vile juggle with my reason here;
I feel I but explain to my own loss
These impulses: they live no less the same.
Liberty! What though I despair? my blood
Rose never at a slave's name proud as now.
0 sympathies, obscured by sophistries!-
Why else have I sought refuge in myself,
But from the woes I saw and could not stay?

As a romantic assertion of the reality of the human emotions, in opposition to the delusory processes of ratiocination, "Pauline" establishes a point of view which dominates all Browning's subsequent thinking.

It should be noted, furthermore, that the poet founds his faith in man's instinctual nature on private insights unsusceptible of demonstration by rational means. So, for example, he maintains that the appeal of Christianity derives from the baffling challenge which Christ offers to philosophic inquiry:

Is it not in my nature to adore,

And e'en for all my reason do I not
Feel him, and thank him, and pray to bim-now?
Can I forego the trust that he loves me?
Do I not feel a love which only ONE . . .
0 thou pale form, so dimly seen, deep-eye!
I have denied thee calmly-do I not
Pant when I read of thy consummate power,
And burn to see thy calm pure truths out-flash
The brightest gleams of earth's philosophy?

"Pauline" contains two additional passages in which the poet calls on his experience of the arts to prove the validity of intuitional experience.

The first of these is the well-known evocation of a painting of Andromeda. The second, deriving from music, is still more explicit. The speaker addresses his imagined mistress as follows:

Be still to me
A help to music's mystery which mind fails
To fathom, its solution, no mere clue!
0 reason's pedantry, life's rule prescribed!

The poet's decision, taken immediately hereafter, to shake off self-consciousness is dictated not so much by social awareness as by an intimation of nobler heights of imaginative being than he has yet attained:

I'll look within no more,
I have too trusted my own lawless wants,
Too trusted my vain self, vague intuition-
Draining soul's wine alone in the still night. . .

Once let the artist turn altruist, however, and the question then becomes how he can best exert influence on the minds of others. In his poem devoted to the pseudo-legendary figure of Paracelsus, Browning first attacks the problem of communication, while still insisting on the primacy of the intuitions over the rational intellect. "Paracelsus" is a study of intellectual pride and its humbling.

The philosopher, conscious of his mission to arouse society with "new revealings," places entire confidence in his individual powers, and thereby repudiates both the guidance of tradition and the support of love, as personified by Festus and Michal. Festus repeatedly warns him of the danger of trying to do without human sympathy: "How can that course be safe which from the first/ Produces carelessness to human love?"; and again: "But do not cut yourself from human weal!" Paracelsus, however, sets off alone on his wanderings, strong in the conviction that he is sufficient unto himself and that ultimate truth has its seat in the depths of his inner consciousness.

"Paracelsus" is divided into five sections to suggest the stages in the hero's tragic progress. In the second part there begins for Paracelsus the betrayal by the intellect, although he continues to insist that this is the supreme faculty:

God! Thou art mind! Unto the master-mind
Mind should be precious.
Spare my mind alone!
All else I will endure. . .

The lyric poet Aprile now enters the scene to emphasize the protagonist's alienation. Aprile compensates for the weakness of his intellect by a capacity for love denied to Paracelsus. Lacking Festus' humble veneration for humanity, however, he loves unrealistically. For Aprile inhabits a Shelleyean world of make-believe where mankind is an idealized abstraction.

In their isolation both Paracelsus and Aprile are self-infatuated, the one by the life of reason, the other by the life of the imagination. Paracelsus realizes that they are "halves of one dissevered world"; but although, having learned to love Aprile, he has begun to move towards recognition of the need for closer communion with his kind, he is not yet ready to renounce his chosen path.

To the dying poet he says:

We wake at length from weary dreams; but both
Have slept in fairy-land: though dark and drear
Appears the world before us, we no less
Wake with our wrists and ankles jewelled still.
I too have sought to KNOW as thou to LOVE -
Excluding love as thou refusedst knowledge.
Still thou hast beauty and I, power.

With the third section disillusionment sets in for Paracelsus. He has found that his teachings are unintelligible to the populace, and scorning the artifices of the demagogue, has taken refuge in aristocratic disdain for his audience.

Aprile's example is for the moment lost on him. In his thinking of the dead poet merely as a devotee of art for art's sake, we can perhaps detect Browning's own rejection of that alluring doctrine:

I cannot feed on beauty for the sake
Of beauty only, nor can drink in balm
From lovely objects for their loveliness;
My nature cannot lose her first imprint;
I still must hoard and heap and class all truths
With one ulterior purpose: I must know!
. . . For other men,
Beauty is prodigally strewn around,
And I were happy could I quench as they
This mad and thriveless longing, and content me
With beauty for itself alone...

Festus reappears to suggest that Paracelsus' difficulties are of his own making, the result of a deficiency in the loving wisdom of the heart; but the philosopher reasserts the supremacy of the individual:

'T is in the advance of individual minds
That the slow crowd should ground their expectation
Eventually to follow . . .

Yet he is not so sure of himself as once; and although without much humility, he is beginning to perceive that his failure may be attributable to pride of intellect:

... were man all mind-he gains A station little enviable. From God

Down to the lowest spirit ministrant,
Intelligence exists which casts our mind
Into immeasurable shade. No, no:
Love, hope, fear, faith-these make humanity;
These are its sign and note and character,
And these I have lost!

Paracelsus next turns his mental powers to unscrupulous

ends, and so betrays himself to the ways of the world. He condescends to magical practices in order to bedazzle his audience. Unwilling to bow to the authority of the magistrates at Basel, he is cast out as a charlatan. Paracelsus thus becomes the first of many compositions in which Browning was to show the enslavement of minds to ambition for material power.

The coarsening of Paracelsus' fibre spreads out from the intellect through his whole nature and leads to sensual indulgence. He falls prey to morbid Satanism: "mind is nothing but disease,/ And natural health is ignorance."

In a final despairing effort to hold onto some remnants of self-respect, he makes the gesture of arrogating to himself godlike infallibility:

I am above them like a god, there's no
Hiding the fact: what idle scruples, then,
Were those that ever bade me soften it,
Communicate it gently to the world,
Instead of proving my supremacy,
Taking my natural station o'er their head,
Then owning all the glory was a man's!
— And in my elevation man's would be.

It is only in his old age, a failure and on the point of death, that Paracelsus under Festus' ministrations finally attains to full recognition of his error.

Man in his slow ascent of the evolutionary scale is to be pitied rather than disdained; his groping, but endlessly valiant struggle to rise is the very thing that makes him lovable. And the superior beings sent to guide the way must possess the faculty of love if they are to fulfill their function.

Paracelsus retains to the end his confidence that he is one of those so elected; but the qualities on which he should have relied, as he now realizes, were his "inborn uninstructed impulses,"-not, that is to say, the reasoning mind, but

perception unexpressed,
Uncomprehended by our narrow thought,
But somehow felt and known in every shift
And change in the spirit, — nay, in every pore
Of the body, even ...

This God-given instinct he has perverted through the selfish desire for individual power; yet he cannot refrain from pointing out the temptation to deal with the world in its own terms:

All quackery; all deceit; myself can laugh
The first at it, if you desire; but still
You know the obstacles which taught me tricks
So foreign to my nature — envy and hate,
Blind opposition, brutal prejudice,
Bald ignorance-what wonder if I sunk
To humour men the way they most approved?

And the poem leaves the reader with the ineradicable impression that in Browning's view the way of the original thinker must needs be a lonely one, since devotion to the best interests of humanity inevitably entails incomprehension and active hostility from all those whom one seeks to serve: "We have to live alone to set forth well/ God's praise."

In theme "Sordello" occupies a position midway between "Pauline" and "Paracelsus." The first sections of "Sordello" trace the growth of a poet's mind, the later ones his career in the world.

As had been the case with "Paracelsus," "Sordello" represents an attempt on Browning's part to gain perspective on his own situation through imaginative treatment of an historical figure sufficiently obscure to allow considerable latitude of interpretation. The hero of the poem is obsessed by the problem of making himself heard.

The theme of the artist's communicative function, emerging from a welter of imperfectly assimilated material, gives the work what little unity it possesses.

Like the speaker in "Pauline," Sordello is motivated in turn by two impulsions, one turning him inward towards self-contemplation, the other driving him outward to a life of action; and like Paracelsus, his career follows a pattern of alternating advance and retreat, as he assumes and is then dislodged from one position after another "vis-à-vis" society.

In total seclusion from worldly affairs Sordello passes his youth amidst the natural beauties of Goito. His imagination is peopled with ideal beings, and he dreams of emulating Apollo, the poet-god. But such isolation, with its inducements to egocentric complacency, is precarious at best; for we are told that

this world of ours by tacit pact is pledged
To laying such a spangled fabric low
Whether by gradual brush or gallant blow.

Sordello's first departure from Goito into a larger sphere of activity comes about under auspicious circumstances. Inspired to spontaneous song, he vanquishes the reigning troubadour, Eglamor, at Palma's Court of Love.

Eglamor is an interesting, though somewhat vague figure. He foreshadows the Pre-Raphaelite ideal of the artist wholly devoted to aesthetic discipline: "Then, how he loved that art!/ The calling making him a man apart/ From men."

Like Aprile, however, his preference for fancy over fact is mitigated by a generous capacity for love; he dies acknowledging Sordello his master. Earlier in the poem Browning had specified two categories of poets. The first includes all those who feel

A need to blend with each external charm,
Bury themselves, the whole heart wide and warm,-
In something not themselves; they would belong
To what they worship. . .

Eglamor clearly belongs to the other category, described as follows:

For there's a class that eagerly looks, too,
On beauty, but, unlike the gentler crew,
Proclaims each new revealment born a twin
With a distinctest consciousness within,
Referring still the quality, now first
Revealed, to their own soul — its instinct nursed
In silence, now remembered better, shown
More thoroughly, but not the less their own. . .

Eglamor, at least, has the virtue of absorption in the technical demands of his craft. Sordello, on the other hand, vainglorious over his easy success, assumes that all he henceforth need do is give unbridled expression to his imagination: "So, range, free soul! — who, by self-consciousness,/ The last drop of all beauty dost express."

At the furthest remove from Eglamor's perfectionism, his sole concern is for popular acclaim- "'t was the song's effect/ He cared for, scarce the song itself." In the outcome he falls between two stools. Lack of worldly experience, coupled with excessive self-confidence, causes him to go astray among abstractions which are meaningless to his audience.

When he attempts to adopt more concrete modes of communication, notably the dramatic, he discovers his temperamental disaffinity to prevailing forms of thought.

The man and the artist split apart:
Weeks, months, years went by,
And lo, Sordello vanished utterly,
Sundered in twain; each spectral part at strife
With each; one jarred against another life;
The Poet thwarting hopelessly the Man,
Who, fooled no longer, free in fancy ran
Here, there, — let slip no opportunities
As pitiful, forsooth, beside the prize
To drop on him some no-time and acquit
His constant faith (the Poet-half's to wit —
That waiving any compromise between
No joy and all joy kept the hunger keen
Beyond most methods) — of incurring scoff
From the Man-portion — not to be put off
With self-reflectings by the Poet's scheme,
Though ne'er so bright. Who sauntered forth in dream,
Dressed anyhow, nor waited mystic' frames,
Immeasurable gifts, astounding claims,
But just his sorry self? — who yet might be
Sorrier for aught he in reality
Achieved, so pinioned Man's the Poet — part,
Fondling, in turn of fancy, verse; the Art
Developing his soul a thousand ways —
Potent, by its assistance, to amaze
The multitude with majesties, convince
Each sort of nature, that the nature's prince

Accosted it. Language, the makeshift, grew
Into a bravest of expedients, too;
Apollo, seemed it now, perverse had thrown
Quiver and bow away, the lyre alone
Sufficed. While, out of dream, his day's work went
To tune a crazy tenzon or sirvent —
So hampered him the Man-part, thrust to judge
Between the bard and the bard's audience, grudge
A minute's toil that missed its due reward!

There ensues a period of withdrawal to Goito and self-renewal at the font which symbolizes the inner sources of Sordello's creative being.

As a result of the illumination received during this time, Sordello vows himself to a career of constructive endeavor in the cause of his countrymen suffering under the wars of the Guelphs and the Ghibellines.

As happened to Paracelsus when he aspired the second time, however, Sordello is seduced by a thirst for power. Finding that Rome is not built in a day, he despairs once more and is ready to exchange his newly assumed mission for the consolations of the imagination. In vain his conscience reprimands him for failure to abide by the choice it dictates:

Only bear in mind,
Ferrara's reached, Goito's left behind:
As you then were, as half yourself, desist!
-The warrior-part of you may, an it list,
Finding real falchions difficult to poise,
Fling them afar and taste the cream of joys
By wielding such in fancy, — what is bard
Of you may spurn the vehicle that marred
Elys so much, and in free fancy glut
His sense, yet write no verses-you have but
To please yourself for law, and once could please
What once appeared yourself, by dreaming these
Rather than doing these, in days gone by.
But all is changed the moment you descry
Mankind as half yourself, — then, fancy's trade
Ends once and always: how may half evade

The other half? men are found half of you.
Out of a thousand helps, just one or two
Can be accomplished presently: but flinch
From these (as from the falchion, raised an inch,
Elys, described a couplet) and make proof
Of fancy,-then, while one half lolls aloof
I' the vines, completing Rome to the tip-top-
See if, for that, your other half will stop
A tear, begin a smile!

Not until after Salinguerra, the ruthlessly practical soldier who acts on instinct, has mocked his feeble vacillations does Sordello come to the recognition that it is the poet's true function to incite his auditors to noble actions:

Thought is the soul of act, and, stage by stage,
Soul is from body still to disengage
As tending to a freedom which rejects
Such help and incorporeally affects
The world, producing deeds but not by deeds,
Swaying, in others, frames itself exceeds,
Assigning them the simpler tasks it used
To patiently perform till Song produced
Acts, by thoughts only, for the mind ...

No sooner has Sordello found the direction in which he must henceforth move, however, than fresh temptations are placed in his way. With the twofold discovery that he is Salinguerra's son and Palma's accepted lover, a career of boundless power opens up for him. In the ensuing conflict between altruism and the will to power, the former wins out, but the price of victory is extinction.

Sordello stamps on Salinguerra's badge of authority and then, emotionally exhausted, dies. Into this somewhat ambiguous denouement Browning steps to confirm the reader's suspicion that Sordello's life is to be viewed as a tragic failure in its twin aspects — both the early immersion in fanciful dreams, the weakness of Pauline's lover, and the later surrender to selfish ambition, Paracelsus' flaw.

Sordello's name is forgotten; his influence, ironically enough, survives to aftertimes in the sole unpremeditated and wholly instinctive utterance of his poetic being, the Elys lyric, as it is sung in fragmentary form by an Italian urchin.

As we have seen, "Pauline," "Paracelsus," and "Sordello" are thematically interrelated by a like conflict; and each leads to the same conclusion: namely, that the artist can only achieve full self-realization through getting into productive communication with the external world. For Browning to embrace this theory, however, was one thing; to illustrate its operation through his own poetry was quite another.

The choice presented to Pauline's lover, Paracelsus, and Sordello is clearly a projection of their creator's own dilemma in the erratic early years of his poetic career. John Stuart Mill's comment on Pauline is well-known: "With considerable poetic powers, the writer seems to me possessed with a more intense and morbid self-consciousness than I ever knew in any sane human being."

This searching criticism made an enormous impression on the youthful Browning, and was perhaps as much as any other single influence instrumental in starting the poet on a succession of technical experiments expressly directed to the formation of a more objective manner.

The attempt to present Paracelsus' spiritual biography in dramatic form was a first step towards externalizing the author's inner perceptions. Fearful, however, that his audience would fail to understand what he was about, and perhaps somewhat suspicious as well of the perfect purity of his artistic motive, the poet took opportunity in the dedication to the original edition to explain the general purpose and method of the poem:

I therefore anticipate his [the reader's] discovery, that it is an attempt, probably more novel than happy, to reverse the method usually adopted by writers whose aim it is to set forth any phenomena of the mind or the passions, by the operation of persons and events; and that, instead of having recourse to an external machinery of incidents to create and evolve the crisis I desire to produce, I have ventured to display somewhat minutely the mood itself in its rise and progress, and have suffered the agency by which it is influenced and determined, to be generally discernible in its effects alone, and subordinate throughout, if not altogether excluded: and this for a reason. I have endeavored to write a poem, not a drama....

In "Sordello," where the mode is narrative rather than dramatic, there is evident, beneath the incrustations of repeated revisions, the author's original intent to employ "an external machinery of incidents to create and evolve the crisis." Yet the principal difficulty which "Sordello" offers the reader is the labyrinthine complexity of the historical events which determine the hero's actions.

In after years, with a better comprehension of where his true talent and interests lay, Browning tended to play down this element in "Sordello" on which he had originally lavished so much care. In dedicating the work to his friend Milsand in 1863, the poet wrote: "The historical decoration was purposely of no more importance than a background requires; and my stress lay on the incidents in the development of a soul: little else is worth study."

Browning met Macready in 1835, and two years later Strafford inaugurated a decade's apprenticeship to the stage. Although Browning's plays were among his earliest productions, while Tennyson did not try his hand at writing for the theatre until the latter part of his life, both men may be said to have turned to dramatic writing out of a desire to reach a wider public. A distinction should be made, however, between the impulses which led Tennyson and Browning to the drama.

The former, secure in his contemporary fame, was looking for new subject-matter of a dignity appropriate to the author of Idylls of the King. Browning, on the other hand, his head crammed with ideas but his reputation all to make, was seeking a manner which would put him into closer correspondence with his age.

Even the most superficial consideration of Browning's relationship with Macready indicates how conscientiously the poet was bent on wooing public favor by means of his playwriting efforts. A "Blot in the 'Scutcheon" was announced to the great producer in the following hopeful way:

"The luck of the third adventure" is proverbial. I have written a spick and span new Tragedy (a sort of compromise between my own notion and yours-as I understand it, at least) and will send it to you if you care to be bothered so far. There is "action" in it, drabbing, stabbing, et autres gentillesses,- who knows but the Gods may make me good even yet?

Despite this readiness to compromise, however, Browning was no dramatist for the stage, as anyone who has looked into his plays knows. Of interior or psychological action there is plenty and to spare; but the poet simply could not translate states of mind into the language of external conflict.

From the first Macready sensed what was wrong. After rereading Strafford, he wrote in his diary: "I find more grounds for exception than I had anticipated. I had been too much carried away by the truth of character to observe the meanness of plot, and occasional obscurity." As if in tacit acknowledgment that this play invited such objections, Browning echoed his estimate of "Paracelsus" in the dedication to "Strafford," where he described the drama as "one of Action in Character, rather than Character in Action."

In fact, one cannot escape the conclusion that, real as was his concern to gain an audience for his work, Browning quite early realized that he had no real talent for the theatre, and as a result inclined increasingly to use the dramatic form as a means for working out problems of artistic expression inherent in his own genius.

In the choice and development of dramatic themes he exercised greater and greater originality out of seeming indifference to the conventions of theatrical representation; and after the completion of "Colombe's Birthday" in 1844, he sent a letter to Domett which announced, in effect, his decision no longer to write for production: "I feel myself so much stronger, if flattery not deceive, that I shall stop some things that were meant to follow, and begin again. I really seem to have something fresh to say."

The later dramas, furthermore, are strongly characterized by the reemergence of certain themes which were announced in "Pauline," "Paracelsus," and "Sordello." It might even be argued that all of Browning's plays exploit a single situation. A choice confronts the protagonist between two lines of action, one dictated by innate idealism, the other by selfish calculation.

The resulting internal conflict supplies the "dramatic" tension of the piece. Like Sordello, Anael, Djabal's lover in "The Return of the Druses," and Mildred Tresham, the heroine of "A Blot in the 'Scutcheon," both die of emotional exhaustion attributable to the clash between their material and spiritual interests.

In "Colombe's Birthday," "Luria," and "A Soul's Tragedy," external action has become almost non-existent, while the speeches of the characters, approximating dramatic monologues, expound with increasing definiteness that master concern in Browning's thinking-the conflict between the wisdom of the heart and the wisdom of the world.

It is too often forgotten that "Bells" and "Pomegranates" included, in addition to the five series devoted entirely to plays, three additional numbers containing dramatic experiments of a very different and much more original kind.

These were: "Pippa Passes" (1841), "Dramatic Lyrics" (1842), and "Dramatic Romances and Lyrics "(1845). In explanation of the symbolic title, "Bells and Pomegranates," the poet wrote: "I only meant by that title to indicate an endeavor towards something like an alternation, or mixture, of music with discoursing, sound with sense, poetry with thought."

Towards this blending "Paracelsus" and "Sordello" contributed as much as the plays. The discipline of playwriting sharpened Browning's dramatic sense; but the kinds of dramatic struggle which excited his imagination, as we have seen, were those enacted within the minds of individual characters.

In the dramatic lyric and its more sophisticated variation, the dramatic monologue, the poet discovered means for dressing his insights in a guise that would pass muster with a public which had been mystified by "Sordello" and bored by "Strafford." Although definitely transitional in character, "Pippa Passes" is the first poem which allows us clearly to identify the thematic motifs and technical methods which characterize Browning's mature manner. The lyric interludes of "Paracelsus" survive in Pippa's songs, but they are now keyed into the story in such a way as to influence its course at climactic moments.

Likewise, while the poet still uses dialogue, dramatic effect is largely engendered through tensions antecedent to action. The subject-matter of the four episodes suggests a striving to fuse the subjective and objective strains in Browning's previous work.

A wealth of incident is present by implication; yet the emphasis does not fall directly on the actions of the characters, but rather on the motives out of which action grows. The psychological analysis of motivation, furthermore, provides Browning with an opportunity for the kind of special pleading at which he was to become so adept. By this means he could endow the creatures of imagination with his own highly individualistic perceptions while seeming to present them as independent beings fully responsible for their own values.

Pippa's refrain, "God's in his heaven-/ All's right with the world!" is often cited as the "reductio ad absurdum" of Victorian optimism. This sentiment, however, is clearly meant to characterize the girl's naïveté and childlike faith, and not the milieu in which she lives. For Pippa's world is given over to the tyranny of church and state, to corrupt officialdom, to envy and malice and wanton cruelty, to adultery and blackmail and murder.

The society which environs the girl from the silk mills of Asolo makes a mockery of lawful love, patriotism, the familial relationships, and art. As she wanders the streets on her annual holiday, she brushes shoulders with pimps, prostitutes, debauched students, informers, hired assassins, and parasites of every variety.

Her immunity to worldly degradation lies in her very unworldliness. She is a child of nature, unlettered, inexperienced, guileless, endowed only with a happy disposition, innocence, and the wisdom of her intuitions. Like Aprile and Eglamor, with whom her kinship is evident, her only means of selfexpression is lyric song. It is through the impact of these songs, so alien to the habits of mind of her auditors, that the theme of the poem comes out.

They are heard by "Asolo's Four Happiest Ones" at critical moments in their lives; and they wholly alter the direction of the lives in question by forcing a choice on the hearers. Pippa's passing awakens the conscience of individuals hitherto enslaved by self-interest, and provokes conduct contrary to the courses of action mapped out by the conscious will.

In each case the ultimate decision negates personal inclination and so discredits the materialistic values endorsed by society. Thus, Ottima and Sebald, having discovered a sense oi guilt, will commit suicide; Jules and Phene will go away together without exacting revenge; Luigi will die in the cause of Italian liberation; and Monsignor will restore her rightful inheritance to Pippa.

Each of the four situations which Pippa influences by her celebration of intuitive feeling hinges on a conflict between individuals and some form of authority. Browning's poems, as we shall see, may be classified into three groups, conforming to the three aspects under which he saw the drama of solitary souls in their strife with the forces of organized society.

One division poses the problem of intellectual assent to established institutions and involves a concept of power: a second poses the problem of emotional assent to conventional morality and involves a concept of love; and third poses the problem of aesthetic assent to artistic traditions and involves a concept of the creative impulse.

All three themes occur in "Pippa Passes," which thus marks out the principal issues with which Browning was henceforth to be concerned.

In the two contrasting panels devoted to the pairs of lovers, Ottima and Sebald and Jules and Phene, Browning advances some of his most characteristic notions about sexual behavior, and in so doing raises issues little in accord with Victorian thinking about such matters.

Confronted by a society which condones loveless marriages, we side with Ottima and Sebald in their splendidly reckless passion, and feel revulsion only after discovering that adultery has led to cold-blooded murder. Pippa's song awakens the lovers to their guilt; but the guilt, be it noted, is for the murder and not for the adultery.

And the act of suicide which follows does not seem an additional crime, but rather a confirmation of love's intensity issued in repudiation of society and its usages. Jules is equally insubordinate to accepted norms of social conduct in his reaction to the cruel practical joke perpetrated by his fellow art students.

To have cast off Phene and then avenged his legitimate grievance was obviously the course sanctioned by custom, and the one to which Jules inclined before Pippa's song educed a nobler impulse.

In turning from hatred of the students to selfless love for Phene, who shares Pippa's natural innocence, Jules flies directly in the face of convention and thereby attains salvation. His escape to the Greek Isles is the traditional romantic comment on the corrupting ways of the world.

The two concluding episodes present individuals under the shadow of institutionalized authority, in the one case governmental repression represented by the Austrian rule in northern Italy, in the other religious formalism represented by the prestige of the Catholic Church. For Luigi, the champion of liberty, it would be easier to remain with his Chiara in Asolo.

Pippa's song sends him on his mission to Austria, and through averting immediate arrest, reserves him for a patriot's death. It is only on second thought that we realise that in order to establish his point the poet is countenancing political assassination. Monsignor in the last episode is a preliminary study for a whole family of cynical worldlings who choose the Church as the surest means of satisfying their thirst for power.

In listening to Pippa's rhapsody rather than to the insidious arguments of the Intendant, Monsignor abandons the riches which would have smoothed his chosen career.

Finally, Jules' calling as a sculptor gives Browning an opportunity to introduce into "Pippa Passes" some of his theories about the rôle of the artist. Overly fastidious by temperament and fearful of exposure to the exacting touch of actuality, Jules has made an ivory tower for himself. Dreaming of ideal beauty, he has fallen into lifeless traditionalism.

He describes for Phene a group of statuary on which he has been at work, the central figure of which reflects his concept of himself as the withdrawn and self-immersed votary of art for art's sake:

Quite round, a cluster of mere hands and arms
(Thrust in all senses all ways, from all sides,
Only consenting at the branch's end
They strain toward) serves for frame to a sole face,
The Praiser's in the centre: who with eyes
Sightless, so bend they back to light inside
His brain where visionary forms throng up,
Sings, minding not the palpitating arch
Of hands and arms...

In Phene, however, Jules encounters the higher beauty of living reality which shows up his past work in its true light.

The resulting break with the dead weight of inherited practice is exemplified in Jules' flight from his studio, and in his determination to find a new mode of artistic expression. We learn of the motives responsible for this decision through the letter which Monsignor quotes in the fourth episode:

He never had a clearly conceived Ideal within his brain till to-day. Yet since his hand could manage a chisel, he has practised expressing other men's Ideals; and, in the very perfection he has attained to, he foresees an ultimate failure: his unconscious hand will pursue its prescribed course of old years, and will reproduce with a fatal expertness the ancient types, let the novel one appear never so palpably to his spirit.

There is but one method of escape: confiding the virgin type to as chaste a hand, he will turn painter instead of sculptor, and paint, not carve, its characteristics . . .

Monsignor is skeptical of Jules' success in a career undertaken after so many years of discipleship to a false vision; but his remarks on the artist's change of heart reflect the value which Browning placed on originality, as over against a sterile traditionalism:

He may-probably will-fail egregiously; but if there should arise a new painter, will it not be in some-such way, by a poet now, or a musician (spirits who have conceived and perfected an Ideal through some other channel), transferring it to this, and escaping our conventional roads by pure ignorance of them. . .

From "Pippa Passes" to "Dramatic Lyrics" and "Dramatic Romances and Lyrics" is only a short step. In progressing from "Paracelsus" and "Sordello" to plays written expressly for the theatre, Browning had been following a blind alley. Now he had reversed his direction, and by so doing, had come in sight of his true destination, the dramatic monologue. In the dedication to "Strafford" he had correctly analyzed the bent of his genius; it was to treat "Action in Character, rather than Character in Action."

But the murky and self-conscious involutions of "Pauline" had shown that the proper field for such action was not the artist's own character. Through his dramatic experiments Browning had learned to project his insights outward and to give them objective embodiment in imaginary characterizations.

Henceforth he would drop the pretense of external action and confine his attention to the portrayal of individuals under the stress of such interior, psychological conflicts as characterized the play of his own complex and boldly original mind. Seemingly so remote from their creator in time and place and circumstance, these figures would thus become Browning's agents for delivering to his age the messages which be had failed to get across in other ways.

Bibliography

Halliday, F. E. *Robert Browning: His Life and Work*. London: Jupiter, 1975.

Markus, Julia. *Dared and Done: The Marriage of Elizabeth Barrett and Robert Browning*. New York: Knopf, 1995.

Ryals, Clyde de L. *The Life of Robert Browning: A Critical Biography*. Cambridge, MA: Blackwell, 1993.

Barrett Browning Dies at Asolo, Italy; Artist, son of the Poets, Robert and Elizabeth Browning, obituary, The New York Times, 9 July 1912

DeVane, William Clyde. *A Browning handbook*. 2nd. Ed. (Appleton-Century-Crofts, 1955)

Drew, Philip. *The poetry of Robert Browning: A critical introduction*. (Methuen, 1970)

Hudson, Gertrude Reese. *Robert Browning's literary life from first work to masterpiece*. (Texas, 1992)

Karlin, Daniel. *The courtship of Robert Browning and Elizabeth Barrett*. (Oxford, 1985)

Kelley, Philip et al. (Eds.) *The Brownings' correspondence*. 15 vols. to date. (Wedgestone, 1984-) (Complete letters of Elizabeth Barrett Browning and Robert Browning, so far to 1849.)

Maynard, John. *Browning's youth*. (Harvard Univ. Press, 1977)

Chesterton, G.K. *Robert Browning* (1903)